Core of
my heart,
my country

Core of my heart, my country

Women's sense of place and the land in Australia & Canada

Maggie MacKellar

MELBOURNE UNIVERSITY PRESS

MELBOURNE UNIVERSITY PRESS
An imprint of Melbourne University Publishing Ltd (MUP Ltd)
PO Box 1167, Carlton, Victoria 3053, Australia
mup-info@unimelb.edu.au
www.mup.com.au

First published 2004
Text © Maggie MacKellar 2004
Design and typography © Melbourne University Publishing Ltd 2004

Designed by Kate Mitchell Design
Typeset in Malaysia by Syarikat Seng Teik Sdn. Bhd.
Printed in Australia by McPherson's Printing Group

National Library of Australia Cataloguing-in-Publication entry
MacKellar, Maggie, 1973– .

Core of my heart, my country: women's sense of place and the land in
Australia and Canada, 1828–1950.

  Bibliography.
  ISBN 0 522 85137 1.

  1. Women pioneers—Australia—History.
  2. Women pioneers—Canada—History.
  3. Women in development—Australia.
  4. Women in development—Canada.
  5. Women—Psychology. 6. Women—Identity.
  7. Australia—Description and travel.
  8. Canada—Description and travel.
  I. Title.

  305.409

For
Robin & Arkie
with love
&
In memory of
Mannie

Contents

Acknowledgements

This book could not have been written without the cast of people that support me. It has been a journey that would not have begun without the intellectual vision of Jan Kociumbas. I thank David Breen for providing me with a way into Canadian history and Richard Waterhouse for encouraging me to think of myself as an historian. Penny Russell has been a mentor, a valued reader and a friend.

I have been privileged to work with Drusilla Modjeska. Without her engagement, energy and commitment to the processes of writing, this book would not be. I thank her for providing a space of peace where we would meet over her kitchen table and discuss how to write history, how to reach an audience, how to tell a story with integrity. I realise that the kind of intellectual exchanges we shared as we worked through the manuscript rarely exist in the current publishing landscape. Louise Adler had the vision to see that such a relationship was integral to the production of this book and I am grateful to her for making it happen. Thank you to the editors and staff at MUP, particularly Kirsty Manning-Wilcox.

The title of the book comes from Dorothea Mackellar's famous poem *My Country*. Earlier versions of material in Chapt. 2 and 3 have appeared as 'A Wild Free Life': Susan Allison in response to land and place on the frontier of British Columbia' in *Women's Writing*, Vol. 8, No. 3, 2001, 403–418; 'Looking through the Fawn-skin Window: White Women's Sense of Place in the New Worlds of Australia and Canada' in Kate Darian-Smith (ed.), *Challenging Histories: Reflections on Australian History*, Special issue of *Australian Historical Studies*, vol. 33, no. 118, 2002, 223–238. I would like to acknowledge the Whyte Museum of the Canadian Rockies, Glenbow Museum, Calgary and the Archives of British Columbia, Victoria BC, for their permission to reproduce images from their collection. The author and publisher have made every effort to trace and acknowledge copyright. Copyright holders who have not been found are invited to contact MUP.

My family and friends have provided both emotional and practical support. I want to thank, however inadequate that is, the network of people that have enabled me to write and indeed survive. Catherine Kevin, Clare Corbould, Lyn Forsyth, Kate Gordon, Heather & Roger Gordon, Lisa MacDonald, Cam Mackellar, Duncan MacKellar,

Jan & Andrew Norton, Jacqui Pollock, Olwen Pryke, Kate Salisbury and Zora Simic. Without each of you I would never have finished this book. To my parents—for the different gifts you have given me, but also for your belief—thank you. To Mike, I wish you could have seen the fruit of the support you gave me in order to research this book and write the thesis. I thank you for the journeys we shared on the sides of mountains, down rivers and on the restless back of the sea. I thank you for the memories.

Maggie MacKellar
University of Sydney, 2004

Into the wild

There is a jumble of rocks in the place I call home. A sea of lucerne laps at their feet, its shores formed by the line of the creek and the steep bulk of Malachi Hill. All around stretch the western slopes and tablelands, rising and falling, a vast patchwork quilt of colour framed in heat and stitched through with a brilliant blue sky.

When I was very young, my mother took me to those rocks. She showed me the ledge, hidden by a jutting outcrop, which she had come to as a child. She showed me how to wedge myself into the crack so that no one could see me from above or below. It is a child-sized ledge, a place to sit, she said, just the size to be alone, a place where you might begin to know yourself. She told me that if I were still, the lizards would come out and sun themselves. Sometimes I would see a red fox on his rounds, or the pair of Wedgetail Eagles that lived high on the hill. The sound of the plovers would carry on the wind from the creek, and the chatter of the Willy Wagtails would remind me that the garden was just over the hill.

When I look at it now, the ledge seems small, but it was big when I was a child and remains so in my memory. My mother was wise to give me that place, away from the house, in the paddock, and she was wise to let me go there alone. If I look at the ledge through a child's eyes, I feel very far away from the house, as if I have gone on a great journey to reach this place. If I look at it through a mother's eyes, the house is just over the hill, hidden but there.

I know the surface of that rock; it is an intimate part of me. I can remember every step of the path down to it and the way you have to twist your body to fit into the crack. In memory the view doesn't fade. It is the only place that has come to me as a gift.

I had always assumed that the landscape of my childhood was the only place where I would feel that intimacy of belonging, that connection between body, land and memory that make up the bones of home. Then, in 1996, I went on a journey with my husband into the Alaskan wilderness. Though I didn't know it then, it was to be the beginning of the journey into this book.

On an early June day, we stood at the end of the train line, gear scattered at our feet, and watched as the train pulled away, leaving us on the edge of Prince William Sound. The sting of fine grit tattooed that moment of departure into me. Ahead of us was a month on the water, a 450-mile paddle, through a landscape so foreign that I fought disorientation at every moment. Then two months in the mountains, climbing the peaks I had seen from the plane window as we flew into Anchorage.

Every night I wrote, pushing back exhaustion in an effort to order this experience. At midnight during the summer solstice, with the wind moaning and the light streaming down, I wrote. At 2am the sun still turned the water orange and blue, and I wrote to make sense of days that had no real beginning or end, days that crept toward dimness, then retreated, like breath—so quiet.

My journal became the place where I would try to ease my dislocation in this new land. My dreams were filled with forests of bull kelp plucking at my paddle; of cold water, dark and deep, seductive, in its silken caress.

It was a shock to feel a physical connection with that place so wild and different from country that had always informed my sense of self. Yet, as I paddled and walked that opposite shore of the Pacific Ocean, my sense of place—so local, so specific in its reference to a particular landscape—was expanded. After days of hiking over ancient caribou tracks, carved like contour lines across the steepest hills I had ever climbed, I dreamed that the tracks opened like a great trough in the earth and slowly sucked me down. My feet were no longer shod in heavy boots, but had become sharp, small, conical hooves. I woke confused. How was it that a place of which

I had known so little was taking possession of me? I had no ancestral association with this land, no possession, no childhood memories.

The landscape—its skyline of jagged mountain ranges, its cold colours—all seemed unknowable. With its vast empty spaces and lack of trees, its bears and caribou, foreign flowers, birds, insects, the tundra was an alien land. I knew no names, and though I learned some, they felt awkward on my tongue. Yet, walking this land for months, removed from the physical structures of civilisation, I began to feel a stranger no longer. I experienced a physical response to the network of living things that surrounded me. Without the presence of buildings, air conditioning and massive man-made structures, my body and mind interpreted the land with a new rawness. I came to accept that a response to the land could extend beyond kinship, beyond cultural 'ways of seeing'. My time in Alaska forced an acknowledgement of the deep interconnections between humanity and nature.

My own journeying traced a movement from estrangement to a sense of place. As I returned to Australia from Alaska, I wondered how other women who had journeyed into the wild more than a hundred years before me had made that same transition.

On 6 May 1830, seven months after her departure from England, and very pregnant, Georgiana Molloy finally stood on the beach at Augusta. How could she express the immensity of the estrangement she felt toward the New World? I can imagine her folding her hands over her hard swollen belly and picking her way along the beach, past boxes of cargo lying where they had landed, to the tent her husband had erected for her on the sand. On one side of her, the ocean heaved and sighed; behind her, the hardwood forest towered, the trunks of the trees creating a mental and physical barrier to the land where she would bear her child and make her home. Three weeks later, in the month of May, when in England Spring bursts from every hedgerow, Georgiana lay on a plank of wood in her tent, with an umbrella held over her to keep off the drips that leaked in through the canvas. Outside the rain poured down. There was no sweet scent of Spring; instead, the air was filled with the rank, harsh smell of eucalyptus. Around her the earth opened itself to welcome the winter season. Racked with contraction after contraction, Georgiana fought to give birth to her first child.

Georgiana's journey into the wilderness, 166 years before my own, captures the experience of women arriving in the New World in the early 19th Century. These were women who had literally to remake their homes out of the broken bones of their past.

Whether in Canada or Australia, they had to find ways of making sense of the strange wild places in which they found themselves. For some, like Georgiana, this process was made possible through botany. They sallied forth to collect the flowers and plants of their new homes, fitting them into an order of knowledge that made sense of their presence in the New World. Their letters home sought to capture the New World and establish the legitimacy of their presence in a landscape that often mocked their attempts at transformation.

Their movement was restricted by a culture that defined middle-class women in terms of passivity, lack of utility, and fragility, but despite this definition of their femininity, women still responded to the natural world around them. If the swish of their petticoats confined them to short walks away from the house and garden, the land around them was relatively unchanged by Western settlement. It was almost impossible for them not to respond to the land, whether to recoil in horror at the immensity of it, or to embrace its beauty and its difference and find a sense of place within it.

Settler women travelled out across the land, their thick skirts swinging wide around them, catching the mud and dirt of the new country. They barely saw the tips of their shoes as they walked through the land. Yet the reality of the land clung to them, flavouring their world and influencing their ways of seeing themselves and their new communities. Though the physical experience of the land affected these settler women at every point in their lives, those who wrote about it left only sparse traces of how they built a relationship with this new place, only glimpses of how they remade the bones of home. They wrote of their experience blinkered by English bonnets and Old World notions of picturesque beauty. Yet, despite these restrictions, women walked, rode, touched, smelt, and felt the new reality around them.

Many of them have written accounts of their lives on the frontier of the New World. Their words raise the troubling ambiguity that emerges when we confront them trying to find a relationship to place in a stolen land. Both in Australia and Canada, questions of place have become increasingly about political contesting of land and nation. But in stories of women's relationships with indigenous women, something different emerges. These often intimate portraits reveal a generosity of shared knowledge about place. Women who wrote from the frontier described the different ways of 'seeing' the land that they were given through friendships, however complex and difficult, with indigenous women. They were given a window to see, if only partially, a different and more profound view of the many layers of place where they had to make their homes. In contrast to the triumphant national narratives of the frontier as the birthplace of the nation, women's stories emphasise the family, the local, and the community. They emphasise the connective tissue between self and place, not necessarily between self and nation.

When Susan Allison climbed the steep switchbacks on the trail to the Similkameen River in British Columbia in 1868, she rode into a world already named, mapped and known to the indigenous owners of the land. But for her, riding her mare Cream Kate and following her new husband, this world was unfamiliar, potentially dangerous and very far away from the small settlement of Hope on the Fraser River where she had met him. When Mary Percy left Birmingham, England, in 1929, as a newly graduated doctor, and set out for her practice on the Peace River Prairie, one of Canada's last frontier settlements, she found herself in a world dominated by nature. Her first letters home skate the surface of her displacement as she sought something familiar to describe to her parents. She wavers between uncertainty and the promise of a land she could barely find the words to describe and which, at first, was to her eyes almost unbearably empty. When Elyne Mitchell first came to the Upper Murray Valley in Australia's Snowy Mountains in 1934, and stood on the veranda of *Towong Hill,* she looked out over an unknown landscape.

Coming to write of that moment, she evoked a cold wind that rose from the mountains and whispered of all that her future held. For Elyne this was a prophecy that held both fear and promise.

What these women sought was a sense of belonging, a desire for more than what is: 'a yearning to make skin stretch beyond individual needs and wants'.[1] These moments of expansion, when the borders of our bodies feel permeable, dispel estrangement from a new environment. Women gave shape and form to their experiences on the land by writing about it. Their stories are personal, domestic, and they break down the specific national myths of women's frontier role. If we talk about the pursuit of this sense of belonging in our histories, a pursuit articulated in the stories of the women in this book, then the discussion moves away from the conventional boundaries that form national histories and beyond the adversarial arguments within nations about place.

At the heart of the writing of women such as Georgiana Molloy, Susan Allison, Mary Percy Jackson and Elyne Mitchell lies a physical confrontation between the land and their bodies. It is a confrontation that has been ignored in national histories. This book explores the expression of this embodied experience through language. What surprised me as I researched these women's lives was that the history that emerged was not national in its boundaries, but shared a commonality of experience across race, across space and across time.

In both Australia and Canada, women's sense of place has been represented as reflected strictly within the confines of the home or, by extension, the garden—that is, the private sphere, its margins delineated by the homestead fence.[2] In Australia it has been argued that white women found this alleged confinement to the private sphere intolerable and so departed from the country altogether, as if the whole continent were hostile to women.[3] Randolph Stow has argued that the metaphor of imprisonment haunts Australian literature,[4] and anyone who has read Australian poetry or fiction is familiar with the bitter bush woman.

Yet, when I first came across this imaginary woman, she made little sense to *me*. At the same time, her tenuous grip on sanity in the face of a hostile and repellent land was somehow fascinating. As a student I was strongly influenced by this persuasive tradition and wrote a portrait of a woman on a veranda looking out over dry paddocks as she picked distractedly at the seam of a dress she was hemming. Her hands, the creases in her skin, were embedded with red dust. Her shoes, dress, the very seam she unpicked was covered in a heavy layer of bull dust, so thick that it pervaded not only her home, her clothes, and her skin, but had started to unhinge her mind. She could feel it working its way in; soon there would be nothing left for the drifting dust to claim.

But why did I construct such a woman? Certainly it wasn't from the reality of the older women I knew from rural communities. Though these members of my grandmother's generation were inheritors of a tamed frontier and had the use of electricity and running water, many remembered their lives before these modernisations. They recalled a hard life and a different use of their time and labour, but not necessarily a different understanding of their place in the land.

My mother remembers going 'chipping' with my grandmother every evening. My grandmother would tell me that she would take the children and walk with them out into the paddocks to collect fuel for the old wood water heater. This was an important part of the day for her. It was a release from the house and a chance to walk in the open spaces of the paddocks. Later, when there was electricity, running water, and grown-up children, she continued to walk in the evening, a stout stick and overweight Labrador by her side. Her task was different, but her motivation to be out in the afternoon was the same.[5]

My dust woman represented the popular view of women pioneers in the Australian bush. The portrait holds suffering, relentless labour, hopelessness and the loss of femininity, all of which exist in our histories. But what it doesn't allow is any sort of creative engagement with the land.

When I looked at the diaries and letters of Australian pioneer women, I found abundant evidence for the construction of a fictional woman claimed by the dust.[6] In those diaries and letters, I found her alone, isolated and fearful for her family's survival. She seemed to claw out a home to reflect some part of herself, rather than the incomprehensible land to which she had come. These stories are in our histories, certainly, but like my dust woman, they aren't the whole story. But where were the other stories? Where were the women from whom I had inherited a love of the land, a deep sense of belonging? Women who had lived on the land all their lives, who had loved it, struggled on it, wept over it, but ultimately saw themselves as intimately and creatively connected to it?[7]

There is a picture of a girl riding a horse in the Canadian west in the early 1900s that seems to capture the 'opposite other' to my dust-maddened construction of women's frontier experience. In this picture the girl looks confidently into the camera. She is riding astride, the reins held looped in one hand, a small stockwhip dangling from the other. It is a tall horse she's riding, not big but lanky, a youngster, not yet attained to his full strength of bone and brawn, but ready to make up for it in high spirits. In the photo the horse looks tired, but he is still rolling his eye, and the camera has caught him attempting to slide away from her request to stand still. His movement looks to be on the point of a spin, a duck, a weave, an attempt to unseat his rider. She, in turn, sits him in a manner that suggests that the effort required to unseat her would be considerable. She is completely at home on the back of this youngster as she is in the land that he shifts uneasily over. She is the granddaughter, metaphorically, of the woman exiled in a strange land.

By looking at women's lives and their various responses to the landscapes of Canada and Australia, this book explores the ways in which frontier myths in both countries have served to silence and marginalise white women's experience and their role in articulating how we 'belong'. Far from allowing white women a presence in the new land, chronicles of pioneering and taming the land have represented them as confined to the domestic space of the house and garden, absent and alienated from the drama of nation building.

Canadian history shares with Australia the perceived hostility of the New World to women. This has been called a garrison mentality.[8] Women on the frontier have been represented as garrisoned behind fences and gardens, and within forts, from the strange New World they have come to inhabit. As in Australian literature and history, there is the same fear of imprisonment, a fear residing in women's lack of mobility and reliance on this garrisoned world for survival.

In Australia there has been a fascination with women who have lived in, escaped from or perished in a wilderness prison.[9] The story of the death of Mary Watson is emblematic of this tradition. In 1881 Mary, her husband, their infant son and two Chinese men lived on Lizard Island, off the Queensland coast.[10] The Watsons were engaged in making a quick fortune from the lucrative beche-de-mer industry.[11] In September, during one of Mary's husband's long absences at sea, Aboriginal men returned to the Island to carry out important initiation ceremonies. After one of the Chinese men was killed and the other wounded, Mary loaded her baby and the injured man into a tiny iron tank and paddled them out to sea. Four months later they were found dead only ten miles from the mainland.

Watson's death is recognised by one of the few monuments built to commemorate the lives of individual women of achievement living on the frontier.[12] But she wasn't really a woman of achievement. Rather, her tragic death and the monument commemorating it reinforce the accepted idea that the frontier was no place for a white woman.

Many of the women in this book refute this representation of white women's experience of the land. Rather, their lives and writing seek connections between themselves and the New World. They reach out and claim a sense of belonging to land and community. In writing about how they do this, I have to confront the moral and political implications of the troubling knowledge that, in Australia and Canada, non-indigenous women's sense of place rests upon and may serve to obscure ancestral acts of dispossession and theft.[13] The women in this book cover the spectrum of responses to indigenous land ownership.

Some, like the Métis woman Marie Rose Smith, have an embedded understanding of the impact of dispossession on the indigenous prairie people of Canada. In Australia, Alice Duncan Kemp writes of how her knowledge and love of the Channel Country in South West Queensland is both informed by her relationship with the indigenous people and allowed a voice because of her ancestors' role in dispossessing those same people from their land.[14] Other women, like Elyne Mitchell in the Snowy Mountains, have written of their custodial role in looking after the land, but Mitchell's appropriation of that role, though sensitive to place, slides over the continuing relationship between Aboriginal people and the Snowy Mountains. And yet other women, like Monica Hopkins in Alberta Canada, seemed blind to their role in the displacement of an entire nation of people.

Underneath these responses to place sits the grief of stolen land. Women's place in this process has always been difficult to pin down. In Canada and Australia, we are still trying to find ways of talking about our 'haunted country'.[15]

In Australia, the poet Judith Wright has given us ways of imagining the duality of grief and love over the same land. Wright acknowledges that she was 'born of the conquerors', but still asserts her strong sense of place in the land of her birth.[16] In her poem *At Cooloolah,* she imagines her desire to belong to the land alongside images of the historical reality of dispossession, 'a black accoutred warrior armed for fight'. Ghosts challenge her right to share the calm of the lake, to leave prints in clean sand like those of the birds and animals. Though Wright knew and loved this place, with its Aboriginal name, yet, walking along by the lake, she was made 'uneasy' and felt 'unloved' by 'all her eyes delight in'. Her poem voiced a fear of the land itself—for it recognised no invader, and was neither won nor lost.

Wright's poetry grapples with her own history on the land. Her heritage, descended from a network of pioneer families in the New England area of New South Wales, had given her a privileged upbringing. Such privilege was a direct result of the wealth her family received from dispossessing the Aboriginal people who spoke Aneuwan.[17] Though Judith Wright acknowledged the dispossession that allowed her to walk upon the land, she also responded to the land and found her own self, defined through her sense of place. Her poetry is alert to the double vision that can exist within a sense of place in the settlements of the New World. For Judith Wright, no matter her depth of feeling for the land, there would be a deeply buried unease that a non-indigenous sense of place will always be based on stolen land.[18]

And yet, in these women's stories, there is hope. For their experiences leave us with images of relationships between women of different cultures and between woman and land. Their experiences are our inheritance, stitches in our history that connect our past with our future.

What is a sense of place? Why is a relationship with place so fundamental to our identity as individuals and as communities? A sense of place is a complex connection between land and self. Place is both inside and outside; it takes us beyond ourselves and exists outside of ourselves, yet allows us to make sense of ourselves. Attachments to place are born into us, but they are also formed through movement, through labour, through words. The expression of a sense of place is difficult to pin down. It shifts constantly and eludes precise definition.

A sense of place can arise from alienation and overcome exile, so that a strange land may be imaginatively possessed. But it is not necessary to own land to have a sense of place. Sense of place has to do with the timelessness and universality of myths; it is bound up in stories about ourselves as individuals and the connections we make with each other.

When I travelled to Alaska, I went as a young woman, confident of my own geographically specific sense of place. What I discovered when I got there was a world completely different in every way to the one I had left behind. The extremity of the experience made me profoundly aware of my body in an entirely new way. After a few weeks of living outside, I began to feel as if I no longer stopped at my skin, but extended out into the air around me. I would feel a shift in the wind, a shadow across the sun, the flight of a bird overhead and respond to it before my mind filtered the information I wanted from these moments. It was from this trip that questions arose for me about how we relate to place as individuals and communities, how we need connections to place, both spiritually and corporeally.

In the summer of 2001, I walked slowly with my grandmother around her garden, just over the hill from 'my' jumble of rocks. She had planted this garden over sixty years, and now it was my aunt's. This was her first visit back after a broken hip and a cancer scare. She seemed frail, reliant on her stick, yet our slow movement was overlaid for me with sensations of the strength in her arms as she pushed me on the swing as a child, or dug in the garden. We stood beneath the prunus tree, with its deep purple shade, its strong colour a point of definition against the lighter green of the elms and white cedars, and she talked of the time she had planted the trees and nursed them through the drought. Outside the garden, the paddocks hummed with life. The trees structured the view to the east and west. The garden was a frame for the land beyond it. In the evening's rich light, the sheep were strung across the paddocks like furry cysts. The cattle shone ruby red.

When my grandmother arrived in 1936, the house had been little more than a shed and the garden a bowl of dust. She came as a young woman and faced the task of making this place, this bare spot on the hill, with its beautiful views, into a home. With an architect's eye, she structured the bones of a home that sheltered four children and then another generation of grandchildren. Now, as an old woman, she looked at the covering of love and laughter, grief and loss that was stitched into the land we stood on.

Nine months later we would gather as a family in the big garden and walk down the paddock to the treeline below. We buried her next to my grandfather and cousin, beneath the flowering gums, in the place that she had loved into a home.

Her memories have become my memories, as we have shared the site of their occurrence. I know the places she would tell me about when she used to walk in the paddocks to escape the confines of the house for an hour. I know the sounds she knew: the running beat of drumming hooves, as the cunning old ewes forced the garden gate. I know the shrubs from which they would tear hurried mouthfuls. Our memories are held in *place*. All I have to do to receive a hundred such memories is recall that place.

In the lives of women who have lived on the land, the centrality of place holds their memories of love and laughter, pain and grief, anguish and joy. Place forms an indistinguishable part of themselves, which links them to the land through their bodies, minds and spirits. Despite all the obstacles of gender, of race, of alienation, I grew up knowing women who have always found ways to connect to the world around them. This memory ultimately rejects the stereotype of the dust woman.

And these women's stories show us that women on the land not only suffered, but loved. A sense of place linked them to the land. It provided the means of connection to the world beyond their bodies. Their realities were shaped by place, as the reality of place was expressed through their words. These women could say as the poet Barbara Schott wrote, *I know this land and I know its language.*[19]

The broken bones of home

Georgiana Molloy and Mary O'Brien

Chapter one

At a Deepening
Of the Isingless River
I lie down in stones &
Tea-colored water.
I think: be careful. Do not say
Home. The bones
Of that word mend slowly.[1]

Marie Harris

The poet's words 'I think: be careful. Do not say home', made me pause in my reading and stand in a different place, to see what—distrust? The murmur of the river, of water over stone, whispered, 'be careful, be careful'. Do not give yourself to something that is not known, that could betray at any moment, and spit you out a shell, rattling with the emptiness of a past that has no meaning in this new place.

The restraint in the poem shifted my perspective from the inability of these early women to write about the land, to an appreciation of the brokenness from which they were rebuilding their identities and homes. The poem forced me to take on questions about how, in their letters and journals, pioneer women thought about themselves in response to a new land about which they knew very little, and on which they had staked their future.

When Mary O'Brien and Georgiana Molloy set out from England at the end of the 1820s, both of them took 'the broken bones of home' to the New World. They packed the ideas of home, along with nails, hinges, doors and timber. Just as important as the tools for building a home in the wilderness were the associations that evoked a comfortable space and the activities that enacted home. These elements wove the fabric of their selves and, out of these elements, a home would be rebuilt in an alien land. The philosopher Gaston Bachelard argues that 'all really inhabited space bears the essence of the notion of home ... that the imagination functions in this direction whenever human beings have found the slightest shelter'.[2] The impulse to make a home was one of the strongest themes of women's lives as they moved out along the frontier. As the poet hints, the bones of what had been home and what would become home required careful tending, a deep involvement of a woman's self in the New World around her.

Mary O'Brien (1798) and Georgiana Molloy (1805) were born into a time of great upheaval and change in English society. The end of the war with Napoleon marked the beginning of large-scale emigration to the New World. The lure of cheap land and new opportunities proved irresistible, especially for middle-class families who found themselves in reduced circumstances. In 1815, directly after the

*Mary Sophia Gapper (O'Brien),
Miniature Portrait (1828).*

end of the Napoleonic War, only two thousand people emigrated from England; by 1819, when the majority of servicemen had been discharged and had faced long periods of unemployment in England's depressed economy, that figure rose to thirty-four thousand.[3] It was this movement of people that carried Mary O'Brien to Canada in 1828 and Georgiana Molloy to Western Australia in 1829.

Mary was thirty when she began her journey to Upper Canada[4] with her mother, brother and sister-in-law. Georgiana was twenty-four years old, newly married and three months pregnant when she departed for the tiny colonial outpost of Swan River[5] with her husband Captain John Molloy. Both women grew up in the urban British middle class. They had a lot more in common than the experience of emigration. They were both highly literate, well-educated, genteel women; neither possessed practical skills for pioneering.

Mary had spent a period of her youth in rigorous study at a private school and was a skilled linguist, speaking and translating Italian, German and French.[6] Georgiana experienced a more typical middle-class education. Private tutors taught her in history, geography, literature, sewing, dancing and playing the pianoforte and harp. Both women were taught embroidery, fine sewing, sampler-work, and drawing and painting.[7] None of these skills were of any practical use when it came to grappling with the physical tasks of pioneering.

Yet there was one element of Mary and Georgiana's impractical education that provided them—and many other women in the 19th Century—with a point of access into a hostile and alien landscape: both women were encouraged to study botany. At the beginning of the nineteenth century, it was believed by both layman and scientist alike that God was in everything. Middle-class women were encouraged to study nature, for here the essence of God was revealed.[8] So Mary and Georgiana were taught to *botanise*, that is identify, collect and draw plants according to their botanical family. Botany was considered a legitimate feminine activity.[9] It served as an unlikely point of introduction to the New World for women, an outlet for their curiosity as they combed the land in search of new specimens. It was this skill, learnt in their girlhood and practised with passion in England, that would become crucial to both Mary and Georgiana as they attempted to make sense of the apparently disordered and chaotic new world.

Like many women who journeyed to Australia and Canada, Mary and Georgiana both wrote of their experiences. Their extensive journals and letters were written for a personal audience, with no thought of publication.[10] Though Mary wrote for newspapers and translated German books for herself and her community, her journal was an intimate record of her changing self and her family's daily life.[11] Both wrote to inform their family and friends at 'home' of the shape and texture of their new lives. They also wrote for themselves, as these changes challenged the foundations of their identity as middle-class women. They wrote to make sense of their experience and, through the medium of writing, they sought the connections between what had been 'home' and what would become 'home'.[12]

When Mary wrote to her friend Cara in an attempt to express her enjoyment of the Canadian woods, she was frustrated that Cara could not appreciate her new self in this new place. She wrote, 'The woods where I now am are a perfect garden and I never look at them without thinking of you and wishing I could have you to admire them with me—the great drawback to my present enjoyment is that some of those I love the very best cannot share them or even understand precisely what they are.'[13]

It was this problem of translation that Mary sought to articulate through the entries in her journal.

Mary's journal was one of the first texts that I read when I began to research the experience of Canadian women on the frontier. Her translation of her sense of estrangement, her ambivalence towards the new landscape, and her wonder seemed to reflect my own attempts to come to grips with a foreign country. I could relate to Mary's attempt to describe exactly what she meant when she talked about walking in the 'woods'. I too was fascinated by how difficult I found describing what the Canadian 'woods' looked like in my letters home and how they were different from the 'bush'.

Mary's journal opens on 1 September 1828 with a firmly constructed picture of herself as the thirty-year-old spinster, very much in the tradition of the maiden aunt. The voyage to Canada was to be an interlude, an adventure in the mask of duty; both she and her mother were looking forward to returning to England and picking up the threads of their lives. Her journal provided little snippets which can be pieced together to form a picture of a woman of independent mind, but apparently weakening body.[14] As I read I had to remind myself that she was only thirty. Her first journal entries portray her as a gouty old spinster setting off with journal in hand to see her brothers safely settled in Canada. She would then, she wrote with assurance, return to her life in England.

Through her writing Mary found the images to connect her worlds. 'I begin now to feel that the ocean we are traversing is indeed the pathway to dear Bill and that by only moving my horses' heads it will lead me back again to the friends I have left behind.'[15] This was an unusual metaphor to use. For Mary the ocean was a pathway, the physical means of connection between the two worlds that held her loved ones, rather than an emblem of distance and separation. Though she did not conceive of her journey to Canada as anything more than a visit, her use of this image was an indication of how strongly she thought of herself as the mobile part of her family. As the only unmarried daughter, she was able to move backwards and forwards wherever she was most needed, whether that be Canada or England.

Mary's writing stressed connectedness, and it was through her journal that she sought to hold her two worlds together. 'My highest enjoyment,' she wrote, 'is that of writing my journal for then I feel that Ivy and Cara and perhaps a few other stray friends are in some sort partaking my pleasures.'[16] As her journal progressed, its role as interpreter of Mary's new self became more important as the gap between old and new widened. From the beginning, her journal writing was a priority in her life.

Mary's journey by sea and then overland through upstate New York took a total of six weeks. She wrote as a traveller; observant and eager to record everything she could see, touch, feel and smell. Not all women emigrants responded in this way to what they essentially perceived to be a term of exile. Louisa Meredith, who left England in 1839 for Australia, and whose journey was four months by sea, wrote as a woman in exile from her home.[17] Like Mary, she undertook the journey with every intention of returning to England within five years.[18] Unlike Mary, Louisa, who travelled with her husband Charles Meredith, imagined her journey only in terms of separation, isolation and alienation. She used the powerful image of the change in constellations: the idea that the very sky above was different provided an effective metaphor for emigrants to the southern hemisphere. Louisa wrote:

> I do not know one thing that I felt so much as the loss of the North Star. Night after night I watched it, sinking lower—lower; ... it was like parting from own loved home-faces once again. ... Those stars seemed like a last link uniting us, but it was soon broken—they sunk beneath the horizon, and the new constellations of the southern hemisphere seemed to my partial eyes far less splendid.[19]

For Mary O'Brien, still in the northern hemisphere, the landscape was somewhat familiar both

to her and her audience. The plants, trees and seasons shared shape and cycle with those in England,
and though everything was on a larger scale, it could
all be fitted into a known order of things. Yet she
still scrabbled for the words and images to describe
the land and society for her audience in England. Of
upstate New York she wrote: 'I endeavor in vain to
find a parallel scene; England is too flat and Wales
too barren and both too small'.[20] She tried to fit
what she saw into landscapes known by her audience, but no description quite worked; everything
seemed just beyond her audience's experience.

> Our way lies thro' the Mohawk Valley close by the
> side of the river. I immediately recognised the scenery
> of the Pioneers and found that in fact we were
> approaching it ... the river is a wide, shallow stream
> and a line of hills run on each side covered with
> forest but with so much intermixed that it has
> nothing of wilderness, tho' much of beauty beyond
> anything of the kind that I have seen. If Cooper's
> description has given you as correct an idea of it as
> it did me, my description will be superfluous; if
> not availing.[21]

As soon as Mary landed in the New World at
New York, she was looking for points of comparison, points of familiarity. She was surprised to see
how many English flowers there were 'amongst
many that were new to me'.[22] From the moment she

landed, she started collecting flowers and shrubs and though they were travelling every day, she attempted to botanise at each stop.

> I have done better than I could have expected with botany—I have not however the scientific pleasure of finding a new genus but there is a pleasure distinct from that and not an inconsiderable one, which I take in making new acquaintance with the near relations of my old friends.[23]

This action of collecting plant specimens brought her into physical contact with the new land and gave her an activity that took her out of herself and her preoccupations with her health. Her exploration and documentation of what she saw was not unusual in the writing of middle-class emigrant women. The most obvious limitation to women's explorations as they journeyed was the burden of pregnancy or small children. In 1828 Mary had no children and therefore had the time and energy to take a walk at the end of a day's travel, as well as the leisure to record her impressions afterwards.

Mary's account of her arrival and first impressions of Canada was dominated by two very different factors. Firstly, she had journeyed with her 'dear Mama' to visit her brothers and see them safely settled into their new homes. The beginning of her account was written in the tradition of the travel journal, comparing, contrasting and recording

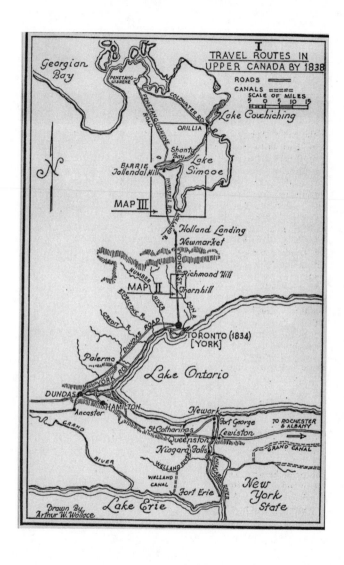

Map of Lake Ontario, Canada, showing
'Thornhill' and Lake Simcoe.

everything that she saw and experienced. Mary's second agenda in writing her journal was to provide the means by which her sister Lucy could be included in the travel experience. As she wrote she built up the scene of a longed-for reunion with her brothers. Mary sampled the New World as a visitor and her early journals have none of the intensity of the settler who, in leaving England, had cut all ties.

In fact, it would be many years before Mary returned to England. However, because she had assumed the mantle of an observer, her writing had none of the breathless, desperate quality that some women conveyed as they battled to find their way in an alien land. Mary was greeted by two dearly loved brothers and a reasonably established and success-ful home. The farm, *Thornhill*, was only 12 miles outside of the major settlement of Upper Canada, the town of York, later Toronto. Mary wrote of her arrival with an almost girlish glee. The tone marked a turning point in her journal as she began to move beyond her role as the invalid unmarried com-panion to her mother, into a more active role as sister and helper to her brothers. In contrast to the tone of despair in many women's accounts of the rupture between their old and new home, Mary's was celebratory:

> Seeing a door open and the figure of a man inter-cepting the light that issued from it, we jumped over some high rails that opposed our progress and

I arrived first at the door. ... We were soon all
seated around Southby's fireside and tea table ...
It was a pleasure to look upon dear Bill again, looking well, though not as young, as at Charlton,
and to hear Anthony's voice with all its wonted
originality.[24]

Mary had chosen her images carefully. The figure
standing in the door was illuminated by a halo of
light; the home was described as a mirror image
of the comforts they had left in England, and their
reunion took place around a 'civilised' tea-table in
front of a blazing fire. She also highlighted her sister-
in-law's pregnancy as a justification that her nursing
skills were needed in Canada, and her decision to
come had been the right one. Again, her journal
served as a link between herself and her sister.
Through the journal Lucy was included in the
reunion, indeed in the whole experience of exploration and adventure. At this stage Mary continued
to write as an observer of the ways of pioneering. As
her relationship to the land changed, she would
move from an observer to a participant.

Mary's early journals were filled with her movement through the land, accompanying her brothers
on trips outside the settled area of their farms. Her
journal was filled with descriptions of the land, as if
it would only then reveal itself in its true form to
her through words. As she continued to write, she
seemed to have an ongoing conversation about

whether she could respond to the landscape and enjoy being in it, as she had in England.

> The face of Nature has been so generally uniform since I have been here and I so shackled in my power of looking on it that I have almost ceased to look till my attention was caught at sunset by the tips of the pines which bound our view to the east— we went out to look ... and found the horizon coloured of the most beautiful chastened purple— But however this may look on paper the fact that in spite of woods and echoes and bugles and axes— this country is not a stimulating one.[25]

Her efforts of description were detective-like in their intensity. Of the land it was as if she asked these things: are you plain, unfinished, picturesque on paper, but lacking in depth, or are you more than I have seen, more than I have allowed; is there something in the depths of your woods that I have failed to see?

As Mary grew in confidence, she began to walk and ride into the cleared fields and gradually entered the woods. At first she accompanied her brothers, particularly Anthony, in his botanising expeditions and then gradually she went alone. Through her botany she was able to transform the alien into the known, both for herself and her audience. This movement gave her the tools to respond, not out of displacement, but from the security of being able to place what she saw into a known order. In a month she had moved from describing the woods as being 'so generally uniform' that she had stopped looking at them, to tapping the maple trees for their sap[26] in work that transformed the way she saw the woods.

> To me the woods are hardly less attractive in the dreariness of their winter aspect (than) in the full luxury of their summer foliage—for still their echoes convert every sound into music and the very air breathes a freedom which I do not find any-where else except on the blue waves of the ocean.[27]

By March of 1829, five months after her arrival, Mary had become so confident that she scrambled in the woods by herself, finding places that became favourite spots, where she would return in her wan-derings. She had moved from a position of curiosity about what the woods might hold to describing their hidden spots and places, where only a bold scrambler could penetrate.

> I scrambled down the banks over trunks of fallen cedars crossing each other or using them for bridges to gain the point at which I aimed where at the foot of the largest tree I sat on the snow close to the brink of the stream which had partially liberated itself from the ice and stole away thro' the dark glen.[28]

As Mary moved through the land, the greater her ease and the stronger her desire to stay. Her earlier focus on her health seemed almost forgotten and, as she crammed the journal with descriptions of her expeditions with her brother Anthony, she learned not to be an invalid.[29] Her keen observation skills and her ability to sketch made her a useful addition to his expeditions. Increasingly, Anthony and Mary had a third companion on their collecting trips.

Mr O'Brien appears in Mary's journal in April 1829, though there is barely a hint of any attraction on Mary's behalf. She dismisses him thus: 'tho' a very intelligent, well informed, decent and gentlemanly man, I missed the high-souled sentiment and exalted principle which seem to carry us above this dirty world. ... A's [Anthony's] bright eyes and glowing countenance however make up for all deficiencies.'[30] After this rather backhanded compliment, the journal makes it obvious that Mary enjoyed O'Brien's company. He made her laugh and think of herself as young enough to have her own family, rather than looking after everyone else's. This unlooked-for romance confused and perplexed Mary. As Mr O'Brien filled more and more of the journal, she still signalled to her family that she intended returning to England in the Spring. But in the meantime, she meant to enjoy every moment of her time in Canada.

In July of 1829 Mary travelled with her brother Southby and Mr O'Brien to Lake Simcoe to locate the backwood lots to which both men were entitled as half-pay officers. It was these backwood lots that made emigrating to Upper Canada so attractive to retired army officers on half pay. They were able to claim the lots simply by 'improving' them. But for Mary, the journey made on horseback and then by canoe and schooner up the lake was significant, for though she could not have seen into the future, this visit was her first glimpse of the lake that she would come to call 'home'.

Over the next few months, she increasingly turned to her journal in an attempt to write out her confusion. In August 1829 she was still writing to her brother Anthony, now back in England, that 'if Lucy does not come out, I think we shall certainly come home in the Spring'.[31] But by December she was going into the woods to seek solace and peace away from the confusion of her thoughts and a torn sense of duty.

> I sat down on a log by the side of the creek to think ... and lay down on a bank at the foot of a pair of hemlocks to employ my mind more fitly in resigning my hopes and fears, my joys and sorrows, my will and ways into His hands—It is so easy to do this in the woods where peace and holiness and mercy seem to reign alone—brought back some

little cedars, &c., which I planted in spite of the frost.[32]

Perhaps this time in the woods brought some clarity to her thinking, for it was less than a month later when she wrote to Lucy in a private letter entered in the journal, asking for a release for herself and her mother from their promise to return to England. In her succinct way she ended her letter with this request: 'Thus then what I would have you understand is this—We should both very much prefer living in Canada but it must be with you.'[33]

There was no compulsion for Mary and her 'Mama' to stay. Their decision demonstrates a remarkable change in their attitude, which for Mary could partly be attributed to the pressure being applied by the Irishman, Edward O'Brien, for her hand in marriage. However, Mary was a loyal and dutiful sister, devoted to her family; she would not consider marriage unless her brothers and sister released her from her duty as a housekeeper and nurse in their respective houses. For Lucy, separated by time and distance, the request would not have come as a great surprise; reading the journal she would have noted the increasing presence of Mr O'Brien.

Mary's decision to accept his proposal signalled Lucy's approval and Mary's commitment to her place in the New World. In May 1830 Mary married Edward O'Brien and moved to his farm only a few miles from her family at *Thornhill*.

At the same time as Mary was writing to her sister, seeking her blessing to stay in Canada, Georgiana Molloy was two-and-a-half months into her journey to the tiny colonial outpost of Swan River in Western Australia. She was five months pregnant, newly married and physically more wretched than she had ever been before.

Georgiana Molloy, Miniature Portrait, (1829).

Like Mary, she was given a choice of going forward into the unknown—or of staying at its edge, waiting in Cape Town, for the birth of her first child. The Molloys had taken twelve weeks to reach Cape Town and the exposed passage between Cape Town and Western Australia was still ahead of them. The temptation must have been strong to accept the invitation of Catherine Bell, the wife of Molloy's old friend Colonel John Bell, to stay until after the birth of her first child.[34] The Cape was rife with reports of disaster at Swan River, rumours that supplies were so scarce that people were on the edge of starvation, grants were unoccupied, and the best land had been taken up by absentee settlers. In short, the colony had failed.[35] Despite this, Georgiana chose to continue, later writing to her family, 'I was determined to follow my husband under all circumstances'.[36]

She could not have foreseen that her decision to follow her husband would mean that she would give birth to her first child on a beach in the pouring rain. Or that they'd have such a task to clear the land and build a house that she could make into a home. When the Molloys arrived at Augusta, they were faced with a forest of trees larger and more magnificent than they had imagined possible. But the settlers did not understand that this abundance did not translate into fertile soil[37]. The immensity of the natural world must have mocked their early attempts to make homes. How much more did Georgiana feel this as she struggled to feed her tiny baby Elizabeth Mary.

The baby had trouble feeding, being too weak to suck strongly. Georgiana had no midwife to show her how to coax the baby to suck, and no older woman to assure her that she was doing everything within her power to help the baby live. Despite Georgiana's fight for her survival, little Elizabeth

Arrival at Augusta, May 1830.

Mary developed blisters and rashes all over her body, and lived for only nine days.

It was over three years before Georgiana was able to write to her friend Helen Storey and relate her distress at Elizabeth Mary's death. Georgiana's despair sits heavy in her letter to her closest friend, who had also just lost a child. Though Georgiana had gone on to have a healthy baby girl, the language in the letter shows how close to the surface the deadening grief sat.

> I could truly sympathize with you, for language refuses to utter what I experienced when mine died in my arms in this dreary land, with no one but Molloy near me. O, I have gone through much and more than I would ever suffer anyone to do again ... I thought I might have one little bright object left me to solace all the hardships and privations I endured and have still to go through.[38]

The Molloys buried their baby in a grave planted with English rye grass and clover.[39] For the settlers, planting English seeds and establishing a garden was an important connection between the Old and the New Worlds.[40] In the same letter to Helen Storey, Georgiana wrote of her baby's grave: 'Its grace, though sodded with British clover looks so singular and solitary in this wilderness, that I can scarcely give you an idea.'[41]

Two weeks after the death of baby Elizabeth, Georgiana started a garden behind her tent. All around the unfamiliar pressed in, and the need to clear the land and plant vegetables and crops, erect fences and build huts was not only a physical need, but also a psychological one. In a landscape empty of the cycles of life by which Europeans defined the seasons and themselves, her garden transformed the small space around her. She planted flowers and shrubs that meant home. There was English jasmine, yucca lilies given to her by her mother, bulbs she had brought from the Cape and a variety of seeds she had packed from England.

However, with the death of little Elizabeth Mary, Georgiana seemed to have become anaesthetised from the world beyond her garden. It was as if she could not see it. She who loved beauty and wildness and saw the hand of God revealed in nature turned away from this new land as if it physically repelled her. Unlike Mary O'Brien, Georgiana asked no questions of it; instead, she seemed to shrink from it. In November 1832, two years after her arrival, she wrote to her sister of the home she had created on the edge of the forbidding Australian bush. It was the domestic realm of the garden she described, dismissing the land beyond that as 'unbounded'.[42]

This is certainly a very beautiful place—but were it not for the domestic charms the eye of the emmi-grant [sic] would soon weary of the unbounded limits of thickly clothed dark green forests where nothing can be described to feast the imagination … Our clime is heavenly, and while you are burning the front breadth of your frock and the nebs of your shoes at an excellent fire of Newcastle coals, I am sitting in the Verandah surrounded by my little flower garden of British, Cape and Australian flowers pouring forth their odour (for the large white lily is now in bloom) and a variety of little birds most brilliant in plumage sporting around me.[43]

Some critics of women's autobiographical writings have argued that the sea journey created a new identity in the emigrant woman.[44] Historians have sought different ways of describing this transformation. Arnold Toynbee in *A Study of History* (1935) first labelled this process a 'sea change'.[45] Toynbee used the image of emigrants packing their belongings onto the ship before they left the shore and then unpacking them before they could make themselves 'at home'. His point was that these 'belongings', which included techniques, institutions and ideas, did not always look the same after they were unpacked in the New World. 'Anything that cannot stand the sea voyage at all has simply to be left behind; and many things—and these are not only material objects—which the migrants do manage to take with them can only be shipped after they have been taken to pieces—never, perhaps, to be reassembled in their original form.'[46]

This theory has been applied to the experience of Canadian emigrant women such as Susanna Moodie and her sister Catherine Parr Traill.[47] It is perhaps more pronounced in the Australian experience, as the voyage was so much longer and more arduous, and the land so different in shape and form upon arrival.[48] If, as Gillian Whitlock argues, emigration 'initiates a new consciousness of the self', then for Georgiana this journey was pregnant with possibilities for her new self as a settler and a mother of her family. Her landing at Augusta, hugely swollen with child, carried through the surf by her husband, and then placed upon the beach that formed the entrance into the land, was the beginning of her new life.

But in many ways Georgiana refused to become involved in any translation of self. Her experience typified other pioneer women's harsh induction into the reality of making a home in a land which, for them, was an alien wilderness. In describing the land as possessed of 'unbounded limits', she described a land both without boundaries and yet held within limits. There was tension in the two images. The land was singularly indistinguishable. She could see no difference in it; sameness piled upon sameness, simply endless wilderness. Mary O'Brien had expressed the same sentiments in describing the Canadian woods as 'genuinely uniform'. Yet the land also imposed limits on Georgiana. Its very bound-lessness, its lack of features, its lack of recognisable limits, and her inability to understand it, had her trapped.

What she could describe, and immerse herself in, was the plot of land around her house. It was her gardening that eventually introduced her to the land. Almost against her own will, she was responding to the new land, as she learned a new cycle of nature. For Mary, who planted three gardens in Upper Canada, the seasons were more powerful in their expression but similar in their cycle to England. The plants that grew wild in the woods may have been unfamiliar, but they were often related to flowers and plants that evoked 'home', plants that Mary referred to in her journal as 'dear friends'.[49]

For Georgiana, all was new, and all was reversed. To plant her garden she needed to understand the direction of the sun at different times of the day, the hottest parts of the garden and those that were pro-tected from the bitter winds. Her garden contained both reminders of the past and a promise of the future; significantly, it contained her present. Through planting and watching and waiting, Georgiana became conscious of the new movement of the seasons as they appeared, even if her response was limited to the small plot of land overlooking the inlet of Hardy's Bay. After two years of settle-ment, her letter to her sister acknowledged beauty, but it was beauty within the boundaries of a transformed world.

By then she had suffered not only the death of a child, but also a miscarriage, alone and isolated from medical attention, before the birth of a healthy baby girl.[50] The rhythm of her days and the tasks she undertook were very similar to those Mary O'Brien was performing on the shores of Shanty Bay. The difference was that Georgiana wished she had never come. Her garden was her garrison against the wilderness in which she dared to make her home. She was dislocated and in exile, despite the breathtaking place in which she lived, despite her comfortable home and healthy child and despite the climate and the promise of a better life for her children. In her letters she sounds exhausted, frustrated and lonely. She wrote to her friend Margaret Dunlop in January 1833:

> My head aches. I have all the clothes to put away from the wash; baby to put to bed; make tea and drink it without milk, as they shot our cow for a trespass; read prayers and go to bed besides sending off this tableful of letters. I wish I had you here to help me. What golden dreams we used to have about your coming to stay with me! How would you like to be three years in a place without a female of your own rank to speak to or to be with you whatever happened?[51]

At this point Georgiana fitted the stereotype of pioneering women; she was alienated and displaced, isolated from friends and family; she was exhausted and burdened by childbearing and hard physical work. Unlike mothers of her social class in England, who would have employed a wet nurse to feed their babies, Georgiana breastfed all her children. She wrote to Margaret Dunlop, 'I need not blush to tell you I am, of necessity, my own nursery-maid'.[52] She only had one female servant at this time, and as well as nursing her Sabina, Georgiana cooked, washed and mended all the clothes of the household. She also undertook a major share of the paperwork generated by her husband's position as resident magistrate.

It was to her garden that she turned for relief from the monotony of domesticity. But although she took joy from her flowers, after two-and-a-half years in Australia, she rarely mentioned the bush, nor ventured into it. It was a heaving presence on the edge of her world, which she blocked out with the profusion of plants in her own garden. Unlike Mary on the other side of the world, for whom many of the flowers, trees and shrubs were 'familiar cousins to dear friends', Georgiana had nothing that was familiar to coax her into entering the bush. Even the wild flowers, which she loved, were alien in their appearance. They were small, insignificant, save in a mass. They had no perfume and their colour 'fled' when she picked them.[53]

Two events changed the way she saw the land around her. In December 1836 she received a letter and a box of seeds from the English horticulturist, Captain James Mangles. Captain Mangles was a cousin of Ellen Stirling, the young wife of Governor Stirling, who shared Georgiana's interest in flowers, and who had suggested her friend as a likely agent for Mangles' project of collecting and categorising the flora of Western Australia.[54] The letter asked Georgiana to accept the English seeds as a gift, and in return, fill the box with native seeds and specimens and return it to him.[55] Through this request Georgiana found her way into the bush.

In the year that followed Mangles' letter, she made more excursions into the bush than she had in her previous eight years of residence. To find what Mangles had requested, and to satisfy her now piqued curiosity, Georgiana had to step outside the boundaries of her known world and leave behind the safety of the domestic realm. She walked through a wall of trees and the deafening beat of the cicadas, which had been an impenetrable barrier, fell like a curtain between her and the small settlement. Beneath her feet and round her body swirled the details of the new world that she had kept at a distance. But armed with a way of thinking that was governed by and reflected the order of the Old World, Georgiana found a way into the New.

To collect the seeds, Georgiana had to develop an understanding of the season when the native plants seeded. She needed to identify the maturing seed and learn the best time to collect. She had to observe closely plants that had seemed monotonous. It was through botany that she was drawn away from the transformed world of settlement and deeper into the land.

When she went into the bush, Georgiana took her children with her. Sabina was five and a half, Mary three, and little John eighteen months. She found them helpful companions and wrote to Mangles of their involvement:

> Sabina I shortly found to be infinitely more au fait at discovering and remembering the abode of differently described plants than I was myself. I have known her unexhausted patience go three and five times a week to watch no. 83 & 74, lest the seeds should be opened and shed. She is six years old! And such a pursuit is highly delightful to her young Mind, besides the pleasing accompaniment of a distant Walk.[56]

As well as learning herself, Georgiana taught her children to look closely at the world around them.

Their excursions into the bush engaged their imaginations with the new land. Though they may have grown up with English stories and read English books, there was a part of their education that connected them intimately with the land beyond their boundary fence. Mary O'Brien was doing the same thing in Canada, taking her children out into the woods to find the rare plants that grew around their home.[57] Both women were actively encouraging their children to understand something of the natural world around their homes.

In November 1837 tragedy again struck the Molloys. Their small son John, who at 19 months old approached life with a joyous curiosity, wandered off in a moment of household confusion and was found moments later drowned in the well. Georgiana was devastated. She wrote a letter to Captain Mangles which, save for the buffer of time and distance and her own unutterable loneliness, she would never have presumed to send. The letter described the death. Words catch at her grief as it slips over and under the pattern of her story. Formal at first, the letter spilt into a confession of grief, guilt and the escape she found in the bush.

> Painful as it is to record—distance of time and place compels me … that lovely, healthy child, who had never known sickness and who had been all mirth and joyousness the last time we beheld him together,

was now a stiff corpse, but beautiful and lovely even in death. ... Forgive me, dear Sir, for thus using toward a Stranger the freedom and minute detail that Friendship warrants and desires.[58]

It had taken Georgiana two-and-a-half months to sit down and write about the death of John. For the first month after he died, she was ill from the shock and the effects of her fifth pregnancy. Everything around her reminded her of John: his cot, the places where he had played, even the well where he had drowned were all part of her immediate world. Death had come to her child within the safe world that the settlers had created. It was only in the bush that she could escape the constant reminders of his brief life. Like Mary O'Brien, who would flee into the woods when she needed a place to think, Georgiana sought the emptiness of the bush as a relief from the strain of the everyday. For her the space that had been 'unbounded wilderness' now offered sanctuary, rather than the order of her small domestic realm. The bush offered no illusion of safety for herself or her family, whereas the sanctuary she had created had proved to be the site of accident and death.

The bush also offered, through the activity of collecting seeds and specimens, a concentration of body and mind. Through the physical movement of searching for rare seeds, Georgiana catalogued difference. By collecting she was not comparing nature with what she had left behind, but describing nature as it was. Slowly she moved from a place where the world outside her garden was limitless in its sameness, to a world that held interest, variety and beauty at every step. She wrote in the same letter to Captain Mangles that, through collecting, she had been given the opportunity to see nature beyond the appreciation of beauty.

> I do not say this vauntingly, but to inspire you with that ardour and interest with which the collection leaves me; and cordially thank you for being the cause of my more immediate acquaintance with the nature and variety of those plants that we have exchanged for productions of our own country; and which also benefits my children, as from necessary avocation, but for your request, I should never have bestowed on the flowers of this Wilderness any other idea than that of admiration.[59]

Like many other pioneering women who worked to establish a home, and invested themselves in a new place, Georgiana was forced to move. From as early as 1830, the settlers at Augusta had known that the land situated to the north of Augusta along the Vasse and Lechenault inlets was better suited to farming, being open, grassy and park-like.[60] From

1835 Georgiana knew she would probably have to leave Augusta: along with other settlers, Captain Molloy had applied for the major part of his grant to be on the Vasse River. From first exploration the area held more promise for settlers than the back-breaking work to clear the heavy wood forests of Augusta. Although the settlement at Augusta was fast becoming a reality of enclosed paddocks, solid buildings and surveyed land, ambitious settlers wanted more land that didn't have to be cleared for their stock to graze.[61]

Georgiana did not leave Augusta until May 1839. When she finally did, it was an upheaval. In a letter to Captain Mangles she compared herself to Eve in Milton's *Paradise Lost*. 'My feelings on leaving my much loved retreat, are best expressed in those beautiful lines of Milton, where he represents Eve driven from her garden in paradise.'[62] The wrench she felt reflected the immense investment of herself at Augusta and the strong sense of place she had come to possess about a land from which she had once felt exiled. Unlike her arrival at Augusta nine years before, Georgiana took with her to the Vasse her hard-won gardening skills and a desire to continue her collecting within a new landscape.

The Molloys chose to travel overland, a journey of two-and-a-half days. Alexandra Hasluck, Georgiana's first biographer, commented that this may be attributed to Georgiana's desire to see for herself the way her husband had so often journeyed.[63] The family travelled on horseback. Georgiana carried baby Amelia, while the two little girls, Sabina and Mary, rode on donkeys. The overland trip afforded Georgiana the opportunity of observing the changing shape and form of the land that connected Augusta to the Vasse. She was able to see for herself the different flora that grew as the heavy forest opened out onto grassy plains.

The Molloys' new home was on the bank of the Vasse River, but after the wide-open expanses of the Blackwood at Augusta, the Vasse was a narrow and sluggish stream, and the country that surrounded it flat and low. There was no open view of the ocean as there had been from Augusta. Instead of the magnificence of the karri and jarrah, the land was dotted with bushy banksia and stunted jarrah. Georgiana resented not being able to see the sky. She wrote that there were no hills or rising ground and they 'were scarcely able to see the clouds unless we look upright'.[64] She could no longer enjoy the beautiful Western Australian sunsets over water from her stone flagged veranda at Augusta.

Georgiana continued to write to Captain Mangles. Her letter thanked him for the box he had sent from England in return for the seeds that she had collected, catalogued and sent from Augusta and detailed the new place where she was to remake her home.

When I last addressed you it was at dear Augusta. I left it with much regret on the 5ᵗʰ May 1839, having on the previous night taken up all my favourite plants and shrubs I could possibly place in the basket which was hung to my crutch.⁶⁵

She recalled the grief they had suffered at Augusta, but also the happiness they had experienced. She wrote of being reluctant to leave and her strong desire to return to her home. Concerning her arrival at the Vasse, she was brutally brief. 'Suffice to say we arrived three days after we took leave of Captn. Cole at the Governor's Bivouac, at the Vasse—a terrible change.'⁶⁶

Georgiana compared herself to the cuttings she had brought with her to start a new garden. She wrote: '[a]fter dinner I sought out a moist situation where I might deposit my poor Plants. Torn from their native soil, they seemed to participate in the feelings of their Mistress, trying through the aid of Water to keep up their natural vigour, but evidently had met with some terrible reverse.'⁶⁷ Georgiana wrote this letter to Captain Mangles nine months after her arrival at the Vasse. She was able to express her feelings of displacement from Augusta at the same time as gradually noting the beauty of the land around the Vasse. Describing the wildflowers, she wrote, '[the] latter end of August the flowers in the Wilderness began to bloom and I was astonished at their loveliness, much finer than at Augusta and many new varieties, some I had never seen there, and vice versa'.[68]

Rather than being the walls of her prison, the bush had become a place of pleasure and freedom from the burdens of domesticity. She wrote to Captain Mangles from the Vasse, after being unable to obtain some specific seeds that he had asked for from Augusta:

> I would with all my heart have rode over myself for them and really have liked nothing better, as being in the Bush is to me one of the most delightful states of existence, free from every household care, my husband and children, all I possess on Earth, about me.[69]

The overland trek to the Vasse marked a turning point for Georgiana. It had awakened a desire for mobility and for the opportunity to explore a much wider area of the new country. Her longing to get into the bush was not satisfied by small walks from her garden. In the remaining few years of her life, she took every opportunity to ride out, 'kindle a fire and stay all night'.[70] Like Mary O'Brien, Georgiana wanted mobility. By the next summer, in January 1841, the family made another excursion, travelling by boat along the coast to Castle Bay. Georgiana wrote to Mangles, 'I spent almost the whole day off Castle Rock on shore gathering seeds etc, as the flowers were very few'.[71] She rode and walked the sixteen miles to Cape Naturaliste, which she described as a bleak and barren headland. The family then returned by boat to Toby's Inlet, where they hoped one day to build a house. They pitched a tent and explored the area for two days, before returning to the Vasse. 'A most delightful trip, this is the clime for such excursions, no apprehension on insecure weather or danger of taking cold.'[72]

The bush had given Georgiana the opportunity to experience an expansion of her identity. Through her collecting she had stepped off her veranda and entered the land. Her eyes, which had been trained by observing her garden, were opened to cycles of the seasons. Her interest in botany gave her the opportunity to explore the land on her terms, within an order that reflected her upbringing and her culture. Her collecting was an attempt to conceive of the land within a system of knowledge that was familiar to her, to know it and to name it. Her curiosity to classify became an artistic response to the new land. Her grief at the loss of her son taught her that refuge could be found in a place that had only represented loneliness, difference and isolation. Finally, her collecting produced a sense of place in the new land, an expansion of herself that was articulated through her longing to 'be' in the bush.

The trip to Cape Naturaliste was to be Georgiana's last major excursion beyond the Vasse. She was pregnant again in March 1841 and on 7 December 1842 her last child, a little girl called Georgiana, was born. With each pregnancy, childbirth had become more complicated and difficult for her.[73] The processes of birth were a constant reminder to women of the tenuous quality of their lives. Georgiana didn't write of her thoughts on approaching each of her pregnancies, and didn't record any feelings of trepidation. Her silence on this subject was not unusual, for few women wrote openly about their feelings of birthing, though it was a major part of their lives.

Yet women did fear giving birth.[74] After the birth of Flora in May 1840, Georgiana nearly died and took many months to recover. The birth of baby Georgiana in December 1842 was again difficult. As with each of her births, Georgiana had recourse only to a drunken doctor. This time she did not recover. She died three months later on 7 April 1843.

Mary O'Brien, who faced her first birth at the age of thirty-three, an age then considered old for a first pregnancy, was initially delighted at the prospect of motherhood. She wrote to Lucy and her friend Cara:

> I had another excitement today of a very different description for I had determined on communicating to Ed., a suspicion which has occurred to my mind

for days past involving the nearest subjects of interest which remain for us to share.[75]

Mary was a strong and active woman. Three days
before announcing her pregnancy in her journal, she
had spent the day making hay in the meadow.
Throughout her pregnancy, she continued to super-
vise the farm during her husband's short absences.
She walked in the woods. She rode into town and
to church. She was still riding when she was seven
months pregnant. She made soap, salted pig car-
casses and packed them into barrels and confided
confidently to her journal audience that she did all
this 'in spite of giving some scandal to our party
who say that this is the men's work'.[76] Perhaps
because she'd already had a significant amount of
midwifery experience, she was aware of the need
to remain as active as possible throughout her
pregnancy.

> I found I wanted some bodily labour, so I asked
> Edward to find me some and we went out together
> to make a pig sty—it was, to be sure, rather cold
> and rather muddy but by the help of my Jack boots
> which I have got into again and hammering away
> with all my might, I got on pretty well.[77]

Mary wrote of consciously preparing her body
for her first birth by being fit and strong, but she
was also aware of preparing her mind and soul. Her

journal provided an important forum for her emotions. When she was six months pregnant, she wrote to Cara, describing her appearance and her state of mind:

> Fancy me then a good deal thinner than I usually was in days past but not quite so thin as when I left England and my appearance giving less witness to my hopes than is usual at the period to which I am arrived, probably about six months—my own feelings however do not fail to remind me almost every minute of the awful crisis to which I am so fast approaching: life, I believe is dearer to me than it used to be yet I know what is passing in my mind is the consciousness of how little I am prepared to enter on another.[78]

Despite or perhaps because of her midwifery experience, Mary went to visit the old Irish midwife, Mrs Munshaw, about her pregnancy, and wrote in her journal that she returned from their meeting comforted. Mary had assisted at both her sister and sister-in-law's births; she had experienced the joy and relief of a safe delivery, and also the despair of delivering a stillborn child for her sister-in-law. Her experience was broad enough to appreciate just how precarious the balance between life and death could be during childbirth.

The journal which described her first experience of giving birth is missing and was probably circulated, as were all her journals, among Edward's family in Ireland.[79] Whatever descriptions the missing journal contained, the next one was filled with baby news, and already the entries were noticeably shorter. Mary had gone to stay with her sister-in-law, Fanny, for her first birth, and from there she received as much help and attention as she needed. A month after the birth she felt ready to go home, a desire she underlined in her journal: 'I have been earnestly longing to take my baby *home*, yet now I feel almost afraid of removing him so much farther from the aid on which we have been accustomed (perhaps too much) to rely and which to speak truth we have hitherto found so effectual.'[80] Mary quickly overcame her lack of confidence in moving around with her baby and by 14 April, she wrote of trying to find a basket that could be fastened to her saddle so she could ride out with her baby.[81]

Mary's first experience of childbirth and motherhood was in marked contrast to Georgiana's. The confidence that she gained from the experience was to stand her in good stead for her second child, who was born in more difficult circumstances.

A year after the birth of their first child, when Mary was five months pregnant with the next, the O'Briens decided to move to their backwoods lot on Lake Simcoe. This move fundamentally changed the framework that surrounded Mary's life. She no longer had the close support of family surrounding her, nor the security of the bustling township of York, fourteen miles down the road. The move to Shanty Bay on Lake Simcoe marks the point at which she faced the challenge of making a home for her family away from the security of her extended family and in a far more isolated position.

At their farm on the York Road, Mary had planted a garden that she described as having beds entirely filled with 'native plants and very much beauty it will have to boast'.[82] Like Georgiana, she had to leave the home and garden she had created but, for her, the move was not so traumatic. She had only invested three years of her life in that home, and there were no small graves to leave behind untended. While she had enjoyed the life that a close community had offered, in her journal there was eagerness to embrace their move to the backwoods. With typical pragmatism, she wrote 'the new residence will perhaps be prettier but it cannot for a while have all the associations which endear this and I am obliged to shut my eyes and harden my heart to all its charms to prevent sorrowing over them.'[83]

Unlike Georgiana, who had seen neither the land at Augusta, nor the land at the Vasse, Mary had visited the Lake Simcoe area before she married, on an expedition with her brother and future husband. At the time she hadn't conceived of a future by the lake, but her impression of it certainly helped her imagine herself living on its shores. Although the area was not settled, the lake and the beauty of the woods had entranced her. When her small family arrived at Shanty Bay, her journal was filled with drama. She faced incidents with bears; she wrote of the ice cracking beneath the oxen as they transported their goods across the lake; she spiced her journal with the presence of Indians in the area and the impending birth of her second child.

Mary was a good storyteller, yet despite the dramas that filled their journey to Lake Simcoe, the journal is remarkably free from any expression of alienation or displacement. Although she did not write with the thought of publishing her experiences, as later women would, she did write for an audience: her journal circle, as she called the close group of friends and family that were a witness to her experience. For them she shaped a narrative and, in doing so, articulated the transformation that she underwent.

When her family finally reached the bank where they would build a temporary shack, Mary described their arrival with obvious pleasure:

> The sun shone so blandly and the air felt so warm on the dry bank where we landed that we hardly felt the want of a fire which the men had begun to kindle. Baby was presently rolling in delighted freedom on the dry leaves, and the men with Edward dispersed on the level above which was still covered

in snow, seeking a favourable position for our shanties.[84]

Within a few days of arriving, Mary was exploring the woods around the shore of the lake. Her journal shows a woman who was enjoying the opportunity of an adventure outside the normal parameters of her life. Edward spent a great deal of time travelling between the new farm and the old settlement, but Mary didn't express resentment at being asked to give up the close community of family and friends she had outside York. It was unlikely that she was putting on a brave front for the sake of her journal audience, as she had never done so before. On the contrary, her journal had commonly acted as a receiver of her most confused and negative emotions. A month after her arrival, she wrote:

> It is now quite late and our people have not returned. I have invited Flora into our shantie lest she should be scared and she has been entertaining us with accounts of her native Islands and here are we two women and two children with no earthly protection but two dogs sitting in the open shanties or walking about the clearings in the moonlight (which by the way is almost sultry) without so much feeling of alarm as to excite the sublime.[85]

In an effort to give a fuller description of her new life, Mary used the perspective of a visitor to describe her new home. Her description provided

delight in the new environment as well as the opposite view that informed her journal circle, of the
magnitude of her undertaking. At this time she was
seven months pregnant and still living in a shanty.
She wrote: 'I walked with him [Captain O'Brien] to
see it [the building site] but our beautiful cedar
wood appeared to him such a scene of utterly deso-
late wildness that I could extract no admiration.'[86]

The O'Briens managed to move into their house
by the end of July and on 15 August, only a few
months after their arrival at the Lake, Mary went
into labour. They had planned for Edward's brother
Lucius, who was a doctor, to assist at the birth, but
he did not arrive in time.

> August 15th to strange and ominous sensations ...
> Ed'd set to work to get the stove up and I lay as
> quiet as I could on the sof(f)a to wait till they had
> finished their work—after dinner, I went into
> Mama's room to get out of their way and from
> thence I did not immediately return for a few
> minutes made me the mother of another son—
> Mama was so completely taken by surprise that she
> had not time to be alarmed and with Ed's assistance
> and Flora's ministrations, she did all that was requi-
> site for me and the baby—such is the way we man-
> age things in the bush.[87]

Mary was up and supervising the household within
three days, remarking in her journal, '(I) feel so well

that I constantly stop to wonder why I cannot do everything as usual'.[88]

Mary's next child was born in October 1834. In the gap between her children, the small community at *Thornhill* had been reduced with the unexpected death of Mary's older beloved brother Southby in 1833 and then their 'dear Mama' in July 1834. This pregnancy was the first one without the comforting and practical presence of her Mama. She wrote of this birth:

> I placed everything likely to be wanted within reach. This was just accomplished when it became, we thought advisable to call in his (Edward's) assistance. In only about ten minutes after, and almost as soon as I became assured that the crisis of my complaint was coming on, the little damsel was in her father's hands, audibly existent. In two minutes more she was lying snugly in my arms till the conclusion of our operations should give us leisure to attend further to her needs.[89]

Mary's journal entries grew shorter and less descriptive as her time for reflection and writing was eaten up by her many roles. She ran an increasingly busy household and a small school, supervised the farm, and often cheated the doctor from his wages by delivering the small settlement's babies. In August 1836 she had another child, again without needing any assistance except that of her sister-in-law. In spite of her busy days, letters and her journal were still so important to her that she wrote after the birth of her fourth child: 'A letter from Lucy arrived a few hours after my baby and I am not very sure which was the more welcome'.[90]

Her journal ended with the birth of her fifth child in June 1837. Like her other births, this one was fast and uncomplicated, and the O'Briens had another healthy baby girl. The journal then just stops. We can only speculate why. Perhaps the family returned to England for a much-planned visit, or perhaps her sister Lucy, to whom she principally wrote, had at last decided to emigrate to Canada. Possibly, with five children under the age of seven, she simply had no time to write. Probably it was a combination of these three things that saw the end of Mary's wonderfully descriptive account of her life in the backwoods.

Both Mary O'Brien and Georgiana Molloy had broken the bones of all that meant home when they travelled to Canada and Australia. Yet both rebuilt, carefully and cautiously, a home in what was often an alien and inhospitable land. They both moved over the land outside of the protective shell of the walls of domesticity.

Mary's and Georgiana's lives have left us with a different legacy of pioneer women's relationship to the new land. The myth of the bush woman trapped in a bush hut or behind the wall of a garrison, afraid to venture out into the unknown, is unsettled by these women's powerful stories. When Mary and Georgiana left the familiar, safe world of England for a journey to the opposite ends of the earth, they fractured the familiar boundaries of space and place, of people and memory that made up home. Mary was able to walk in her brother's boots and ride in his saddle, and all the while she revelled in the freedom of movement that the land had brought to her. As Georgiana moved through the bush, bending, peering, picking and learning, she found peace where previously there had been only fear. Botany gave them the tools to assemble a sense of place that reached beyond their beautiful gardens.

Mary and Georgiana both moved from a world where their physical presence was only legitimated when expressed through a sense of belonging to a delicate, refined, gentle, domesticated, extremely feminine world. In the early settlement of Australia and Canada, no such world existed. Homes were rude shelters. There was very little time or space for women such as Mary and Georgiana to practise the art of their femininity. Apart from their knowledge of botany, their education made very little contribution to their ability to survive in the uncivilised spaces of the frontier. Arriving in the New World, both women were comforted by the trappings of their culture. They wore this like an insulating coat against the heat and cold of the physical presence of the land.

Both of them faced a physical confrontation with the New World when they arrived, and both, with varying degrees of success, rebuilt the bones of home through their creative responses to the land around them.

Looking through the fawnskin window

Susan Allison and Marie Rose Smith

Chapter two

'And so began ... my wild, free life.'[1]
Susan Allison

In the 1870s and 1880s, Marie Rose Smith lived the semi-nomadic life of the Métis, the great trader nation on the Canadian prairies. She wrote in her memoir that in preparation for the winter on the prairie, families would choose a suitable place and build small homes of logs chinked with mud and hay and roofed with turf. These houses were low and dark and, in an effort to let in some natural light, women would take the skin of fawns and tan them ever so gently, their fingers following the tiny grain in the leather, until they were strong and supple. These skins were stretched to impossible thinness across the window openings of the dark log homes, so that during short winter days, some of the snow's brightness would be allowed to enter. It was through filaments such as these that relationships were mediated between indigenous, Métis and white women on the colonial frontier.

The metaphor of the fawnskin window offers a way to talk about the view of the land white women were given through their relationship with indigenous women. The view is partial, distorted even, but it is outwards, for information did pass between Métis, First Nation, Aboriginal and settler women in frontier societies[2]. Looking through the window offered white women access to an indigenous interpretation of place that grew out of a relationship with the land. It was a way of seeing that did not rely on a foreign system of knowledge, or idea of nation, to understand the land.

Writing a memoir is an act of creation. It is an interplay between the experienced past and the imagination of the memoirist. As an historian I constantly run up against the limitations of the memoir as a way of reading history. As a reader I embrace its fluid boundaries and its imaginative reconstruction of the past. Reading women's life stories as history works against the singular narrative offered by a national history. Literary theorist Marcus Billson argued that the memoir served as the means through which women could 'rescue' themselves from an obscure past and publicly claim their lives as unique.[3] Of course these women's stories are subjective. No matter their intention, they cannot escape from the ideas that shaped their worlds. Yet it is this that makes them interesting. Their identity, as they carefully construct it, is a statement of their role, their importance at particular points in our histories.

When Susan Moir came to Hope, British Columbia, she was fifteen years old and a true daughter of the British Empire. Born in Ceylon, her early childhood was spent in the mountainous highlands of Kandy in Upper Bulatgame, Central Province, where her father owned several coffee plantations.[4] There she was exposed to the sight and sound of an utterly different culture and language. Probably it was here, among the giant teak forests, that Susan first learnt to ride. After her father died in 1849, she returned to England with her mother and sister. Eight years later, Susan's mother married Thomas Glennie and agreed to emigrate to British Columbia with him.[5]

The family arrived by ferry steamer at Fort Hope on 18 August 1860, Susan's fifteenth birthday. It had been a slow journey up the Fraser River, which was sluggish in its late summer flow. Susan scrambled up the riverbank, and before her was the township slowly fanning out from wooden fort of the stockade. Fort Hope was then twelve years old, having come into existence in 1848, after the signing of the Oregon Treaty between Britain and the United States in 1846. This treaty ratified the 49th parallel, the 'Medicine Line', and effectively forced the Canadian Hudson Bay Company to reroute its fur brigades away from the Columbia River, which now lay in the United States, and instead converge on the Fraser River in British Columbia.[6] From 1849 the brigades from the districts of New Caledonia, Thompson River and Fort Colville brought the furs by packhorse to Fort Hope, where they were shipped down the river to Fort Langley.[7]

In Susan's memoir, Hope was a 'charming, busy little place, nestled in the mountains'.[8] It consisted of a church and parsonage, a courthouse, hotel, saloon, two stores, a butcher shop, blacksmith and sawmill —all still dominated by the Fort. The family spent their first few days within the stockade but, for Susan, its exotic associations all spoke of a world beyond. From the door of the shack they occupied while their new home was being built, she could watch the pack trains come in from Colville, Keremeos and other places. She remembered the stampedes where 'pack trains would disrupt. Horses and men could be seen through a misty cloud of dust, madly dashing all over the Hope flat, lassos flying, dogs barking, hens flying for safety anywhere.'[9]

The Fort and the men associated with it represented another world which, for Susan, was filled with romance and excitement, far away from the protection of the walls of the Fort and the social conventions of the town. When she wrote of first sighting a brigade train led by the Hudson Bay factor, she portrayed herself as the white woman incongruously placed in a wilderness setting. Restrained by her lack of a horse, she was out of place, pushing the boundaries of her position in the community in the only way she could—by wandering up the trail that led to this other world, alone:

> I had gone for a stroll on the Hope-Similkameen trail … I heard bells tinkling and looking up I saw a light cloud of dust from which emerged a solitary horseman, the most picturesque figure I had ever seen. He rode a superb chestnut horse, satiny and well groomed, untired and full of life in spite of the dust, heat and long journey. He himself wore a beautifully embroidered buckskin shirt with tags and fringes, buckskin pants, embroidered leggings and soft cowboy hat. He was as surprised to see me as I was to see him, for he abruptly reined in his horse and stared down at me, while I equally astonished stared at him.[10]

On the 'golden shores' of British Columbia, Susan had been ushered into a shadow world of the settler's making. From the moment she stepped from the steamboat and walked up the bank of the Fraser River, she was confronted with two worlds jostling for prominence in the new land. There was the tenuous new settlement of the Fort, with its walls and silent gun. Then there were the mountains, their massive presence both threatening and beckoning.

Her early memoir tells stories of short journeys out from the sheltered world of the Fort into the land, her words a river of frustration as she sought to push beyond the restrictions of the tiny colonial society.

In 1867 Susan started a small school with her mother for the children of the successful and increasingly prosperous settlers around Hope, and it was while teaching there that she met John Fall Allison. He had immigrated to New York in 1837 from Yorkshire at the age of twelve. His education had included some medical training, but he had left his hometown of Oriskany following the stories of fortunes earned on the California gold fields. From 1849 to 1858, he had worked variously as a miner, manager and storeowner on the gold fields; when he heard of the Fraser River gold rush, he headed north. He liked what he found and settled on the south fork of the Similkameen River, about seventy-five miles north-east of Hope. From there he mined gold, traded with the First Nation people and ran a small stock ranch. He regularly drove cattle to market through Hope on his way to New Westminster. On one of these trips, he met Susan Moir.

The arrival of John Allison into Susan's life presented her with an opportunity to change the predictable direction of her future. 'Mr Allison brought in a cream mare for me to use,' she wrote, 'and we often rode out as far as Lakehouse with him on his return trips to the Similkameen.'[11] For Susan, who described herself as 'dancing with joy' at the opportunity to see 'more of the country', the chance to leave behind the dull, respectable life of a schoolmistress was not to be missed. Even so, she alerts us to the risk she was taking; her mother refused to make her home with them as she 'had heard such wild stories of the Similkameen and the horrors of the trial that she would not think of it'.[12]

After a quiet wedding in September 1868, the small party of Susan, John, and three native guides rode out of Hope, heading north-east into the mountains. Susan rode side-saddle, dressed in an English riding habit. Even allowing for creative embellishment in her recollections, the trail they travelled was wild. No white woman had ever ridden across the mountains and, as Susan's editor notes, only a Mrs. Marston had crossed the Hope Mountains before Susan—and she had been so terrified that she had refused to ride and had walked the whole way to the Similkameen.[13]

Susan was not terrified. She was intoxicated. The air was crisp to her skin. The country she rode through was covered in hemlocks and firs, with needles scenting the ground beneath her horse's hooves. The earth stood on its end as she climbed higher, and her mare strained beneath her to keep her footing. Susan cautioned herself not to look down and kept her eyes on the guides ahead. 'Then began my camping days and the wild, free life I ever loved till age and infirmity put an end to it.'[14]

In September 1998, a hundred and thirty years after Susan had climbed the steep switchbacks on her mare Cream Kate, we drove the road blazed by John Allison. It follows the fat lazy banks of the Fraser River and then climbs swiftly into the mountains. Above us the sky was a peerless blue, and I could see peak stacked upon peak. Reaching the Similkameen, we stopped for a cup of tea, and looked at the map of the original trail used by the Allisons to link their ranch with the outside. There were twelve river crossings that Susan would have had to negotiate, trusting Cream Kate and the knowledge of their native guides. Sitting in the weak fall sunshine, I felt I was in a fairytale land. The earth was covered by the first fall of snow, enough to dust the fir trees white. It had taken us two hours to reach a point that was a day-and-a-half ride for Susan Allison. Two hours from the city, a heated car, snow-ploughed highways and picture-book scenery can take away from the reality of the isolation that this land was—and is—capable of. Still, as we sat on the edge of the Similkameen, with the music of the river pushing aside thoughts of return, I could feel the smouldering immensity of the land beyond.

On her first night in the wilderness, Susan wrote of brushing her hair and washing alone in the darkness by the side of a mountain creek. She wrote of returning to camp and relishing the fresh trout, grouse and bannock, of drinking tea out of tin cups.[15] Her first night as a wife was spent sitting round the fire and listening to the stories of the land. 'We sat and talked till late, the Indian boys sitting with us and telling us stories of the place. Here, Yacumtecum said, one of the Big Men (giants) lived, and had been often seen.'[16] She was eager to hear the stories of the place, instinctively recognising an existing and ongoing relationship between the land, the stories and the Indian men. She also knew that if she were to find a place for herself in the mountains, then she too must understand the forces and stories that belong to the land and the people.

Despite her use of their names, her labelling of the Indian men as 'boys' shows the deeply entrenched colonial mindset. On the one hand, she was relying on these men to guide her, to interpret everything she saw, and on the other, she diminished their manhood. She slept, that first night of her new life, on a bed of spruce branches, covered in a buffalo robe.[17]

Susan's journey into the mountains had taken her from the safety of the small settlement that had grown out of the Fort into an area where the indigenous population far outnumbered the white settlers. The Indian men had spoken English to

Susan as they travelled, but within two weeks of reaching her new home, she was confronted by the silent isolation of her situation. There were people around her, but she could understand no one; her recollection of the first months at the Similkameen is infused with vulnerability.[18]

As the winter closed in and her husband was absent for weeks at a time, driving cattle to market, Susan was virtually alone. When the niece of Quinisco, the 'Bear Hunter' and Chief of the Chu-chu-ewa tribe, came to visit, she was at a loss as to what to do. She remembers details of the woman's clothing, but nothing of the exchange between them, except an awkwardness that increased her sense of isolation.

> She was dressed for the occasion, of course, in mid-Victorian style, a Balmoral petticoat, red and grey, a man's stiff starched white shirt as a blouse, stiff high collar, earrings an inch long, and brass bracelets! I did not know my visitor seemed to think she ought to sit upright in her chair and fix her eyes on the opposite wall. I think 'Cla-hi-ya' was the only word she spoke. I was not used to Indians then and knew very little Chinook. I felt very glad when the visit was over. I know now that I should have offered her a cigar and a cup of tea.[19]

In those early days, Susan doesn't mention the presence of the indigenous women in her life, except for this painfully uncomfortable meeting in the kitchen. She had already proved unfriendly and inhospitable through this clumsy handling of the overtures of friendship being offered by the women; her only comment was that the women were not as friendly as the children.[20]

The birth of her first child was to change all this. Susan had fourteen children between 1869 and 1892; for twenty-two years, birthing was a major part of her life. All her children lived which, for this period, was a significant achievement. However, her memoir only relates the first birth, which marked the beginning of a relationship with the native women that enriched and ultimately saved Susan's life.

This first baby came two months early. Susan had no mother, sister, aunt or community midwife—no white women at all within three days' ride. The Allisons had planned to return to Hope for the birth. Instead, John administered castor oil and painkiller —most probably an opiate, which would have inhibited Susan's uterus contracting and slowed the labour. Susan fell asleep exhausted, and awoke screaming, worse than before. Her husband, now truly frightened, ran for the Indian ranch to see if a woman would come and help his wife. Suzanne, one of Chief Quinisco's sisters, came. She smoothed the bed, administered whisky for the pain and prepared for the birth. Across the birthing bed, these two women met and, though their cultural experiences of birth were starkly different, a friendship was formed. 'Suzanne was very good to me in her own way,' Susan wrote, 'though I thought her rather unfeeling at the time. She thought I ought to be as strong as an Indian woman but I was not.'[21] The next morning at 9am, Susan and John's first son was born.

Through this meeting Susan began a relationship that lessened her sense of isolation. 'Suzanne was a perfect treasure and so was her boy, Hosachtem, and I always feel grateful when I think of the kindness I received from them.'[22] Shortly after the birth, Susan made friends with some of the other Indian women. She resolved to speak Chinook. Ability to communicate was not only imperative to overcome her loneliness, but it would also be an aid to her survival. 'It was about this time I first really became acquainted with the girls. They came to see the baby.'[23] Through their friendship Susan gained a language and a way out of loneliness. The women taught her stories and myths about places around her house, many of which she scribbled down in the back of the store book. They taught her the native names for plants and their medicinal uses. They shared their knowledge of survival skills and different methods of birthing. They taught her how to gather food and prevent it spoiling. When the baby was born, they made her a little birch-bark basket to carry him safely on horseback and presented it to her as a gift.[24]

She exchanged recipes and taught them how to bake her cakes, which they loved.[25] But her need for their skills and friendship was greater than their need for her, and her memoir didn't make a point of relating stories where the Indian women relied on her, most probably because they didn't. She wrote letters for the Indian men, especially letters to the government on issues of land use and management. She traded milk and butter for fish and fresh meat. She had begun to look through the fawnskin window.

When one of the Indians camped near the Allison's house became sick, the native doctor was called. Susan crept from her house and hid behind a log, watching the drama of a powerful woman doctor at work. The night was filled with the rhythmical beating of the tom-tom. The fire surged, and a crescendo of chanting carried the magic beyond the circle around the fire. Susan wrapped her shawl closer, and tried to make out the intricate movements of the doctor. 'I saw the woman afterwards in our store—such a nice-looking pretty woman. I could hardly believe it was the frenzied creature I had watched in the night. I told one of the young women that I had watched and she said I ought to have come over and sat with the others.'[26] Susan learnt that the doctor had removed a snake from the body of the patient, who was expected to recover. 'They use a force or power that we know little or nothing of,' she wrote, 'you may call it animal magnetism, telepathy, or give it any name, but it was something very real.'[27] This respect for their beliefs and willingness to believe in the power of their medicine marked her out from her contemporaries, most of whom refused to see the connection between the land and the culture of the First Nation people.

In 1873 John Allison approached his wife with the proposal that they move from the mountains down to the Okanagan area to establish a cattle ranch. Once again Susan was eager to embrace the change. 'In spite of my growing family, I agreed to the plan and never have I repented the decision.'[28] She made the journey with three small children, pregnant with her fourth.

On the two major journeys recorded in her memoir, Susan recalled stories shared around the fire about the place to which she was going. '[M]y husband always laughed at the Indian yarns but I did not, for I thought there must be some foundation for what they said. They told me more than they told most white people.'[29] These journeys and the stories she gathered on them formed an important thread in Susan's memoir as both an introduction and a rite of passage to a new place.

Susan Allison wrote her memoir at the age of eighty-two, but her recollection of her life as a young woman on the frontier in British Columbia

Looking through the fawnskin window

sparkles with warmth and intimacy. She had written short pieces for the Okanangan Historical Society and then a series of stories of her early life for the *Vancouver Sunday Province* in 1931. It was the public response to these short sketches that encouraged her to write a memoir.[30] In 1967, thirty years after Susan's death at the age of ninety-two, Margaret A. Ormsby prepared the manuscript for publication. Although Susan never saw her memoir published, she still wrote with an audience in mind. Before she introduced her readers to the new place, she would tell them a story of the area. The effect strengthens the presence and meaning of her relationships with the Indians.

When Susan reached the Okanagan, she found that no house had been built as promised and that the country was in the middle of an 'Indian' uprising. The 'Indians were stirred up', she wrote, by stories they'd heard of a great chief called Joseph who was fighting the Americans across the Medicine Line. This was Chief Joseph of the Nez Perez, whose reputation as a mighty warrior had worked its way northward as he fought an increasingly desperate battle with the well-equipped American army in the south[31]. In Susan's opinion Joseph was not a rebel fighter and troublemaker, but 'a really good man, fighting as a chief for his people's rights'.[32]

On arriving at the dwelling that was to be her house, she found herself in the midst of a rattlesnake plague. She came upon snakes everywhere, in the pots and pans and every crevice in the house. Her isolation from white society was even greater than in the mountains. Yet for all this, from her first glimpse of the lake, Susan loved it. They arrived in November, when in the mountains the snow was starting to fly, and the land was stilling itself in preparation for winter. On the Okanagan, the land still smelt of summer. The rye grass was shoulder-high on horseback and, though there was a hint of frost in the air, the sky was blue, the mountains were close only in their reflection in the still water, and she enjoyed the sight of the late swans on the lake.[33]

At the Similkameen Susan had been 'condemned to keep store'; at Okanagan she had time to be with her family. Though she was busy with the house-hold, her energies were not taken up in trading and bookkeeping. At *Sunnyside*, the name the Allisons had chosen for the ranch and by which the town is now known, she had time to teach her children. 'I don't think they ever forgot what they learned at Okanagan, though they learned little enough after.'[34] Susan learnt, too. From the indigenous people she learnt to fish and cure fish; to dry venison; to gather straw and grass to make hats for the children; to mend boots, make moccasins, cut rawhide into strands and make lariats to lasso horses. She des-cribed her life there as 'perfectly ideal'.[35]

Susan's log house is now the Quails Gate Winery, and has been restored to host wine tastings. It is a simple log cabin, but the view is extraordinary, and the sun streams down all day. Susan loved this place. She had four more children, exactly halfway in her family. The house is on a hill about a kilometre above the lake, far enough not to worry about small children falling in, close enough for a view, and a midday expedition. Today the eye is drawn across the lake to the land beyond, its gentle folds so unlike the majesty of the mountains. The predominant colour is blue. Even the air appears blue. This land is easier, simpler, quieter to the eye than the country around Similkameen River. A breeze reaches the house and cools the air around. Above the smell of the asphalt carpark is the scent of water. No wonder Susan wept when she left.

But leave she did. The winter of 1879/80 was the worst the Okanagan had experienced since settlement. The snow lay deep on the ground. When it finished snowing, the cold arrived and the snow froze hard; then a thaw and a fall of rain and quickly another freeze, and there was a thick layer of ice over three feet of snow.[36] To keep their stock alive, the Allisons hand-fed hay for a month and, when that ran out, the cattle died. Faced with massive stock losses, John Allison sold the ranch and moved the family back to the Similkameen.

The regret in the memoir is enormous. Susan 'begged him to keep our little home and argued the long, long, winters at the Similkameen and scarcity of winter feed, but his mind was made up and that was that.'[37] For John Allison, the regular income that running the store at the Similkameen provided was paramount in his decision. Susan's frustration at leaving the Okanagan came from a different relation to place. For her, beauty, self-sufficiency, and the availability of time not spent on commerce were uppermost; her desire to stay came from the home she had made for her family, the garden she had ploughed and planted, the rosebushes where the hummingbirds nested, the mountain stream that brought their water full of the earth's strong flavour, and the harbour where she and the children would row and fish.

Both Mary O'Brien and Georgiana Molloy had faced this same challenge of establishing a home and garden and then uprooting themselves, like the plants they transplanted to their new homes. It was not an unusual challenge for pioneer women, who knew that they'd have to re-establish themselves in a new place, learn its mysteries, understand its moods —if a husband saw greener pastures on a further horizon. Like Georgiana, Susan was forced to leave a place she had come to love.

Susan returned to the Similkameen to find her old home destroyed by the weight of the snow on the roof. Once again she had to house and feed her family without a roof or a stove, and the resentment in the memoir lasted for years. 'I longed more than ever to go back to Okanagan in the fall of '81 when the cattle started back. I hated store-keeping. The poor little children, I felt, were neglected but it had to be.'[38]

Away from the Okanagan, the tone in her memoir changed. Her longing to return to the Okanagan took the colour out of her observations of the Similkameen. One of the last stories she includes was of a fire in the middle of a winter night that destroyed all they owned. The story shows she hadn't lost her resourcefulness; she fed and housed her family with no shelter but an abandoned cabin, and no food save some flour and yeast. She built an oven of river mud and stones, as she had seen the native women do. She wrapped the children in horse blankets and, after five days, help arrived.[39]

When it came to writing her memoir, Susan Allison knew she had an insight into the pioneering years that was different from the standard histories of fur traders, Indian wars and the Hudson Bay Company. All of these were mentioned in her memoir, but it is her role as a woman that she claims as different.

Her openness demonstrated a choice. She chose to learn. Certainly there were circumstances that

Susan Allison and some of her family in front of their house on the Similkameen River, 1893.

made that learning imperative to her survival, but she also seemed to gain something beyond survival in her desire to know Indian place names and the stories associated with those names. For Susan, the transformation of the landscape into something more recognisably 'European' was not fundamental for her to imagine herself 'at home' in the New World. She recognised the façade of the use of place names that represent somewhere else. She wanted to know why Trout Creek, where they camped on the way to the Okanagan, was really called Look-look-shuie. She respected the fact that though the chief In-cow-mas-ket had been given the name Moses by the Roman Catholic priests, his name was In-cow-mas-ket. Her recognition of the careless assumption of place through naming was typical of her partial perception of the appropriation of place by the whites. Through her acknowledgement she found a way around the shallowness of nostalgia for the Old World place names imposed upon the New. It was through her relationship with the First Nation people that Susan learned to look.

Her writing still leaves us with questions. The heaviest comes with the silence from the indigenous side of the frontier. Though Susan gives us names, characteristics and events of her interaction with the First Nation women, we are left looking out, with little idea what Susan looked like to the women for whom the Similkameen Valley was their home.

Susan's memoir adds to the body of literature written by pioneer women in Canada. Her sense of her
audience has broadened, unlike Mary O'Brien's intimate 'journal circle', to the local communities of
British Columbia. Her writing claims her life as important to the growth of these communities; her
words uncover an uncelebrated history—a history of
individual exchange, of relationships around family
and domesticity that shaped the face of settlement.

※

*Marie Rose Smith and
Charlie Smith, and
daughter, c.1910.*

As a Métis woman, Marie
Rose Smith (1861–1954)
offered no justification for
writing her history. She
recognised that her understanding of the land around
her was informed by a radically different perspective
than that of the white settlers, and it was with pride
that she wrote about her
place in the changes on the
frontier, where she lived variously as a nomadic trader,
a rancher, a small-business
woman, and a community
midwife.

Some of Marie Rose's stories of her early life on the prairie were published in *Canadian Cattlemen Magazine* in 1948–49; as with Susan Allison, this encouraged her to expand into a memoir.[40] Then in 1977, twenty-three years after Marie Rose's death in 1954, her recollections were published by her grand-daughter as *Fifty Dollar Bride: Marie Rose Smith, A Chronicle of Métis Life in the Nineteenth Century.*[41] In this book the narrative voice has been changed, so her story is told in the third person. The material has been heavily edited, with no reference to how or why the changes have been made. It is a strange mix of biography, written by Jock Carpenter, and memoir, written in Marie Rose's words, with no distinction made between the two voices. Marie Rose's manuscript, entitled *Eighty Years on the Plains,* is now held at the Glenbow Archives in Calgary, Alberta, Canada. Though it deals with the same material as *Fifty Dollar Bride,* the tone and specificity of detail make the manuscript a far more interesting source than the book.

Marie Rose's memoir, written in the 1940s, is historically located on both sides of the cultural frontier in the Canadian West and reads like a season on the trail. She did not keep to a chronology; instead, her story meanders through her life, spending a lot of time on some aspects and hardly mentioning other areas. She moved confidently between the different cultures of Indian and white, and she tells her story, if not from the 'other side of the frontier', then certainly from an interchangeable and unique perspective.

For Marie Rose the land was home. It sustained her family and was the one constant in a life of movement and change. Her memoir, like Susan's, was written in old age. Her memories were filtered through time and imbued with nostalgia. Her life was hard, she worked long hours with little help, yet she writes with a positive tone. She often commented on the cold, but frames the short, winter days with sparkling affection. Winter was one of the easiest times to travel on the prairies, if one knew how. Sleds drawn by horses or dogs could negotiate frozen lakes, rivers and boggy roads that were difficult obstacles in spring and fall. *Eighty Years on the Plains* is punctuated with family reunions, New Year festivities and community celebrations, which all took place while the wind outside howled and the world froze.

Because of the language and the nostalgia in Marie Rose's memoir, it is easy to read it as the rose-tinted recollections of an old woman. Yet Marie Rose writes with an urgency that carries the weight of what she is trying to reclaim. She stressed again and again that her life was lived beyond the settlement society and before the introduction of private ownership of land, fences and laws. Her memoir can also be read as a political statement about identity. For Marie Rose, the stories of her life before settlement articulate the depth and importance of the Métis cultural heritage.

Marie Rose's memoir was different from white women's recollections of their life in the New World, for she recalled the land without comparison to someplace else. Because she was neither an immigrant, nor a daughter of an immigrant, there was an absence of a comparative analysis between life in the New World and life at 'home'. For Marie Rose the land she lived on and wrote about informed her version of herself and was her only reference point. Her text is unique in the interplay she presented between her semi-nomadic childhood and her transition to the life of a settler's wife. Travel, movement and mobility are vital to her construction of her younger self. The knowledge to survive in the land came to her from her culture. Unlike Susan Allison, Georgiana Molloy or Mary O'Brien, it was not knowledge that had to be grafted into her world.

The degree of self-invention involved in these memoirs can only be acknowledged, not measured. Like Susan, her response to land and place was written through the refraction of hindsight. Both women were recalling a time in their lives that was exciting. It was their girlhood that sparkled with liveliness and mobility. For Susan Allison her perspective was perhaps governed by a longing for inclusion, a desire to romanticise closer links with the native

women than necessarily existed.[42] For Marie Rose
Smith the links with white women are tenuous, and
she found more in common with the society of
Indian women, though her skill as a midwife was in
much demand by the white women of the area. The
stories they tell highlight aspects of their personality
or experience that they wish to celebrate. They
exhibit courage and heroism in the face of danger,
resourcefulness in overcoming life-threatening situations, and a willingness to experience the new, the
strange, the exotic, the other to their conventional
world.

Marie Rose was born on the White Horse Plains,
just out of present-day Winnipeg, on 18 August
1861. Her mother, Marie Desmarais, was born in
1838 and had grown up in the Métis settlement on
the White Horse Plains. Marie's mother was the
daughter of Frenchman Joseph Desmarais and
Adelaide Clairmont, an Indian woman of the Saul-
teax. Marie Rose's father, Urbane Delorme, was a
Métis, born in 1835; his grandfather was a Frenchman and his grandmother an Indian woman. By
1763 there were at least thirty thousand Métis living
on both sides of the border, west of the Great Lakes.
As a nation they were becoming a significant cultural and political force in western Canadian history. John Kinsey's descriptive history of the Métis

described them as 'wanderers of the wilderness—the best boatmen, best guides, hunters, trappers and traders ... Their knowledge of the country ... made them indispensable in the development of the West, as did the fact that most of the Indians welcomed them as relatives and friends.'[43]

The Métis, which in French means 'mixed blood', spoke three languages; they used French as their 'official' language, English when dealing with whites, and Cree in their homes.[44] Marie Rose spent her early childhood travelling with her family as they traded with the Indians all the way to the barrier of the Rocky Mountains in the West. She was educated at St. Boniface Convent School for four years and learnt to write in both English and French. She also spoke Cree fluently and kept the three languages throughout her life.[45]

Her memoir opens with a tableau of waking on the morning of one of her family's great trips west:

> 'Wake up!' I was very excited as any other little girl might be, who, at the early age of ten years, was embarking on a winter trip over the great western plains, from the Great Lakes to the Rocky Mountains.[46]

Their journey would take them west, where they would seek out the largest of the winter Indian camps and settle down to trade. In preparation, Marie Rose's father gathered together a convoy of over forty Red River carts, seventy-five head of horses and outriders, all of whom would be led by the covered *democrat* (the Canadian term for a horse-drawn vehicle, generally a buggy or spring-cart), which her mother drove with the five children. The convoy went east first to St. Paul's for supplies such as prints, knives, guns, ammunition and axes to trade for furs, buffalo hides, bladders, grease and *pemmican* (smoked buffalo meat, pounded and mixed with berries and buffalo fat). If journeys form a key motif in Susan Allison's writing, then they were a way of life for Marie Rose. Once they left the settlement on the White Horse Plains, there was no hurry; they generally made between eight to eleven miles a day, stopping to camp each evening whenever they found good water. 'There were no fences, gates or law to impede us on our way.'[47]

The Red River carts served as ships to cross the prairie. They were made entirely of wood, which was usually oak from Winnipeg, and held together by buffalo rawhide. No iron was used, and the carts, if broken, were easily repaired. The traders carried extra wood, as the prairie had no trees to replace a broken axle. The rawhide was strong and always finished the journey. The sound of the carts' creaking and groaning carried for miles across the horizontal world of the prairie.[48] They must have looked like a swaying caravan, another world making its way westward toward the Indian lands.[49]

Though they lived a trading life that had a twist of profit at the end of it, the Métis moved in accordance with the seasons. It was a life that ebbed and flowed with the requirements of travel—day after day, month after month, living on the wild game that was plentiful. They had little financial outlay. They made their carts, their homes, and their clothes; the buffalo and the land they travelled over provided all their material needs. After a season's trading, or perhaps two or three, Marie Rose's father would return to Winnipeg, where he sold the furs for cash. Having little need of the money, he banked it, leaving his children a 'considerable fortune' when he died.[50]

Marie Rose wrote of the prairie as both garden and wilderness. In her girlhood it was a place through which her family moved and was sustained.

Wild food was abundant; when camped near a lake we gathered wild duck eggs by the bucketsful and hard boiled them to eat while travelling. This would make a change from pemmican and dried buffalo meat of which we always had a plentiful supply.[51]

They also ate wild ducks, prairie chickens, antelopes, badgers, skunks and wild cat or lynx. Bear meat was a particular treat. The hunters would track down the bear and those in camp would prepare for a feast. Any meat left over was always dried by the women and packed away for future meals.[52]

These stories give voice to a different history of the prairie than those offered by white settlers on the plains. Marie Rose never speaks of the land as a place to be feared and, although she drew on a literary tradition that took its roots from European pastoral culture, she wrote of a land that had no need of transformation in order to sustain her community physically or emotionally.[53] Her family found everything they needed in the land. 'Sometimes we younger ones dug a white root, which grows wild and resembles a carrot in shape which also tasted much the same, eating it raw like any little girl who has just visited her mother's garden'.[54]

In Canadian history the prairie was evoked in images of the 'Great Lone Land'.[55] It was the prairie as wilderness, a hostile and alien space without boundaries or refuge, that was dominant in white consciousness.[56] For white travellers and settlers, the only places of respite from the massive skies and open spaces were the forts built by the Hudson Bay Company and the Great North West Company. In her opening pages, Marie Rose referred to this territory in these terms: 'The wild, lone land/Into this wilderness we were preparing to penetrate'.[57] These phrases were the tropes of the white explorers.[58] But after these remarks, Marie Rose never used this language again.

In identifying the prairie as a garden, a nurturing space, a place of freedom outside white law, Marie Rose aligned herself with a way of life that was being destroyed during the years she travelled. By writing about the prairie as 'wilderness' and as 'great lone land' into which her family prepared to 'penetrate', she called attention to her ability to understand how the white culture had interpreted this same space as hostile, threatening and alien. Her experience reversed that recorded by the white explorers and settlers, who described the land as empty until transformed by settlement. Her memoir captures the change from the prairie as a garden to the prairie as empty space. Her images are powerful. The Canadian geese that migrated south each year were so numerous that the beating of their wings as they rose from the water of the lake was like the sound of distant thunder. 'Sometimes it is difficult to convince new arrivals that so much wild life was formerly in evidence and when one claims to have seen acres of ground literally covered with wavies and grey geese, their look of unbelief is far from flattering.'[59]

There was comparison in her writing, but it was between cultures and ways of living on the land. Her memoir interprets life before white settlement, with Marie Rose located between the semi-nomadic life of the traders and the sedentary life of settlement. She finds points of contact and exchange between her understanding of Indian culture and white culture.

Young mothers, too, when on the trail, vied with one another in seeing who could make the prettiest Ti-ki-na-kan (baby beaded bag) which is the cradle of the papoose and is strapped to the mother's back when travelling. We were just as proud to 'show off' our bead work on the baby bag as you are to display your knitting or embroidery.[60]

In Métis society women played a major role in food gathering and preparation. Like many well-meaning white women, Marie Rose wrote of this with an ethnographical instinct, but her point of recording the processes of culture was different. She was not like Susan Allison, a privileged observer separated from the activity by her whiteness; rather, her knowledge was essential for her survival. Her memoir includes detailed descriptions of how the women made their staple food of pemmican and of how they would travel in family groups and share their resources.[61] She was particularly aware of the exchange of knowledge between her people and the Cree. From the Cree they learnt how to use every part of the buffalo.[62] When a herd of buffalo was sighted, the caravan was stopped and the men would hustle about catching their best horses.

It was a grand sight to see them as they galloped away, their beaded shoulder straps glittering in the sun, as each loaded his gun while on full gallop, pouring in powder from the powder horn, ramming it down and dropping in the lead ball—several of which he was carrying in his mouth.[63]

While the men hunted, the women and children would empty the Red River carts of their loads and harness the horses to be ready to drive out to the kill site and bring the meat back into camp. It was the women's work to cure the meat and dry the hides, many of which would be tanned. Their camp would look like a small village of leather tepees made from buffalo hides.

Marie Rose noted that though the traders bought their lead shot from the eastern stores, the Indians saved the lead from the big Hudson Bay Company tea chests. They melted the lead in fry pans, poured it into long strips, then cut the strips into small pieces and chewed them into balls. Even the children would help with the shaping of the shot. In 1885 the Métis would use this method during the war against the British.[64] It was through the accumulation of such technological details that Marie Rose portrayed the exchange of knowledge between the First Nation people and the traders.

When her family travelled across the prairie, they would often spend time with the Cree tribe, led by Chief Crowfoot. Marie Rose's parents held Chief Crowfoot in high regard; he was an important person in their world.[65] When they met they would sit and talk late into the night. Crowfoot was regarded as a man of insight, and these meetings had a strong effect on Marie Rose. She remembered him teaching them to care for the land: 'When you leave camp in the morning gather up all rubbish, burn or bury it; do not spoil the land or destroy its beauty.'[66] She included a quote, which she attributed to Crowfoot, in comparing the way of life of the Indian and that of the white man:

> I have heard many white men preach of their goodness and truth, but to the Indian, White Man's religion is love of money and fear of death. White Man thinks his reading and writing has lifted him above the native of the prairie and made him clever. He learns from books, but the Indian learns from nature.[67]

Marie Rose's reconstruction of Crowfoot's words emphasised her desire to communicate the tone and texture of life on the prairies before the land was opened up for white settlement. Her recollections of this relationship strove to demonstrate interdependence between her family and the Cree: 'We were glad to learn what nature had already taught the native tribes'.[68]

Unlike Susan Allison, Marie Rose never faced the silence of an unknown land or a lack of language to describe that land. Rather, her unhappiness and isolation came as a result of her marriage to a 'white man' twenty years her senior.

Marie Rose was sixteen when her family first met with the Norwegian trader, Charlie Smith. Marie Rose described him as a 'big raw-boned Norwegian of very fair complexion'.[69] He had left his native land at the age of twelve and worked as a sailor, travelling to foreign ports, until he came to the Canadian west to live as a trader. Marie Rose married Charlie Smith on 26 March 1877. In her description of her courtship, she described him as 'Mo-ni-ash' (white man).

> It was settled between my parents and Charlie right then and Charlie gave my mother a present of Fifty Dollars. Was I not sold for that sum? ... So I a little girl of sixteen years, was forced into a marriage with a man twenty years my senior, and of whom I knew nothing.[70]

The use of the term 'Mo-ni-ash' distanced Marie Rose from Charlie. She writes of him as an outsider to her family, her experience and her culture—all of which he was. Her memoir stresses a double betrayal, for not only was she sold into marriage, but her husband was a white man.

Marie Rose recalled the first year of their marriage as the unhappiest in her life: 'Day after day I went away by myself and cried; surely God would perform some miracle on my behalf'.[71] She was saved from despair by her parents' decision to travel with them over the summer. By day she could be with her brothers and sister, but at night she was alone with her new husband. 'When night came and I was alone with my stranger husband, alone in a camp of our own, such fear seized me, that I bound my clothes about me with raw hide ropes.'[72] Her husband was advised by the other men in the community to beat her into submission, but she wrote that, instead, 'Charlie was patient and determined to win me through love'.[73]

Marie Rose's first baby was born 12 July 1878 at Chicken Prairie, North West Territories. Her second child was born on 3 January 1880 at Frenchtown Montana.[74] She doesn't give any detail about the births. She had seventeen children over the twenty-six years between 1878 and 1904.[75] Her first two babies were born on the trail within a close community; her other children were all born after they had settled and Marie Rose no longer had access to the community of women that supported her on the trail.

With the coming of the railroad in the early 1880s and near extinction of the once mighty buffalo herds, Charlie Smith recognised a change in the way the western economy would be run. In the late 1870s, the Smiths and other Métis families had travelled to Montana 'following the Treaties',[76] and trading with the Indians. On their return Charlie brought cattle back across the border and selected land in Alberta.[77] In the fall of 1880, Charlie took up land to ranch in a sheltered spot on the banks of Pincher Creek, where it winds its way out of the foothills of the Rocky Mountains. The Smiths' move to settle in what was then known as the North West Territories was part of a larger movement of Métis people. In 1870, 80 per cent of the population around Red River was Métis; by 1884, after the Riel Rebellions against the British, the proportion had halved to 40 per cent, as the Métis moved their communities westward.[78]

The land around Pincher Creek is searing; it is dominated by two forces: the mighty Rockies, which fill the western and southern horizons, and the power of the Chinook wind. It is an electric wind; strange things happen when the Chinook blows.[79] Sid Marty, a modern-day writer who lives near Pincher Creek, not far from where Marie Rose and Charlie Smith settled, writes of the Chinook:

> Everywhere you look in Chinook Country, you will see the marks of the wind on the earth. It is there in the permanent lean of the aspen groves, those white tree trunks all leaning northward as living wind-vanes indicating the prevailing southwest winds. It is there as a current of energy wavering through the grain fields and through the sweep of the remaining prairie grass.[80]

The Smiths built their long, low wooden ranch house in a coulee[81] to escape the Chinook. They called it the Jug Handle, after the brand Charlie used on his cattle.[82] Marie Rose gave birth to fifteen more children in this house, the first permanent building she had lived in since she had left her convent school.[83] At first it consisted of just one room, made of logs, with the gaps between them chinked with mud, and roofed with bark. There was no floor, but hard-packed dirt, and the windows were constructed of small bits of glass. They made all their own furniture, but Marie Rose had 'a fine stove' to feed her huge family and the large number of people who stayed with them. Her cupboards were boxes nailed to the wall and 'though dishes were few, food was plentiful'. The house was decorated with a few picture calendars, which 'lent a spot of brightness to the place'.[84] At one end there was a hammock, which Marie Rose had made with two ropes of rawhide, 'with blankets and pillows placed between the ropes as a bed for my baby'.[85]

Unlike most white women immigrants, who often had intermittent help in the house, Marie Rose had none. She used many of the skills she had learnt on the trail in order to survive the daily grind of raising young children and running a ranch house, but time was so pressured that she didn't even sit down to nurse her babies: '[I] would stand beside the high hammock until the baby nursed his fill, then covering my breast and giving the rope a push, I went about my work while the swinging cradle lulled the

Looking through the fawnskin window

Jughandle ranch house, where Marie Rose gave birth to fifteen of her seventeen children, c.1900s.

baby to sleep.'[86] Like Susan Allison in her use of a birch-bark basket to carry her babies on horseback, Marie Rose used many of the Indian techniques in baby care. She bought moss from the women of the Stoney Nation. She would heat this in a frying pan as her mother had taught her, to drive out or kill any insects hiding in it, and then use it in her baby bag as a natural nappy.[87]

> I also used an Indian baby bag to wrap my newborn babies in. Three times a day, my baby was unwrapped from his bag, and when he felt the freedom about his legs and arms, how he did stretch! This was his exercising period, and he enjoyed it for perhaps an hour each time.[88]

The land the Smiths had moved onto was turbulent with racial tension. The First Nation people had little choice but to move onto government reserves, following the extinction of the buffalo. There was a very large indigenous population that was still moving over much of the land around the homestead. As a child travelling over the prairies, Marie Rose had only feared the Sioux. The traders considered the Sioux treacherous and often cruel, though Marie Rose gave a reason for their hostility. 'As the white traders and their families moved further and further west, the Sioux feared they had come to take the plains away from them, robbing them of their free life and their natural mode of living.'[89] She contrasted the Sioux with the Cree, who mixed more freely with the Métis; her comments highlight her knowledge of the difference between the Indian nations.

In contrast to Susan Allison, who was facing the same racial unrest on the other side of the Rocky Mountains, Marie Rose was informed about which people presented a threat to her and her family, and why they were aggressive toward the settlers. She understood the devastation caused to them by the hunting to extinction of the buffalo. She understood, in ways Susan could not, the extent to which the First Nation people were reliant on the land and the way the land defined their identity. In contrast to Susan, she never eulogised the First Nation people as a dying race unable to survive in the face of technology and civilisation. She knew that the people died because their land had been taken from them, and they had been forced to live on tiny parcels of reserve land unwanted by the white settlers.

Marie Rose was comfortable with large groups of indigenous people in and around her house. Her attitude towards them was markedly different from Susan Allison's uneasy portrayal of indigenous gatherings. Marie Rose often fed extra people, and her house was something of a meeting place. Charlie, she wrote, was 'an open-hearted fellow', who never refused anyone a welcome at the Jug Handle; 'no one left the place hungry, whether he be White man or Indian.'[90] Marie Rose would often be faced with groups of twenty or more Stoney Indians passing through the ranch, and she remembered often being tired and angry at having to feed so many people. Still, she was able to use the contact to her advantage.[91] She made an arrangement to buy fine buckskin from the Stoney women and made gloves and clothes. Her industry purchased her independence, as her buckskin gloves were renowned for their quality and good fit. She eventually made enough money through the sale of her buckskin products to buy a house in Pincher Creek after Charlie's death.[92]

Marie Rose's independence and self-sufficiency gave her mobility and, therefore, a degree of control over the isolation of her situation. On one occasion shortly after they had settled on Pincher Creek, Charlie left Marie Rose and the three small boys—the youngest a babe of four months—alone on the ranch. 'When the hired man began to get "fresh" and wanted to kiss me,' she wrote, 'I knew I would rather suffer hardships on the trail than be subjected to the ugly attentions of this hireling.'[93] It was a large undertaking, to travel alone with three small children in charge of five horses, but that is what she did.[94] Fortunately, she met up with a neighbour, Mrs. McGilliss, who was also travelling on her own with her two small children as far as the Cypress Hills on the border between Alberta and Saskatchewan. An old man, Joe Brown, made what Marie

Rose referred to as 'a pleasant addition to their party'; he played the fiddle well and was going all the way to Winnipeg. The trip didn't go smoothly. Their horses were stolen, which held them up for a month and, because of the delay, they were forced to travel in the spring thaw.

> Day after day ... the wagons sank into the mud traps up to the hubs, and the horses got mired, the children became tired and began to cry, how I longed for Charlie's help and the chance to cast the whole burden onto him.[95]

When she finally reached Winnipeg, she found that they had passed Charlie somewhere on the trail and would have to return alone.[96] With the money her father had left her, Marie Rose bought a well-matched team of brown mares. She was pleased with her purchase as the mares were 'really quiet', a virtue that was essential for her to make it safely home again without an escort. She travelled with her sister as far as Batoche; from there her mother and stepfather decided to accompany her to see the country where she had settled.[97] Marie Rose had left the Jug Handle in early May, as soon as most of the snow had melted off the prairie. She returned in a snowstorm. She had been travelling for six months.

On another occasion, despite Charlie's opposition, Marie Rose set off driving a gentle team, heading westward with a packed lunch for the children.

She had heard that there was a crew of men cutting logs up in the foothills. 'Baptiste Boone and his wife were a part of this crew', she wrote. 'I knew Mrs. Boone would welcome me and looked forward to a day of pleasure.'[98] The camp was much further than she anticipated, and darkness threatened before she had reached Mill Creek. The country into which she climbed became progressively wilder and more thickly covered in timber. The hills, though gentle to begin with, became steep for a team and wagon filled with children. She found herself on one precarious hill after another, with sides as 'steep as teepees' [sic], until it was too dangerous for the children to remain in the wagon. Taking them out, she left them at the top of the hill, and guided the horses down the steep gully, 'not for a moment daring to think what would happen to those children up there if I failed to reach the bottom, right side up. But heaven was with me!'[99]

She tethered the horses at the bottom of the gully and scrambled back up the hill to bring the children down. She could find no wagon tracks out of the gully, only a single horse's trail. She had not brought a shelter with her, or any wraps for the children; she had nothing except a pillow and blanket for the baby. With little choice but to trust that she was within walking distance of the camp, she unhitched the team, and put the children back in the wagon. Having given them their lunch of sandwiches and doughnuts and warned them not to move or fight, she left them and set off to find the camp.

> Down the single trail I ran and ran! Then in front of me loomed another hill which I must climb. At the top I again found a dim trail. It was getting darker and darker; I was running further and further away from my babies along that trail. At last, breathless, flushed and crying, I stumbled into camp, with breath enough only to gasp, 'The children; the team', and pointing back along the trail I had just come over. Then flinging myself into the friendly arms of Mrs. Boone, I sobbed my hysteria away.[100]

Baptiste Boone saddled his horse and rode back along the trail, returning with the team, and the children—though not the wagon. Although she had momentarily feared she was lost, this story highlights Marie-Rose's ability to find a place she had never been before and to navigate safely through unknown country; it also highlights her desperation to visit another woman.

Another skill that ensured her family's survival was her ability to interpret the weather. On a Sunday in the winter of 1883, Marie Rose decided to take her children to church, although the snow was drifting badly. She dressed them warmly in fur coats and then wrapped them in badger robes. On their return journey, still six miles from home, the wind picked up and they were nearly blinded with snowdrift. Because she had her children wrapped warmly and a quiet trustworthy team of horses who knew the trail, she was able to find her way safely home. They were passed by a miner who, she judged, would have been very cold 'perched so high on the back of his horse'. As Marie Rose guided her team into the coulee where the homestead stood protected from the wind, she called to the miner to come into the house and get warm. He refused. Perhaps he underestimated the weather, or perhaps he didn't want to associate with a Métis family. He was later found dead of exposure not much further along the trail.

Marie Rose's ability to keep her bearings in a blizzard and to choose when it was safe to push on home and when it was best to overturn the wagon and take shelter beneath it had been learnt from her time journeying over the prairies.

As she reaches the end of her memoir, she writes of burying twelve of her children. With an emphasis on her local community, she also writes of her battle with the government to practise as a midwife, and rages at the injustice of having to send her sons off to war for Canada. Her memoir ends with a simple wish to live out her days beneath the shadow of the Rocky Mountains, 'along the beautiful Creek that flows forever from those lofty hills'.[101]

It has been argued that for settlers in the New Worlds, asserting ownership meant that they renamed places that already possessed names. They renamed people who were already named. They blocked their ears and refused to hear the sound of the words that already described the land they had come to.[102] They made for themselves a world transformed into a recognisable likeness of the Old World they had left.[103] Reading these two memoirs of women's life on the frontier complicates our impression of relationships between the immigrant and the indigenous. Susan Allison, in her eagerness to learn, and her isolation from her own language, was open to the native names of people and places in a way many of her contemporaries were not. She recorded many of the Indian legends and stories of the places she had lived and began to map, albeit partially, the web of relationships on the frontier which were invisible to most settlers. Without her interaction with the native people, she might never have moved beyond the appreciation of moonlight on snow. Without the women, she wouldn't have had language to begin to understand the connective tissue that can grow between self and place. Landscape writer Barry Lopez wrote, 'One learns the landscape finally not by knowing the name or identity of everything in it, but by perceiving the relationships in it—like that between the sparrow and the twig.'[104]

It is these connections that emerge in the stories of Susan and Marie Rose and demonstrate the shallowness of a 'garrison vision' of white women's relationships to the land and indigenous people. However blurred their differing views out beyond the fawnskin window might have been, they each found a way of seeing—and of writing about what they saw—that was independent of the men and connected to the indigenous women who entered their memoirs with names and children and skills and stories of their own.

Jumping the fence

Alice Duncan Kemp, Monica Hopkins
and Mary Percy Jackson

Chapter three

... straight from the bed in which I was born to the back of a horse with no perambulator intervening.[1]

Miles Franklin

For many women, learning to ride was a necessity from an early age. For writer Miles Franklin, riding formed her earliest memories and, in *Childhood at Brindabella*, she recalled that '[t]he rhythm of horses came to me earlier than walking'[2]. Miles' mother, seven months pregnant with her, had ridden over seventy miles from her new home at Brindabella to her family's home at Talbingo station. Miles wrote of her mother's journey: 'She went by impossible tracks negotiable only by a mountain-bred horse, at such angles that those unaccustomed could not retain a seat. For miles the horse plunged to the girths in snow.'[3]

When Miles was three months old, the family rode home again, this time by a different route. Miles rode on a pillow made by her mother that was stuffed with feathers and had an outer case of purple sateen. The pillow was placed in front of the saddle, and baby Miles was carried home by the rhythmical long stride of a 'Waler'[4], 'with no perambulator intervening'. The movement of a horse was a foundational motion in Miles' life. She wrote that in those moments when 'a sense of actuality has been slightly loosened', when she was physically exhausted, or in the grip of a high temperature, it was this memory which became the rhythm of her world.[5] Miles shaped horses as a key part of her consciousness as a young child, and she remembered no time when she did not feel that they were an important part of her world: 'My confidence and pleasure in horses was inborn'.[6] In *Childhood at Brindabella*, she wrote of the sensation of a 'well bred horse being released or about to be released into action'[7] as a foundational memory; from birth she had been steeped in the movement of a horse.

In the words of women who wrote of their everyday lives, of their activities and tasks, and of the land that informed their identity, it's easy to miss the impact of their daily contact with the horse. That moment of reaching out and touching *horse* was often hidden behind a screen of more immediate information. As an historian I would ask many questions when I read the common phrase, 'saddled the horse'. Where are you going? Or whom are you going to see? Or, how far do you plan to travel? Even, what are you wearing?

Rarely did I acknowledge the challenge before a woman of the latent power that stands quiet beneath her touch. In that moment of stillness can be traced the artistry of line, the compliance of a head lowered to receive the bit, the lifeless touch of leather and iron. Messages transferred, language without words: tension, caution, eagerness or peace and solid dependability. Questions are asked and answered along the line of the reins—questions that shoulder aside anything but the immediate moment and require knowledge and skill to interpret. Will you buck, or spin? Will I feel you gather yourself to whirl away? Or are you quiet, well-broken and schooled, unlikely as a rock to tip the world from beneath me? So many moments missed in the phrase, 'saddled the horse', yet on the frontier, woman's relationship with the horse defined the boundaries of her world.

Many women have felt the stretch and snatch of the stride of a horse at full gallop. When, in letters to their parents, Mary Percy Jackson and Monica Hopkins sat down and wrote about their day, they held in their bodies the memory of movement. For Alice Duncan Kemp, riding was her vehicle into anthropology. Riding required a presence of mind that placed women in the moment, their senses open to the world around them, their imaginations engaged through the motion of the horse they rode. In both Australia and Canada, riding gave women independence and access to a more nuanced understanding of the connections between their bodies and the places in which they lived.

The ability to ride is a sudden departure from the pedestrian world into a place where your body's capabilities are extended by the horse. Riding gave women a physical equality with men that they had in no other arena of life. Even today, equestrian events are the only Olympic sport where men and women compete on equal terms. For women in the Nineteenth and early Twentieth Century the mobility of the horse and the ability to communicate with the horse, regardless of strength, counterbalanced gender difference on the land. Riding a horse not only added physical status to a woman, but it served as an equaliser on the frontier.[8]

Yet for elite nineteenth-century women, the mobility offered by horse-riding had to be mediated via the side-saddle. By the end of the nineteenth century, the question of whether respectable white women rode side-saddle or astride was a hotly debated issue, with discussion focused on the effect of the latter method on women's health, sexuality and bodies. It was a debate that was part of the reconceptualising of women's bodies, movement and clothes that occurred around the end of the nineteenth century. As with the bicycle, riding astride was linked to 'images of female emancipation'.[9]

Riding straddle was also taken to be a sexual display. When a respectable woman rode a horse side-saddle, her legs were covered by her long habit that swept to the line of her boot. When women began to ride astride, though they rode in long divided skirts, the existence of their legs could not be denied. The more overt display of women's legs, especially clad in riding trousers and boots, was taken to signify a blurring of distinctions between the sexes and thus a threat to male power.

In 1844 Annie Baxter (1816–1905), the wife of a New South Wales grazier, wrote in her journal of altering her husband's pantaloons to ride in them. Annie enjoyed nothing more than a day's riding after cattle, an activity that came as naturally to her as more conventional feminine pursuits. 'Yesterday we all rode out to see the cattle—and brought home three cows and their young calves ... Mr. du Moulin paid me the compliment of saying that he would as soon have me with him as a man! Indeed that I was quite as good as a Man!'[10] For Annie the speed and exhilaration of galloping behind the cattle was a release from an unhappy domestic situation. She wrote, 'There is a great excitement in cattle hunting and I glory in it'.[11]

Annie was renowned as a good horsewoman. She often hunted dingoes and kangaroos, riding out on a 'splendid horse' with two or three big dogs, armed with a horse pistol. Annie's ability to jump the fence was quite literal. She recorded in her journal that Mr Black had shown several ladies a fence behind his house and challenged them to jump their horses over it. They all, perhaps prudently, refused. Annie relished her reputation as the one woman who would put her horse at the fence and clear it easily.[12] But Annie rode side-saddle, and apart from altering her husband's pantaloons to ride in, she does not record riding astride. This is not to say that she didn't ride astride, just that she didn't write about it.

Mary O'Brien in Canada was not so shy in recording her experiments in riding astride. As early as November 1829, she recorded in her journal, 'I made my first essay on Anthony's saddle and succeeded so well that I shall try it again'.[13] Although she doesn't say whether she sat sideways or straddle, a comment later in her journal seems to confirm that not only was she prepared to be seen in public riding astride, but she also enjoyed the shocked response she would elicit from those she met while out riding: 'At the Parson's we met [Dr Daly] again and he observed that I had changed my horse—I told him no—only the saddle which was in fact the change he had noticed but scrupled to mention till I did so … Thus you see our wild ways are not acknowledged by all Canadians but we are determined to stand stoutly by them whatever attempts any newcomers may make to infringe our liberty.'[14] But Mary was certainly not evangelical in her decision to ride astride; rather than challenging the definition of femininity, she was responding to the lack of side-saddles and horses broken to side-saddle.

Isabella Bird, the famous English traveller, was one of the earliest and most vocal supporters of women riding astride. In the flyleaf of the 1880 edition of *A Lady's Life in the Rocky Mountains*, there is an engraving of her in her infamous Hawaiian Riding Costume. She is holding a dancing horse, whose curved neck, foam-flecked hide and fiery eye contrast with Isabella's restrained respectability. The depiction

Isabella Bird in her Hawaiian Riding Costume.

of the horse carried the movement and wildness in the picture. The horse was restrained by Isabella as, in turn, Isabella was restrained by expectations of her behaviour and the boundaries within which she had to stay if she were to continue to profess to be a 'Lady'. The purpose of the picture was to prove both the respectability of Isabella's costume and her decision to ride astride.

In the second edition of *A Lady's Life in the Rocky Mountains* (1880), she reacted to criticism from a review in *The Times*, which accused her of donning 'masculine habiliments for her greater convenience'.[15] She wrote:

> For the benefit of other lady travellers ... the American Lady's Mountain Dress ... a half-fitting jacket, a skirt reaching to the ankles, and full Turkish trousers gathered in frills and which fall over the boots,—a thoroughly serviceable and feminine costume for mountaineering and other rough travelling in any part of the world. I add this explanation to the prefatory note, together with a rough sketch of the costume, in consequence of an erroneous statement in the Times of November 22nd.[16]

Isabella was aggressive in her demand that her audience accept her femininity within the terms she set of functional dress and mode of riding. Throughout the book she called attention to the occasions when her life was saved by the increased mobility and security of movement her costume allowed her.

If a mountain lifestyle offered Isabella an escape from the restraints of Victorian respectability, it also offered the freedom to experiment with her femininity. Nowhere was this more clearly expressed than in her defiance of riding side-saddle. Her willingness to ride astride, a decision partly based on health reasons and partly because it was so much safer, allowed her a far greater range of movement over the landscape. When she entered a settled area, however, she observed convention: 'I rode sideways until I was well through town, long enough to produce a severe pain in my spine, which was not relieved for some time even after I had changed my position'.[17] On another occasion she compared herself with men who came into Denver from the mountains. These men, she said, 'find [it] hard even for a few days or hours to submit to the restraints of civilisation, as hard as I did to ride sidewise to ex Governor Hunt's office'.[18] Isabella effectively reinforced her gentility through recording her visit and reception at the ex-governor's office. Yet like the frontier men who rebelled against the restrictions of civilisation, she too was chaffed by the restriction on her method of riding.

Her attitude to the land and reverence for it had something to do with her access to the mountains through her mobility. She mustered cattle, often riding over thirty miles in a day and working with herds of up to a thousand head. When she wrote of her experience, she used images that are anything but stationary and feminine:

> The great excitement is when one breaks away from the herd and gallops madly up and down hill, and you gallop after him anywhere, over and among rocks and trees, doubling when he doubles, and heading him till you get him back again.[19]

Hester McClung, who travelled in 1873 in the same area of the Colorado Rockies as Isabella Bird, wrote of the moment when she first rode astride.[20] In contrast to the famously independent Isabella, she was travelling with her family, who had come to the mountains as a health cure for her youngest brother. Entrenched in her role of unmarried sister, thirty-year-old Hester was much more dictated to by convention than the radical Isabella. Hester was shocked when she realised that she must ride astride: 'It seemed an impossibility at first, but we were encouraged by the refined Mr. M. who said ... this was the only safe way'.[21] She made it clear that she was only encouraged to ride astride by the obviously genteel Mr M. Her record, however, was delightfully free of fear and inhibition. The party had travelled up to spectacular waterfall and river rapids, a round trip of only twelve miles. Hester wrote of their return:

> Our homeward ride was pleasant, not only because of the mountain scenery but also on account of the

mere pleasure of the ride ... I think that letting a
ballot slip though my fingers into the ballot box—
that ungraceful, unwomanly act that is to convert us
some day into masculine beings—I think that even
that will not make me feel more free, more unfet-
tered, in plain language, more man-like than I did
that day while galloping on my great black charger.[22]

For women on the frontiers of Australia and Canada,
the ability to ride with confidence and comfort often
set the boundaries of their experience of the land. If
they mastered the horse, or even just *one* horse, a new
level of mobility and independence was available.
For those who relied on their men to harness a horse
and drive them, getting off their property was a matter of chance and factors outside their immediate
control. Riding gave women an opportunity to connect with the natural world that was less restricted
in its vista, wilder in its outlook and somehow inter-
connected with the movement, instincts and understanding of the animal being ridden.

When Monica Hopkins (1884–1974) came to
settle in the Canadian west in 1909, she could not
ride and was unfamiliar with handling horses. Monica
was the daughter of Reverend Joseph Thomas L.
Maggs, a Wesleyan minister, and Amy Elizabeth
Maggs. Her childhood and education had prepared

her for a comfortable, stationary, middle-class existence, and for a marriage to a minister or professional. She was born in Dorset, England, a landscape
of softly rounded hills carpeted in a rich and verdant
green and dotted with sheep—a world away from
the Canadian West, with its rolling prairies, massive
mountain ranges and endless vistas.

Monica had lived in Canada before, having travelled with her family from England to Montreal in
1900, when her father accepted the position of principal of the Wesleyan Theological College at McGill
University. On board the ship on the trip over from
England, she had met a young Irishman, Billie
Hopkins from County Wicklow. After years spent
working at sea, Billie was on his way to the Canadian
West to seek land on which to build a homestead.
Monica, at only sixteen, found much in common
with Billie, and when the Maggs family returned to
England in 1903, Billie and Monica continued to
write letters. Monica's parents disapproved of any
suggestion of her marrying the Irish rancher. Her
father believed she was not strong enough 'and not
suited for the life that I should lead in Canada and
also that the life would be very different from what
I had been used to'.[23]

Billie refused to be put off by parental resistance
and slowly built up his horse herd, improved his
homestead by building a log cabin and fenced some

of the property to make it habitable for Monica. When it was ready, he returned to England. They married on 25 August 1909 in Leeds, County York. Monica's first letter to her parents was dated a month later and was written in the three-room log cabin Billie had built on the banks of Fish Creek, in the foothills of Alberta, nine miles south east of the tiny township of Priddis.

The country around Priddis is pretty. It's a slightly smaller version of the giant open spaces further south around Pincher Creek and north of Peace River. The hills provide a pocket of protection against that feeling of being naked under the sky. When Billie and Monica set off on the final leg of their journey from Calgary in their new green democrat[24], it was probable that Monica had never seen such huge mountains. Something of the excitement of moving through this country seeped into her early letters. As they bumped along under that massive sky and felt the power of the wide open spaces, Monica experienced a mixture of fear, intimidation and intoxication at the life she had travelled so far to lead.

When she sat down and wrote of her journey, she framed her account with details of the weather. It was her uncertainty in the face of the land and her lack of skills and materials to cope with it that expressed the burden of her alienation. When they got off the train at Calgary, she wrote:

The rain was coming down in buckets and all the protection I had was a white lace sunshade … it vindicated its existence by keeping me dry in spots as I made my first appearance in Calgary, holding my white lace sunshade over my head at 2.30 in the morning of a very wet day.[25]

As Billie was anxious to return to the ranch, Monica had little time to look around when she arrived in Calgary. She bought some postcards to send home to her parents, providing evidence of 'civilisation'. The postcards show scenes of the hospital (which she failed to mention would be over thirty miles away on rough trails), the electric streetcars and Indians dancing the Sun Dance.[26] Perhaps Monica had hoped that the fact that the Indian ritual of the Sun Dance was now depicted on a postcard as a tourist attraction would demonstrate to anxious parents the extent to which Indians were no longer a physical threat to white settlers on the frontier.

The couple left for the ranch around two in the afternoon and again Monica wrote of feeling out of place, uncertain about how to react. As they drove across the prairie, she caused the horses to bolt:

The country was open and the sun beat down on us … I leaned down and fished up my sunshade that was lying on the floor near my feet. Its pristine glory was already beginning to fade somewhat, but I opened it and held it aloft something after the manner of Grannie when she drove in Hyde Park. Unfortunately, our horses are not quite as well schooled as hers were, for with a startled snort away they went, nearly pulling Billie over the dashboard. I hung on for dear life, still holding the sunshade over my head. I could hear Billie yelling but was far too occupied in keeping myself in the democrat to listen to what he was talking about, until one extra loud roar reached me, 'Put that damned umbrella down!'[27]

From her high seat on the democrat, she looked back at the last shack on the way out to their ranch and admitted to herself a certain vulnerability: '[F]or the first time I had a funny feeling inside me, not exactly afraid but not quite so sure of myself. England and all my people did seem so far away.'[28]

Monica's letters give a vivid account of her first two years, as she gradually found her place in the foothills. The letters were reworked and expanded by Monica after she and Billie left their farm in 1943. She entitled the manuscript, *A Log Cabin and We Two*. It was given to the Glenbow archives in Calgary and published with an Introduction by archivist Sheilagh S. Jameson in 1981, seven years after Monica's death. It is only possible to guess how Monica touched up these letters, what she expanded on and what she left out. Their importance doesn't lie in how truthful an interpretation they were of Monica's early years; what they offer

are the opportunities, situations, places and responses to the land that Monica, as a woman of
fifty-nine years of age, considered retrospectively
important to her transition from minister's daughter
to rancher's wife, from alienated newcomer to
established and accepted member of the community.

Reading Monica's record of her first impressions,
it's easy to lose sight of the difficult transition she
faced. She told her story with such self-depreciating
humour, yet beyond the humour are repeated pictures
of her as out of place in this new physical world.

> The men are haying about four miles away, cutting
> wild hay on the range[29]. For the first few days I went
> with them, Billie not caring to leave me alone and,
> to be strictly truthful, I wasn't anxious to stay alone
> either. But it was a nuisance for everybody.[30]

Those first days spent accompanying Billie out to cut
hay set the limits of Monica's world. Her ability to
move about in that world was reliant on her confidence in handling horses. After meeting several of the
neighbouring women, Monica was quick to understand this:

> Several of them have ridden over alone, others have
> come in all sorts of vehicles and one arrived in a
> wagon with a small baby bumping around in an
> apple box … they all live so far away and those that
> do not ride and are dependent on their menfolk to
> take them about evidently do not get taken out very

much; I've decided that I'm not going to be depend-
ent on anyone so I ride nearly every day, generally
just around the place but I have been out on the
range alone.[31]

For Monica to be independent she had to ride well
enough to get herself safely about the range, into
town or to visit neighbours. She soon became skilful
enough to be useful in helping bring down the cattle
from the mountains, or in the bi-annual round-up
of horses from the hills. She was able to ride into
Priddis, 'eighteen miles there and back', to collect the
mail, instead of having to wait until one of the men
were free either to drive her in, or go and collect it
themselves. She learnt to ride well enough for Billie
to take her camping up into the mountains, and to
go out onto the range by herself.

Because of these trips, Monica could look from
her vegetable garden across to the mountains and
imagine the sound of a bustling stream through
which she had ridden. She could see the wind scud-
ding the clouds across the heights and know it would
be moaning in the spruce forests of the foothills.
Her view was broadened and her awareness of the
landscape deepened with her movement over it. Her
response to the land and her obvious happiness in her
new life did not preclude attacks of homesickness.[32]

I love the mountains, but today I would willingly
have never seen them again if only I could have seen

the sea in their place. I closed my eyes and pictured myself standing on the cliffs at Eype, and I could almost hear the splash, splash of the little waves as they broke over the beach. … I don't often get such an attack of nostalgia but when I do I get down to the very depths. But I bounce back up just as quickly and today by the time I reached the little log cabin I had quite recovered.[33]

Her homesickness was partly quelled through the busy cycle of ranch life. Without children, Monica was able to fully involve herself in the running of the ranch. Like Susan Allison on the other side of the Rocky Mountains, who was dealing with Indian women in her kitchen, Monica found it hard to be homesick when she was caught up in the immediacy of the task at hand. Women's labour brought them into an engagement with the present moment that shouldered aside the emotions of homesickness.

[Billie] has given me Dolly, his saddle mare, to ride. … She is lovely to ride, so easy and up on the bit. She can turn on a sixpence and has nearly had me off a couple of times for she knows a great deal more about 'running in' horses than I do. Yesterday when we were out and the bunch we were after made a break, she seemed to know exactly what to do. I let her have her head and between us we turned the horses in the direction that Billie was waiting for them and he was able to drive them into the pasture.

I must end this epistle now ... Tomorrow we are
planting potatoes and it behoves me to have a good
night's rest.[34]

For Alice Duncan-Kemp, who was born in 1901 in
the Channel Country of South West Queensland,
riding was part of her earliest education. She and
her sisters first rode bareback with only a halter for
a bridle. They found this difficult and fell repeatedly,
but the stockman encouraged them back on and,
eventually, Alice was good enough to be given her
own stock horse:

> Will I ever forget the excitement and thrill of that
> day when I was given a stock-horse for my own, to
> ride at musters and to look after, along with a saddle
> and bridle which were my own? And the thrill of a
> thoroughbred horse, probably a lot more intelligent
> than I, galloping beneath me, weaving among a mob
> of seething cattle and by some sixth sense, made more
> acute by intensive training, bringing out the right
> cow and the right calf from the midst of a thousand
> head of milling bellowing beasts.[35]

Horses and riding were a central theme throughout
Alice's recollections of her childhood on her family's
cattle station, *Mooraberrie*. Her ability to move freely
over the land in the harsh and often dangerous
Channel Country was made possible by two factors:

her relationship with the indigenous people and her ability to ride well. The two were intertwined and, when she wrote of her experiences, she acknowledged the value of the lessons she learnt from the Aboriginal stockman who taught her horse husbandry and riding skills.

Like Marie Rose Smith on the Canadian prairie, Alice Duncan-Kemp (1901–1988) shaped her recollections around journeys across the land. She described her home as 'a place where heat, dryness and cold are alike unbearable and where food is almost and water, except in good seasons, quite non-existent.'[36] Her experience on long cattle musters gave her an insight into how narrow the boundary was between life and death in the waterless and unfenced stretches of land. Often the only buffer between her life and that boundary was a good horse.[37]

> One of the charms of the outback is the fascination of travel in the open, over a country teeming with native history, under the stars, kissed by sun and winds. When the motor-car and aeroplane take the place of the horse and camel and the physical laws and necessities no longer regulate our journey across the country that glorious feeling of being one with the land ... will have passed from our ken for ever.[38]

An awareness of what Alice called the physical laws of nature was needed to travel safely. In the desert country, water dictated travel, and knowing the country intimately and intelligently was the only way a person travelling on horseback could survive. Travel in cars and planes cushioned the occupants from the heat of the sun, or the cold of the wind. In motorised transport the land is interpreted through glass. The climate is controlled by air conditioning or heating, and we travel at speeds outside the natural rhythms of the landscape. As Alice said, we are removed from that 'glorious feeling of being one with the land'.

Being 'one with the land' was something that characterises Alice's rather complex memoirs. Like Susan Allison in British Columbia and Marie Rose Smith in Alberta, Alice Duncan-Kemp relied on indigenous skills and labour to survive.[39] Her life was also enriched by her mobility and her friendship with the Aboriginal people who worked for her parents. Alice's father, William Duncan, had arrived in Australia in 1876 and had first come to *Mooraberrie* in 1886. He began managing the station in 1894 and, shortly after this, married Alice's mother Laura. Alice was the second of their children, born on *Mooraberrie* in 1901. Her memoirs are written in four volumes, published over thirty years, from 1933 to 1968. Though they are all concentrated around her first thirty years, each book was written at a different point in her life, and the changing tone across the four volumes demonstrates the different perspectives she brought to her memories as she aged. The most notable change is the increase in anthropological information.

Writing, as she was, on the fringe of the anthropological world, Alice's memoirs sit awkwardly between autobiography and ethnography. Her expertise comes from her personal relationships with the Aboriginal people, but her observations were not considered 'scientific' enough for publication.[40] Dr. Winterbotham, who was an amateur anthropologist and founding member of the Queensland Anthropological Society, showed some of Alice's material to the Professor of Anthropology at Sydney University, A. P. Elkin. Elkin was said to have found Duncan-Kemp's information 'tantalisingly incomplete' and suggested to Winterbotham that he consider critically editing and arranging the material against a background of Aboriginal social structure, rituals and philosophy. This was never done, and Alice used the letters as a source in the last three of her memoirs.

The anthropological influence is most marked in the last two volumes, *Where Strange Paths Go Down* (1952) and *Where Strange Gods Call* (1968). Both these books emphasised that her interpretation of Aboriginal customs and ceremonies had been made possible through her close relationships with the people and her understanding of the language. By publishing her anthropological material in the guise of autobiographical writing, Alice protected herself and her informants from any potential abuse of her information by professional male anthropologists[41]. In this she was successful.

However, it is the anthropological information in her books that make reading her experience of the frontier so difficult. The lens through which she wrote of her relationship with the Aboriginal people was ethnographic. Her material is both autobiographical and ethnographical. Alice makes little effort to distinguish between the two perspectives, and this makes for a double sense of distortion in her writing.

The importance of her memoirs is that in contrast to other women anthropologists, writers, settlers' wives in Australia, Alice makes the connection between her understanding of place and her relationship with the indigenous people.

> One of the most important people in my early years was our nurse ... Mary Ann, who ... for the first years was my chief companion and instructor on walkabouts and fishing expeditions. She taught us the lore of her tribe and the whispered language of nature.[42]

Like Marie Rose Smith, Alice spent large portions of the year outdoors: 'for days we rode through the country mustering, following mobs of cattle and camps from place to place'.[43] She wrote very little about the homestead and garden. 'The clean sweet smell of the casuarina blooms, the sweet drenching scent of wild boronia and green herbage greeted my

nostrils, a soft breeze carried a fresh earthy damp-
ness up from the waters. How good it felt just then
to be away from roofs and walls!'[44]

Alice had been taught to ride and to move through
the bush safely by the Aboriginal stockmen and
women. Her appreciation of the skills and knowledge she was given by Aboriginal women like Mary
Ann is a strong theme in her writing. But she also
received something more from them, an idea that
her body was connected in some way with the world
around her through her daily interactions with
people, animals and land. What Alice was taught by
her Aboriginal teachers was to learn to 'see'; to
understand that the earth would speak to her and
that she could learn to listen.

> We were taught to judge the fall and the lie of the
> land, to listen to, and to interpret, the 'talk' of the
> many different types of country which comprised
> various sections of our run and adjoining runs. This
> 'talk' or sound-reaction we listened to as we walked
> or rode on horseback over the land, taking care to
> note landmarks and certain tree and plant charac-
> teristics, contours of hills and sand-ridges in daylight
> and darkness. All this knowledge makes up the 'talk'
> of the land, and in our youth we absorbed it, and
> much else, like a sponge, with the result that by
> maturity we were fair bushmen; any type of country
> 'talked' to us and we learnt much that was a closed
> book to the casual or untrained observer ... this

part of our education proved extremely valuable and of absorbing interest. We realised that when moving with the aborigines we entered their world.[45]

Alice was acutely aware that her view was partial. She was in effect, like Susan Allison in British Columbia, looking through a fawnskin window. She could see out, but often she was not sure of what she was looking at or why. Her understanding of different Aboriginal dialects helped her comprehend, but she was also aware that many words and concepts that made perfect sense to the Aborigines were incomprehensible to her.

Aboriginal words like wai-mou-yan and European interpretation do not mix satisfactorily either from the aboriginal or European point of view. In honest fairness the same rule applies to aboriginal life and ritual in all its phases, as interpreted from the European standpoint, no matter how kindly disposed and understanding the European or the aboriginal for that matter.[46]

Nevertheless, what Alice received from her contact and relationships with the Aboriginal people was an awareness of land and a sacred understanding of the places around her that changed the way she understood her *self*. From her Aboriginal mentors, she learnt to take nothing for granted; rather, in her riding and walking over the land, she must listen to the country and respect, celebrate and care for places.

Amidst much dubious scientific racial theory popular at the beginning of the twentieth century, Alice records intimate images of the land: of a savage staghound-dingo loping through spear grass; of sensing the flight of migrating birds in the darkness high above; of the sounds of a rutting wild camel, too close for safety; of seeing flickering lights far across the plain where there was no one to carry them. She wrote of being so affected by the power and spirituality of the country that she was turned from a stone-ringed hillock by a force as real as a knife blade.[47] Her writing about the land was affected on every level by her relationship with the Aboriginal people and her ability to ride. Without the example of Mary Ann, and the Aboriginal stockmen in Alice's life, she would never have received this embodied understanding.

> It was friendship with the lonely land, and with its people white and black that tied me to its body with an unseen umbilical cord and seemed to throb its life-blood through my own body ... The true relationship of this deep friendship was one of those subtle mysteries of the human spirit which defy attempts to pin them down in words.[48]

Her images are physical, her body connected to the land. She spoke in terms of friendship with the land, of mutual obligation, taking care of the country, of acknowledgement and respect. She was given the means to see the land in this way through her upbringing, her movement over the country, but ultimately through the generosity of the Aboriginal people who surrounded her and shared their world.

This body-to-land connection that Alice talks about has informed the writing and lives of many women living on the land. It is a connection that is accessed through their labour. Alice's ethnographic recording of Aboriginal legends and language, like Susan Allison's less professional note-taking of the indigenous legends around the Okanagan, provided both women with an independent, intellectual life outside of their normal workload. This was not work that was paid or 'needed' but, like Georgiana Molloy and Mary O'Brien with their botany, extended into a world outside of the domestic sphere and it widened their understanding of place. It was work that had no expectation or requirement, so that even though Alice collected her data on mustering trips on her family's property, she was making something of it that was for her own mind. As a woman of the twentieth century, Alice did not have to jump the fences of nineteenth-century convention that Isabella Bird was faced with. Although she never questioned her freedom to ride, Alice's intellectual freedom was more curtailed. Her interest in the science of anthropology and her desire to publish her work in this field were never realised.

Dr Mary Percy Jackson came to Canada from England, having had little experience with horses. Before her arrival in 1929, she had taken up riding as a hobby on her half-day off. She quickly discovered that the small amount of riding she had done in England for exercise was completely inadequate as preparation for the kind of riding she needed on the frontier in Canada.

Mary was born in 1904 in Birmingham, England. Her mother was a teacher and her father was a director of a woollen manufacturing company. Her parents believed in providing a good education for their daughters as well as their sons, and so Mary entered the medical program at Birmingham University and graduated in 1927. That year she won the Queen's prize as the best all-round student and told the editor of her letters, Janice Dickson McGinnis, that winning the prize was one thing, but 'beating all those men' was better.[49]

Mary, twenty years Monica Hopkin's junior, was inheritor to the vision of the New Woman. Although the New Woman had emerged as a figure of feminist rebellion in English fiction and social commentary as early as the 1880s and 1890s, it wasn't until after the First World War had expanded opportunities for women's work outside the home that the term had a more popular application.[50] The New Worlds of Australia and Canada were openly promoted as places of opportunity and adventure. For Mary Percy such potential was not to be found in Birmingham. She sought a wider arena for her talents. After replying to an advertisement in the *British Medical Journal* by the Canadian Ministry of Public Health, Mary was appointed the first doctor to the community of Peace River in Northern Alberta. Women doctors were wanted as government doctors in the new settlements in Western Canada. The Minister for Public Health argued at the time that most of the patients were women and children, and therefore a woman doctor would be better suited to the job than a man.[51] However, there were more economic justifications behind the Canadian government's drive to employ female doctors.

Women doctors cost less than males, could be relied upon to do the nursing as well as the doctoring and were considered easier to recruit, having fewer opportunities available to them than their male contemporaries. So, at the age of 25, with seven years of hard study behind her, Mary left Birmingham, a safe job in the hospital, and her family and friends, and travelled to Northern Alberta to the Peace River to be the first white doctor in the area.

The Peace River Prairie, further north than Edmonton and well within the Arctic Circle, is high and spare and wild. The winters are long, with temperatures regularly reaching below minus forty degrees Celsius. Though Mary arrived in 1929, the harsh land and extreme conditions created a settlement removed from the technological advancements of the post-war years. Fur traders who travelled into the north in search of fresh trapping territories had dominated the early European history of the Peace River area. In the 1880s and 1890s, the Yukon gold fields had boomed, and the Peace River had become home to a few miners who were defeated by the climate and conditions on the long and difficult over-land route from Edmonton to the Yukon. The First Nation and Métis populations that lived in the area had attracted the attention of the Roman Catholic Church, which sent priests to set up the missions. However, none of these forays into a landscape of open prairies, endless muskeg and stunted forests of spruce and elder had brought with them white women.[52] The Peace River Prairie was the last area in Canada to be open to free homesteading, a govern-ment policy whereby land could be taken up by living on it and improving it. Homesteading required the labour and commitment of women. In her letters home Mary emphasised how new the area was to settlement:

> Most of the white women up here only came in this year certainly but Mrs Robertson has been up here over 3 years. She and her daughter were the only white women here for two years—and they came up in the days when there wasn't even a trail and they had to cut their way through the bush. And there are

women who came up in 1922 when you couldn't even make it on a saddle horse. The only way was on foot, 100 miles.[53]

Most of the settlers were very poor and many were emigrants from the Ukraine and other parts of Europe, seeking a new start after the devastation of the First World War. Because the land was free, they required little capital to homestead. Homes were built out of the prairie sod, and the land was farmed with a horse and plough, rather than the mechanisation that was changing the face of farming in the 1930s in more settled areas. According to the government, Mary's district covered 250 square miles; according the locals, it was upwards of 350 square miles. Midwifery and dentistry dominated the medical practice described in Mary's letters. She also mentioned frostbite and infectious diseases, including tuberculosis. She treated a range of accidents that were a result of the physical labour of homesteading. Often it was not the difficulty of the diagnoses or the treatment that were the focus of her narrative, but the extreme conditions she faced in reaching her patients. Her shack was in the middle of her practice, which made her accessible to as many people as possible. Her transport methods were various and often bizarre. Mostly she rode her own horse and, when he was exhausted, she borrowed others. She also rode in cars, a steamboat, wagons, sleighs, dog sleighs and cabooses.[54] Once she travelled behind a caterpillar tractor for two days, an experience she never wished to repeat, as the noise and the crawling pace nearly drove her mad.[55]

Mary's letters, written predominantly to her parents between 1929 and 1931, form a record of her first few years on the Peace River. They have been edited by Janice Dickin McGinnis, with an introduction, giving context and biographical material. The letters themselves are largely unchanged, though Mary did request the exclamation marks be removed. Dickin McGinnis begged for them to stay, believing that they added expression to how Mary was feeling and how young and enthusiastic she was.[56] They stayed with permission. Mary told her tale with verve and a breathless energy that reveals the difficulties she faced in such an isolated and hostile environment. Letter writing was a way of coping; she kept up a prodigious amount of correspondence. Her writing acted as an anchor, connecting her to her family as she reacted to the new country and life she was leading.

My last letter to you only left yesterday and here I am writing again. I hope you won't get tired of my effusions. Really if I wrote all I wanted, you'd be getting about 20 pages a day! I hope you'll keep my letters. I should rather like to have them myself in my old age. They take the place of a diary! I meant to keep a diary but soon discovered that life was too short to write down all the interesting things that happened.[57]

The letters form an almost continuous narrative of her adaptation to the Peace River area. She was particularly positive for her parents' sake, as was Monica Hopkins. This optimism, that of itself draws the reader into her world, also reveals the strain. In searching for the good fortune, the happy times, the beautiful scenes to describe in their letters, both Monica and Mary left silences that hint of the hard, aching tiredness, the loneliness, and the battle to belong in a new land.[58] A fortnight after her arrival Mary was able to write a positive picture of her home and a humorous account of her struggles to learn all that was involved in looking after her horse. In drawing attention to the improvements, Mary hinted at the condition of the shack upon arrival. The scene she was greeted with when she first opened her door on her new home was only written in the shadow of the list of changes she made:

> It's a fortnight all but two hours since I arrived at this shack and no one would know it for the same place. Cupboards, shelves, a bookcase, curtains at the windows, curtains at the doors, cushions, pictures and the windows mended are the most obvious differences. My horse Dan'l (I suppose it's spelt Daniel

but that's how everyone pronounces it) is fastened about 100 yards from the window. May he remain there. It's the first time I've had to do the tying myself![59]

Mary had arrived at Battle River on the same boat as the letter announcing her appointment. A meeting was called at the town store for all English-speaking settlers not only to meet the new government doctor, but also to elect a committee to look after her wood and water supplies. The appointment of a government doctor was very important to the growth of a district, and many families made the difficult trek to the Peace River on the strength of comfort that a doctor in the area offered. The district was obliged to keep Mary in wood and water and provide a horse for her. A hat was passed around and thirty-one dollars collected towards a horse. Mary recorded the long debate over what type of horse she should have, a technical discussion that furthered her dislocation from the situation, as she had no idea what they were talking about. She reported that a stallion apparently was out of the question, a mare was considered suitable but a difficult proposition because of all the loose stallions running round the district, so a gelding was settled upon.[60] Mary, who at that stage, did not know a gelding from a stallion or mare, was to be faced with more evidence of her lack of horsemanship. She quickly realised she must learn not only to ride properly but to feed, water, and saddle the horse that was to be her constant companion for the next three years.

Mary's approach to riding around her practice was initially somewhat naïve. She didn't appreciate the magnitude of the challenge she faced, which was probably fortunate. Before her arrival at Battle River Prairie, she wrote to her parents of taking every chance she could to ride, in readiness for the challenges she faced at Battle River.

> I had a most exciting ride yesterday evening, bareback at a gallop! Then they found a saddle for me and I went for a long ride. It was really great. I've never ridden so fast in my life, but as I was being taken by a boy of about fourteen, I didn't dare slow down![61]

Two weeks after she arrived she again wrote to her parents about the horse she had been given and the challenge she faced both in looking after him and controlling him.

> He's a very nice horse, well broken and very comfortable. He ran away with me this evening but that was my fault for letting him trot down a steep hill. Please don't get worried. I don't mean that I couldn't have pulled him up with an awful effort. I think I could have but he merely went off on a gallop without any stimulation from me.[62]

These two extracts make interesting reading. In the first, written at Jarvie, she wrote of the excitement and exhilaration of riding fast for the first time. She was confident of her abilities and proud of being able to ride bareback, which she had never done before. Her focus was on having enough riding so she would not be stiff when she started her new job. The second extract, written two weeks after her arrival at Battle River, was still positive and light-hearted, but much more cautious in her summary of her ability. There was an underlying awareness of just how much she had to learn. Now she had been run away with, and though she wrote that she thought she could probably have pulled up if she had really wanted to, she was confronted with the reality of her lack of experience. She had no choice but to get back on and try again, as her horse was her only form of transport. At the end of the letter, she gave herself some incentive to improve: 'When I've learned to ride properly, I am going to get some leather chaps, coloured leather preferably, then I shall look the real thing!'[63]

In England Mary had paid for the privilege of riding a well-schooled quiet horse, a horse that had been saddled and bridled and stood ready for her to mount from a mounting block. She would then ride quietly along pathways, perhaps with the opportunity of a short canter on a nice flat section of park. In Canada she was expected to feed, groom, tether, and tack up her own horse. She was expected to be able to ride across open country and contend with natural obstacles such as creek and river crossings and steep hills that had to be climbed and descended. There had been no bears or moose to negotiate in the relative safety of an English park. She wrote from Battle River after her first ride in public:

> People are awfully funny about my riding. Of course, everyone here rides. Children can ride as soon as they can walk. So, I carefully didn't say more than I 'could ride after a fashion' when I was asked. One man looked at me the first time I went out on a horse here. 'Oh yes—you can ride—but you'll know a whole lot more about it in 6 months!' He was about right too.[64]

In her next letter she was expressing surprise at how much she had already learnt:

> I can hardly believe that I'd never been on a horse 6 months ago. And I suppose in another 6 months I shan't even be able to believe that I didn't know all about feeding, watering and saddling a horse. I'm getting much quicker at saddling already. It only took me 20 minutes this morning to go and untie him (he is tethered by a rope about 30 feet long and gets it tied round and round everything within easy reach), water him, saddle him and get him off to church. I may say that I was an hour later, the service began an hour late and lots of people arrive an hour late![65]

As the letters progressed, there was an observable relationship between riding and beginning to feel comfortable, rather than intimidated, on the land. It was often after an exhilarating ride that Mary wrote very evocatively of the land that she was coming to call home. In a matter of months she had moved from not being able to manage a horse trotting down a hill, to being able to control a horse that tried to run away with her. 'But it's a great sensation galloping across open prairie.'[66]

This image is in such contrast to her earlier descriptions of riding on the prairie. It was with delight rather than apprehension that she wrote of the sensation of the challenge from her horse to control him. As she travelled to treat her patients, she received an idea of the immensity of the land she rode through:

> I ride sometimes for hours with no sound but Dan's hoofs thudding on the ground and the creak of my saddle, seeing nobody for 10 miles at a stretch. It gives you a sensation of being absolutely <u>alone</u>, quite a different sensation from loneliness. I wonder if you get my meaning? ... I love it. And these weeks of hard riding, in the open air from morning till night, have made me browner and fitter than ever I've been. That Krushen feeling [according to a well-known advertisement, a rush achieved by taking Krushen mineral salts] is a feeble description of the sensation of unlimited energy I get when I go galloping across a big prairie and Dan is full of oats.[67]

Within four months of her arrival, Mary was talking about not wanting to leave the harsh North West of Canada. As she described a ride to a patient in horrendous conditions, her love of the wildness of the land overwhelmed the difficulty of travelling after nine inches of rain had swamped the roads and swollen the rivers.

> ... I'm more in love with this country than ever. You can't imagine how fascinating it is—and I can't describe it.[68]

Mary's developing love for the land comes across strongly in her letters, yet it also puzzled her. In a letter written on her way to Edmonton in January 1930, she reflected on the beauty of the country in which a colleague worked. The land she was travelling through had a more conventional beauty than the Peace River. As the train chugged through picture-book scenery of lakes, mountains and 'real forests', Mary wrote, 'There is a certain thrill in being right up north absolutely cut off from civilisation and railways'.[69] Later in the letter she expanded on how the country had captured a part of her:

> They tell me that wherever I go after this, however beautiful and warm the winter is, I shall get homesick for the snow and cold winters for the rest of my life. I think they may be right.[70]

In her journeys to and from her shack, in her crisscrossing of the land to treat her patients, Mary experienced nature in a very raw way. She wrote of returning home from seeing a patient and, taking her hand out of her glove to open the door to her shack, receiving a nasty case of frostbite. She was aware of the land at nearly every moment of her life; it pushed its way toward her; it was almost impossible to find a retreat from it. In the winter Mary would go to bed at 11pm and get up at 4am to stoke the fire. If she slept through, she would wake to a frozen world: her blankets, clothes, bread and every drop of water in the house would be frozen until she could get the shack warm enough for it all to thaw.

As she rode huge distances, her movement seemed to impart something of the essence of the land. Living and travelling alone in a landscape largely free from the transforming hand of European settlement, she could sense something of its mysterious magnitude and struggled to convey it to her parents:

You can't think how weird it feels at night, living all by myself in this little house. I've got the whole valley to myself. There's not a light to be seen. All around are old burnt-off tree trunks, very white in the moon-light, and the Spruce trees are intensely black against the sky and make a noise like the sea in this wind. The sound of the river has almost gone, now its freez-ing over. It feels as though Brutus [her dog] and I are utterly isolated in the middle of this immense country.

... That's something queer about Canada. I keep noticing it—not only that it is big but that you can't help feeling all the time how big it is. Even though you can't see more than a mile or so around, you still feel that it goes on for thousands of miles. I can't make out the cause of it. It seems to be something apart altogether from one's knowledge of geography. Do you know what I'm driving at or does it sound merely mad?

Kettle's boiling. I'd better wash up.[71]

Mary's letters keep trying to articulate her place in the new land. She balances the detailed, everyday moments with something much larger, more profound, something beyond geography. Her attempt to articulate her emerging response to place separated her from women such as Georgiana Molloy or Susan Allison, who were limited by 19th-Century definitions of femininity, both in their movement over the new land and their expression and understanding of the freedom that that movement offered them. Mary's experience reflected a new level of opportunity for women to broaden the registers of independence in work, leisure and their thinking.

In March 1931 Mary married farmer and fur trader Frank Jackson. Her decision to marry signalled her commitment to making her life in Northern Alberta. Her letters end with her marriage, but her role as doctor to the district was expanded as she moved a hundred miles north to Keg River. From there she continued to work, but as her editor notes, the government refused to pay her. Instead, she set up a laboratory in the basement of the farmhouse and, with the farm income supplementing her need for equipment, she continued to practise as a doctor.

Mary has become a well-known figure in Canadian medical history. Her story works on many levels—as a pioneer doctor, new woman, working mother, rancher's wife—but it is her response to the land as something apart 'altogether from one's knowledge of geography' that challenges the tired myths of women permanently alienated from the land in frontier places.

Cutting steps

Freda Du Faur and Mary Schaffer Warren

I climbed on Graham's shoulders and grasped an ice-axe dug into the upper lip of the schrund and by its aid pulled myself into safety on the slope above. Then I cut a big step to stand in and another beside it, and pulled up the other women one by one, cutting a step for each as they arrived ... I soon had them ranged out in a neat row beside me ...[1]

Freda Du Faur

The essence of life is stripped to the essentials of survival when a climber is faced with a mountain. To step high upon the back of a mountain is to leave behind all the elements of ordinary life. The sound of the wind is not softened by the whisper of leaves or filtered by growing things. Up high the wind screams, scouring the rocks, sending plumes of snow high in the air. Unshackled, it is shaped by peaks so mighty they split the funnels of air that circle the earth. There is no smell of earth up there, no whirl of insect life. Instead, only the creaking and groaning of giant rivers of ice, the crash and boom of falling rocks and the reverberation of avalanches both near and far. It's a catastrophe of sound, a great pageant of movement.

Going up into the mountains is all about coming back again, so in many ways, it defines the security of home. It is the mythical cyclical journey of quest and return; the forced shedding of the ordinary and everyday. It is the movement beyond the normal elements of society to a place and space where experience is filtered through the physical receptor of your body, where success is ultimately measured only in terms of survival.

Mountains have always held mythical qualities for human society. They are places of the imagination, places that can peel back the layers of life.

Women's accounts of moving through the mountains as climbers and explorers are as little known as those of botanists. When they do break into the public world through being published, they tend to sound staid, even when the women's words as much as their bodies are cutting steps into a relationship with the land that goes way beyond the ordinary. To begin to understand the extraordinary experience of these women, imagine for a moment your body as the prime receptor of the information that mediates your survival. It is through the sensation of hanging over space—anchored to the side of the mountain—by a rope or just the strength in your fingers and toes, that you feel the pull of the earth's gravitational forces and the permeable boundaries of your own body.[2]

Imagine in that moment the strength you'll need as you stretch beyond yourself and suck in the mountain, face pressed against rock, your fingers like sightless eyes searching blindly for a crack, a fissure in the hard face of the mountain. The weight of your body might be reliant on one foothold, and your breath comes in gasps with the fear and the effort. If we can imagine the physical experience of moving through the mountains, the feel of ice and rock against the skin and hand, then perhaps we can gain insight into the women who wrote of the power of mountains.

Why have some women returned to the mountains again and again, pushing themselves physically and mentally, depriving themselves of comfort and exposing themselves to danger for weeks on end? Removed from the cladding of civilisation, their accounts of journeying through the mountains reveal a changing comprehension of their bodies and minds in response to the land.[3]

For women such as Freda Du Faur, an Australian who climbed in New Zealand between 1906 and 1913, and Mary Schaffer Warren, an American who explored the Rocky Mountains in Canada between 1898 and 1913, the mountains provided opportunities to test their abilities as well as the boundaries imposed on them by convention. Both women rebelled against the barriers placed on their behaviour by 19th-Century ideals of femininity, while their writing locates them firmly within the colonial context of which they were a part.[4] There is a strange oscillating tension in both their accounts of the mountains. Colonialism demanded intrepid and fearless behaviour, while femininity demanded passivity and a concern for relationships.[5]

Both women move uneasily between the masculine rhetoric of the explorer as conqueror and a more feminine response that sits awkwardly alongside the popular memoirs of climbing and exploring. But it is through their rejection of the role of the isolated individual triumphing over all, that they find in their experience an interconnection with place.

Freda Du Faur was born in Australia on 16 September 1882. Her father was one of Australia's first ardent environmentalists. His passion was the preservation of the bushland around Sydney as a site of national significance. Eccleston Du Faur was responsible for the Ku-ring-gai Chase area being gazetted as a reserve in 1894, and for promoting the use of land around the Hawkesbury River area as a National Park.[6] Freda's mother was Blanche Woolley, the daughter of John Woolley, Professor of Classics at the newly established University of Sydney.[7] Freda had a privileged and essentially urban childhood. She was educated at Sydney Church of England Grammar School for Girls under the headmistress Edith Badham, daughter of Charles Badham, Principal of Sydney University. Alongside this middle-class education, Freda had access to many of the ideas of early feminist thinkers through her aunt Emmaline, who was a close friend of the vocal and influential Rose Scott. Emmaline gave Freda John Stuart Mill's

The Subjection of Women (1861)[8] and a way of thinking that she drew upon throughout her life.

From 1899 to 1904 Freda lived with her mother and father on the edge of the newly formed Ku-ring-gai National Park.[9] Though she had no access to the sort of climbing she would later do in New Zealand, her exploration of this reserve challenged her mind and body as she faced some complicated rock-climbing problems. She wrote of being 'lured' by wild flowers deeper into this sandstone labyrinth, often finding herself trapped by the cliffs and faced with a steep climb to gain the ridge again. These un-structured explorations developed in her a love of adventure and exploring and 'a self reliance which caused my parents some alarm'.[10]

Freda had spent family summers on the North Island of New Zealand, but it wasn't until 1906 that she went to the South Island to visit the Christchurch Exhibition. It was here that she saw her first picture of Mount Cook and met people who'd visited the Southern Alps. Her curiosity was aroused and, though she had no thought of climbing, she decided to cut short her time at the exhibition and travel to the mountains.

Freda described her first view of the Alps as something akin to a religious experience:

> From the moment my eyes rested on the snow clad Alps I worshipped their beauty and was filled with a passionate longing to touch those shining snows, to

climb to their heights of silence and solitude, to feel
myself one with the mighty forces around me.[11]

To feel as one with the mountains was a challenge
that could not be gained by walking in the foothills
or staying at the hotel and enjoying the view. For
Freda, the desire to belong to the mountains came
from a need that could only be met by immersing
herself in the land. She used the language of romance,
as if she were seduced and wooed by the mountain.
The sexual metaphors of conquest and possession
are popular ones in the language of exploration and
mountaineering. But when women used these metaphors, they evoked a different kind of possession—
one in which the woman was subsumed by the
mountain, rather than conquering it.

> My chief desire as I gazed at them was to reach the
> snow and bury my hands in its wonderful whiteness,
> and dig and dig till my snow-starved Australian soul
> was satisfied that all this wonder of white was real
> and would not vanish at the touch.[12]

From the moment she arrived at the hotel, Freda
actively sought the means to climb. She joined a
group, led by guide Peter Graham, to climb the Sealy
Range. Though she recalled little detail from the
climb, she came away convinced that she would
'never be content to worship the mountains from a
distance'.[13] This brief experience of the mountains

left her with the knowledge that she must return. She was also left with questions about her ability to climb. She wrote that she knew she had an inborn love of climbing, but felt overwhelmed by doubts about her physical ability and her courage.

Freda did not want the gentle day trip of the typical woman tourist; she dreamt instead of climbing to the highest peak in New Zealand and being the first woman to do so.

It is the ability to 'read' a mountain, to understand it and anticipate its different conditions that distinguishes technically good climbers from great mountaineers. Freda wrote about this desire to be part of the mountains, to possess them and be possessed by them, from her first experience of climbing. When she returned to Mount Cook in 1908, she spent two weeks climbing with small parties led by head guide Peter Graham. She was usually the only woman in these parties, and she was careful to be the most enthusiastic and fittest member. On one of the last days of her trip, she climbed with Graham to a pass immediately below the third summit of Mount Cook. It was the highest point she had ever reached and, as she stood on the summit, all the questions she had asked of her ability to climb two years before appeared to have been answered.

Silently she gazed at the thin jagged ridge stretching beyond her. It was a knife-edge of ice and rock rising into a background of blue sky. At that moment she reached a decision that would change the course of her life:

> I decided I would be a real mountaineer, and some day be the first woman to climb Mount Cook. When I made this decision I was half afraid of it ... I knew how trained men and guides had been beaten back time and again, and how fierce the struggle of those few who had succeeded.[14]

She wisely said nothing of her ambitions, but approached Peter Graham and candidly asked his assessment of her capabilities to return the next season and train for some high climbing. Graham willingly agreed to train her in ice-and-snow climbing, of which Freda had no experience. Neither of them mentioned the silent challenge she'd received that day when staring at the ridge leading to Mount Cook.

When Freda returned to New Zealand in December 1909, she wrote that the mountains made her 'tingl[e] with joyous excitement ... and free and irresponsible as the wind that stung my cheek'.[15] Before she was allowed to start any of the bigger climbs, Peter Graham suggested that she complete a couple of minor excursions to 'get me in touch with the mountains again'.[16] This was a theme that she would return to over and over in her climbing accounts. On one of her longest trips in the mountains, she wrote of lying in her bivouac on a patch of rocks at 7000 feet, staring up at the western ridge leading to the third peak of Mount Cook. As she stilled herself in preparation for the climb, she listened:

> Some stone falling from the heights, the gurgle of an underground stream, or the wind sweeping into a hidden cave and raising an echo from the distant ridges—clear and distinct it comes, this call of the mountains, sometimes friendly and of good cheer; but often eerie, wild, and full of melancholy warning, as if the spirit of the mountains bade you beware.[17]

Surrounded by the presence of the mountains, and drawn by their 'call', she took this message of caution with her as she prepared to climb the next day.

Freda's philosophy of climbing drew a distinction between feeling a sense of belonging on a mountain and climbing for the sake of notoriety, of being the first to the top. Peter Graham had told Freda that he could easily guide her to the top of Mount Cook without any more experience, but it would not be a climb that she could acknowledge as her own:

> Climb Mount Cook at once, and you will have done what is considered the biggest climb in N. Z. ... You probably won't enjoy the doing of it, or be fit to appreciate your success when you have gained it. Except the mere notoriety of being the first woman

on the summit, you will gain nothing, and stand to lose the best of a wonderful experience, because you tried to grasp it before you are ready to appreciate it in all its fullness.[18]

For Freda the processes of climbing, the journey that she undertook to reach the top was more important than the destination and achievement. She was ambitious and she had the ability to climb Mount Cook, but her decision to wait until she was ready showed an attitude of mind that spoke of humility in seeking a relationship with the mountains. Her journey into the mountains was not really completed until she sat down several years later to write about her climbs.

Before Freda could climb any mountains, she had to overcome the prejudices and restrictions placed upon her by the other women staying at the hotel. She was the first unmarried woman to climb in the New Zealand Alps. There was no precedent for a single woman to go out alone with a guide, and women staying at the hotel implored her not to throw away her reputation for the sake of climbing a mountain. But Freda saw herself as a pioneer, a woman going where no woman had gone before. Her first serious climb of Mount Sealy required an overnight bivouac immediately beneath where they would make a final attempt on the summit. Such a break with conventional climbing practices for women was met with fierce resistance.

> In vain I argued ... that I had come to the mountains to climb, not to sit on the veranda and admire the view. If I were to limit my climbs to occasions on which I could induce another man or woman to accompany me, I might as well take the next boat home. At the moment there was no one in the hotel who could or would climb Mount Sealy ... only women who found a two-mile walk quite sufficient for their powers. This they could not deny, but they assured me with all seriousness that if I went out with a guide I would lose my reputation.[19]

For a moment Freda rued her lack of what she called 'that useful appendage to a woman climber, a husband'.[20] But then she concluded that if she did possess one of those [a husband], he would probably consider climbing 'unfeminine', and therefore make her state worse than it already was. Eventually, a compromise was suggested in the form of a porter accompanying her and Peter Graham. Freda was not pleased that she had to pay for someone to come with them and carry the packs: 'I would like to see a man asked to pay for something he neither needed or wanted'.[21]

They reached the summit of Mount Sealy at 8:15 am. Freda noted with satisfaction that Peter Graham had to help the porter more than herself; this had been her chance to prove her stamina, courage and skill. As a result of this higher and harder climb, she convinced Peter Graham to train her for Mount Cook.

Mount Sefton was a turning point for Peter Graham as well. After several more training climbs, including a difficult traverse of Mount Malte Brun, he decided that Freda was ready to tackle Mount Cook. The man they had employed to work as a second guide had poisoned his arm and could not accompany them; Peter planned the climb for them alone. His decision to climb with only two on a rope was based on the approach to the summit he had chosen along a route that included long sections of exposed rock face; it was his confidence in Freda's rock-climbing ability that enabled him to make this choice.

The decision raised a storm of criticism and disapproval. 'Everyone was against us', Freda wrote; 'they came at us separately and together to say it was "madness" or "an unjustifiable risk".'[22]

Jack Clarke, a senior guide and highly respected member of the party who had first ascended Mount Cook, was vocal in his opposition, and Freda had to fight him over her right to make the attempt. Her account of the clash seethes with the injustice of his position:

> [Clarke] must acknowledge that a traverse of Mount
> Malte Brun such as we had made, not only by a new

and difficult route, but in the fastest time on record was a reliable test as to my powers of rock-climbing and endurance ... [I]f he would simply ignore the fact that I was a woman, and judge me as an individual on my climbing merits, the case might appear to him in a less alarming light.[23]

Freda and Peter Graham left on 21 January 1910 for Freda's first attempt of Mount Cook.

On the evening before our team's attempt to climb Mount Silverthrone in the Alaskan Range, I crawled into my sleeping bag. That night the wind whistled down the glacier and shook the nylon of the tent as if to emphasise its thin defences. Morning brought a frozen stillness. I fumbled for boots and, as my fingers fought with laces stiff with frost, I felt a knot of tension settle deep in my stomach. Unlike the experience of kayaking on Prince William Sound, where I often paddled in tandem, the climb today would require total commitment from my body. My husband would be on the rope team, but he would be no buffer from the extreme physicality of the experience. Climbing, I had found, was a profoundly individual journey.

As Freda and Peter climbed through the ice field to reach their bivouac at 8000 feet, they were confronted with a crevasse over twenty feet wide. Graham searched in both directions for a snow bridge to span the crevasse and returned with the news that the only possibility was a tiny fragile bridge—so narrow that the only way to cross it was to straddle it. Freda described the crevasse as another world. Its sheer sides glistened with blue-green ice, and there was no discernible bottom:

> I don't know how I got on that bridge, it seemed to take ages; I was so frightened of not distributing the weight properly and breaking through, and the black abyss below me was not an encouraging thing to fall into.[24]

They crossed the crevasse, and the next day climbed into a dead end. Freda's disappointment was heavy. 'It was one of the bitterest moments I ever experienced, and mere words were useless. We must have stood there for half an hour, knowing it was hopeless, yet hating to leave.'[25]

They returned to the hotel, dragging the weight of their failure behind them. But they also took back with them valuable knowledge and experience of what it was like to camp at 8000 feet with the wind howling and the barometer falling. The climb had given Freda exposure to that most alien of landscapes, the ice field.

> Nothing was what it seemed to my untrained eye in this strange frozen world ... helplessly I began to

wonder if there was a solid yard on this horrible mountain strong enough to bear my modest weight. My mind was chaos, my nerves on edge.[26]

Freda described her first ice field as the most mentally intimidating space she had climbed. In this alien space she experienced the overwhelming fear of her own insignificance in the face of the glacier's indifference. She had not yet learned to read the ice and negotiate her way through the labyrinth of cracks and crevasses. As she gained in experience, the ice field became less disorienting, and though she was never comfortable moving through such a dangerous and constantly shifting space, the paralysing terror that she had felt on her first encounter was replaced by a deep and alert respect.

Freda returned to New Zealand in November 1910 to make another attempt at Mount Cook, after three months of hard physical training back in Australia.[27] This had given her a mental and physical edge; she felt 'fit for anything, and with a reserve fund of endurance to draw upon which may mean all the difference between success and failure on a difficult and possibly dangerous climb'.[28] On arriving back in the Alps, her program was to complete a week of minor climbs to put her 'thoroughly in touch with the mountains again'.[29] She and the Graham brothers, Peter and Alex, left the hotel on 30 November 1910 to try for Mount Cook. Bad weather struck, and they were trapped by a blizzard for the whole of the next day. By 11am on 2 December, they reached the last bivouac from which they would attempt the summit on the 3rd. That night, with the temperature well below zero (Fahrenheit), Freda broke with convention and asked the guides to join her in her tent. It was a pragmatic request; with three people in a tent, they'd have a better chance of warmth and, therefore, sleep.

> I decided that having walked over most of the conventions since I began mountaineering, one more would matter nothing; so I suggested to the guides that they abandon their tent and save me from shivering in icy aloofness till morning.[30]

It was a different kind of courage that she needed to write about these breaks in convention. She could have hidden these details from her audience, instead of using them as a testing ground for the limits imposed on femininity. In many ways her record of these moments was as potentially dangerous to her future as the adventures on which they were based.

The three climbers set off at 2:45am. Freda described their start beneath crisp starlight: 'We put on the rope, lit two lanterns, and started away … the snow was frozen very hard, and in the dim light seemed to slope away to fathomless depths.'[31] The rock they found on the western buttress was good, and well within her ability. But a thousand feet from the top, they struck rotten shale, covered with a thin film of green ice. The ice acted like glass, making it hard to find secure hand and feet holds. As they picked their way over this rotten rock, they saw the summit ahead, 'dead-white … gleaming above us'.[32] When they were within a few feet of the summit, the Graham brothers sent Freda ahead, and she found herself on the top of New Zealand, with the world below her. Instead of feeling triumphant, she felt 'very little, very lonely, and much inclined to cry'.[33]

She stood on top of the mountain and failed to feel as a conqueror. Her desire to cry, to feel little and lonely—that is, unimportant and insignificant—could be taken as a very feminine response to her achievement. She made the climb and wrote of it in an anti-heroic way. She admitted vulnerability just at her most triumphant moment. As the Graham brothers joined her, she swallowed the feeling of insignificance and laughed instead. They had made the summit by 8:40am, beating the previous record by two hours—'and I a mere woman'![34]

They had returned safely to their bivouac by five-thirty pm. Freda had been climbing for fourteen-and-a-half hours; six hours up, two hours on the peak and six-and-a-half hours back down again. When she came to write about the climb, her recollection was very physical, as if she remembered it first through her body. Her description of waking in the early hours of the morning pulses with the reality of the mountain pushing against her body. She wrote of winding frozen puttees around her legs (these woollen strips would protect and support her from knee to ankle), of fitting her feet into heavy leather boots. We are with her at the eerie start in flickering candlelight, with the snow crunching tight and compact beneath nailed boots, and the ring of iron on ice as she climbed. As she wrote, it is as if her fingers, swollen and throbbing, were once again remembering the texture and tone of the rock, solid and exhilarating, or flaky and alarming—numbed fingers on death-cold rocks.

> [T]he sure foot, muscle and brain pitting themselves against the mightiest forces of nature as when life flows wild and free in the beginning of the world. All the primitive emotions are ours—hunger and thirst, heat and cold, triumph and fear—as yard by yard we win our way to stand as conquerors and survey our realm.[35]

She certainly used the masculine rhetoric of colonial exploration, of which she was a part, occasionally speaking of herself as conqueror of the mountain, but there is a tension between the thrill of conquering a mountain and respectfully acknowledging its separate supremacy. For Freda, the engagement with the mountain required a surrendering to the process of climbing. These attitudes exist side by side in *The Conquest of Mount Cook*.

Freda Du Faur, Peter Graham and Alex Graham after their successful ascent of Mount Cook, 1910.

Through her climbing Freda was given a radically changing perception of the landscape of the mountains. From the stance of those below, mountains covered in cloud offer no view at all. From above, there is an entirely different understanding as the clouds close in. In cloud, the mountains have no depth. They no longer appear to be made of solid rock, ice and snow. In cloud, they are shrouded in mystery, revealing nothing of themselves and giving no answers. The world they create is perfectly illusionary. Freda wrote of sitting on Tucker's Col at one of these moments of change:

We were startled by a puff of icy wind, and ten minutes afterwards we were enveloped in a great bank of clouds that had been drifting quietly up from the sea. There we sat, alone on a few square feet of rock, with a precipice on either side, while the mists blotted out the world. The sensation was extraordinary; we were the only solid objects in a world of wraiths. We sat very still, afraid to move.[36]

After climbing for about two hours, my breath was coming in ragged sobs. The mountain filled my vision and pushed its whiteness into me. My hand scooped snow and caught nothing solid. It seemed only the pain in my lungs and legs that claimed me as real. Moving up the mountain, I was finding it difficult to feel the edge of myself. The boundary of my body seemed blurred: where did I end and the mountain begin? In coming to find something, I was in danger of losing myself.

Sitting in my tracks at 15 000 feet, swapping snowshoes for crampons, it occurred to me that climbing is a frivolous adventure. For Freda climbing was leisure, but it also allowed her a freedom of movement and an expression of herself that she could not access anywhere but on the side of a mountain. The mountains judged her as a climber, not as a woman. Sitting on the side of Mount Silverthrone, I had to ask myself why I was there.

The early women climbers, from the 1890s through to the 1930s were vocal supporters of female emancipation, yet climbing historians have argued that they climbed in ways that ultimately reflected and reinforced the values of the patriarchal society they sought to change.[37] At first this can seem a plausible argument, yet after reading Freda's narrative in *The Conquest of Mount Cook*, it's clear that she wanted to make a distinction between herself and the male climbers she accused of climbing for the sake of conquering, rather than the love of the climb. After she had climbed Mount Cook, she contrasted her experience with another climber who had come back to the hotel after a successful ascent:

> His attitude to the climb amused me somewhat; it seemed mainly thankfulness that it was over. So far as I could discover the doing of it, instead of being a pleasure, had been merely a monotonous grind. ... For the hundredth time I was up against the problem as to why men who were not merely seeking notoriety should climb at all, when they apparently enjoyed the doing of it so little.[38]

What overwhelmed me when I sat down to write about Freda's climbing were the details embedded in her story. Reading her memoir, it is not the magnitude of the climbs, the numbers and figures, that remained with me after I finished, but a sense of the journey that she had undertaken. She had written at the outset of her desire to belong in the mountains. It seemed that this, as much as the incredible achievements of her climbs, sets her story apart from the masculine tradition of climbing memoirs. Despite this difference, Freda's account is one of a very serious mountaineer. She asks to be read first as a climber and then as a woman. What is so interesting is the way she negotiates the space between these two concepts.

Although Freda was undoubtedly ambitious, she climbed for the experience, rather than for her reputation, and her accounts of her climbs are richly peopled with her guides' presence and personalities. She always gave the credit of her success to the guides that found the routes up the mountain.

Freda's relationship with the Graham brothers was very close. She had difficulty imagining herself climbing without one of them. The intensity of the moments they shared when life seemed to hover on the strength in Peter Graham's arm or the ability of Alex to read a changing weather pattern had developed a level of trust between the three of them that Freda found difficult to explain. Freda had been taught to climb virtually from scratch by Peter Graham, and their relationship went beyond the normal professional arrangements between guides and clients. This was part of the reason Freda's record of climbs in New Zealand is so extraordinary. But it also meant that she found it very difficult to climb without them beyond New Zealand. Freda was Peter Graham's rather brilliant protégé, and their climbing relationship was more egalitarian than the more normal hierarchy between client and guide.[39]

*Freda climbing the rocks of Mount Nazomi (Heart's Desire),
1911. Note her short skirt, puttees to protect her legs, large hat
and scarf to protect her from sun and wind. Her clothes are
very different from those she posed in formally after
the ascent of Mount Cook.*

Over three seasons, Freda climbed all the most challenging mountains in New Zealand. She made five first ascents and named Mount Nazomi, Mount Pibrac and Mount Cadogan. These mountains were named after those things that were most close to her. Nazomi was a Japanese word for heart's desire, Pibrac was the name of the Du Faur family home, and Murial Cadogan was the love of Freda's life.[40] On 4 January 1913 she accomplished the feat for which she is most famous, the first grand traverse of the three peaks of Mount Cook, with guides Peter Graham and David Thomson. This Grand Traverse is still considered the classic climb of the New Zealand Alps.[41]

After completing all the major climbs in New Zealand, Freda had hoped to continue her climbing career by travelling to Canada and the Himalayas. She decided to move to London to start to plan for these trips. She travelled with Murial, whom she had met at the Dupain Institute in Sydney and who had been responsible for training her for her ascent of Mount Cook. Before she could climb again, however, Freda had a contract to write her book, a task she confessed to finding more difficult than the climbs themselves.[42] Her writing became a way of processing what had happened in New Zealand, and also a way of farewelling the mountains and the relationships she had formed there. The sensitivity to place that had developed through her climbing is lovingly

The western face of Mount Cook, showing the route taken by Freda, Peter Graham and David Thomson of the first Grand Traverse of the three peaks of Mount Cook. X marks the bivouac where they slept the first night, and the dots mark their route (January 1913).

193

crafted into her descriptions of the mountains, but the book failed to attract the sort of attention she had enjoyed after her triumph in New Zealand. The reviewers anointed her as an extraordinary climber, but not as a writer.

In London Murial and Freda became lovers and lived together until Murial's descent into mental illness and death in 1928. Freda never recovered from this, and she did not climb again. She battled with mental illness herself until 1935, when she neatly arranged her affairs and gassed herself in the oven of her small home on Sydney's northern beaches.[43]

Freda's writing never received the attention that Isabella Bird had garnered when she challenged Victorian conventions in *A Lady's Life in the Rocky Mountains* (1879). Like Freda, Isabella had written of the mountains as consuming her thoughts and imagination: 'they [the mountains] are gradually gaining possession of me. I can look and feel nothing else.'[44] In 1873 she climbed Long's Peak, the mountain that dominates Estes Park in the Colorado Rockies. This peak had been climbed for the first time five years earlier, a fact that was no doubt something of a disappointment to the ambitious Isabella, who had a good eye for the commercial possibilities of nearly every experience. Her ability to convert experiences into saleable stories was another defiance of

*Freda Du Faur on Mount Dampier ridge, facing the North
West rocks of Mount Cook. Note the rope around her
waist, connecting her to Peter Graham in the lead. This was
the first ascent of Mount Dampier (1911).*

convention. Most female climbers were women of independent means, and Freda was able to fund her climbs without having to write about them. But, for Isabella, money was more of a problem. By making her travels adventurous enough to sell books, she purchased her freedom. So although she confessed to having 'no head and no ankles, and never ought to dream of mountaineering', she arranged for a guide to take her to the top before the end of the season.[45] Having found her guide, she treated her audience to a tableau of her riding out of Estes Park with the guide and two other young men. They took only saddle horses and carried enough food to last them three days. We are left with the image of Isabella riding towards the mountain, horse's tail swinging as she found her seat in her big Mexican saddle, her bright quilt draped over her shoulders to warm her at night, *flashing* between the trees like some exotic bird.

She later claimed that she would never have attempted the climb had she known that it was a 'real mountaineering feat'.[46] It was typical of Isabella to perform a remarkable physical feat and then write about it as if it were an accident that she had achieved such a hard technical climb.[47] The effect was to distance her feminine self from the activity as if she had somehow been miraculously transported to the top without any sweat or undignified effort. In this way,

she retained her feminine gentility even in as masculine an arena as climbing.

Thirty years later, Freda had none of Isabella's
false modesty, and was far more aggressive in her
demands that her climbs be recognised as significant
achievements; she staked her publication success on
her reputation as an outstanding climber and not as
a lady. She refused to let the fact of her sex diminish
the difficulty of the climb. Isabella, in contrast, wrote
of being 'humiliated by my success',[48] and, in many
ways, she was, for she and the two male tourists that
formed her party would never have reached the top
if it had not been for the skill and strength of their
guide, 'Mountain Jim'.[49]

It's possible to read Isabella's humiliation in
another way. Climbing a mountain is a humbling
experience. Physically, it is exhausting, pushing your
body far beyond its normal limits; mentally, you are
challenged by discomfort and danger: *Why are you
here? Can you make it to the top? Will your body
perform this feat for you?* Such questions haunt you
all the way up. When Isabella left Estes Park with
two young men to climb the peak that dominated the
valley, she reeked of confidence. Her letters present
her as a woman filled with self-assurance, but she
returned 'humiliated' by her climb. The action of
climbing had diminished her perception of her capabilities. In the face of the mountain, she had learnt

the extent of her physical limits, an uncomfortable sensation for a woman as confident as Isabella. In the face of physical limitations, it is hard to maintain the confidence of the heroic individual conquering the mountain. Yet Isabella also returned exhilarated, for she had gained something from her climb: 'I would not now exchange my memories of its perfect beauty and extraordinary sublimity for any other experience of mountaineering in any part of the world.'[50]

Halfway up Silverthrone and space—blue space—yawned on either side. This was a huge crevasse. I stood still, weight distributed as evenly as possible, as the guide probed the bridge in front, seeking a continuous layer of ice to support our weight. I peered into the depths of the glacier's heart, and was lured to look further. It was so blue, so terrifyingly beautiful. Is this the sublime?

I have returned to that moment when it was as if time stood still and I hovered between spaces. In that place I felt invincible and powerful, exultant that I had arrived, yet insignificant and so terribly out of place, as if I had no right to look there at all.

Laying in my tent that night, my body carried the memory of a wind that shrugged us off the side of the mountain. We'd sat on the col with only a hundred feet to the summit and watched the whiteout blast toward us. The memory of the climb was already fading into that white. Still at last and warm in my sleeping bag, my body hummed with the push and pull of the wind. From the edge of exhaustion, my mind slid back and forth over the day. Through the night, it was the icy blue heart of the mountain, stretching back beyond geography, beyond history, beyond my ability to know it, that infiltrated my dreams.

The Rocky Mountains in North America stretch the length of a continent and link three countries. The first fur traders moving across the endless openness of the Canadian prairies called them the 'Shining Mountains'.[51] The Blackfoot Indians called them 'the Backbone of the Earth'. As you cross the prairie heading west, they are always before you, earth's skeleton laid bare, filling the western horizon. They creep into the edges of your dreams and form a new landscape in your mind.

Mary Schaffer Warren's first view of the Canadian Rockies was from the luxurious appointments of a Pullman car. Like Georgiana Molloy and Mary O'Brien, an interest in wild flowers was the catalyst for a journey that would take her from the world of the insulated tourist into unmapped territory.

Mary Shaffer was born in 1869 into a wealthy Quaker family in West Chester, Pennsylvania. Her childhood was privileged, and she received an excellent education in mathematics and languages, probably at the Friends' Select School in Philadelphia. She excelled in art and was taught painting by the renowned flower artist, George Lamden. She was also encouraged in the study of natural history, and this led to an interest in botany and the attention to botanical detail that was evident in her later illustrations.[52] Mary had always travelled as a leisure activity. She had taken her first trip west in her mid-teens when she journeyed with her family by train to California. Her second trip took her further away from the settled frontier; this time the family travelled by freight steamer up the West Coast of North America to Alaska.[53]

As a child, Mary had overheard a conversation between her father and her cousin Jim, who was an officer in the United States Army. He'd told many stories about the West: of settlers heading out across the prairie in covered wagons, and of buffalo hunts. What appalled and fascinated Mary were the stories he brought back of the war between the Indians and the United States government. On this particular night, Jim told of the complete destruction of an Indian village, including the women and children. Mary later wrote:

The baby face, the dead mother, the smoking tepees remained in the child's mind forever after and governed many an act as she grew older. She never spoke of what she heard that night, but the shadow of the story always hung on her horizon.[54]

Mary wrote of this experience in the third person, and it adds to the sense of its strange, disturbing effect on her young mind, as if even now she could not bear to place herself in the situation of hearing that story again. Perhaps it was this fascination with a world that had been so ruthlessly changed that pushed her to take the first steps outside the normal conventions of her world. The high, untouched landscape of the mountains was a counter to her memory of the destruction wrought on land and people by her government. When she later wrote about her travels and explorations of the Canadian Rockies, she always included an acknowledgement that the land was known and mapped by the Indians, and that she was following trails they'd used for thousands of years. Her first publication was called *Old Indian Trails* (1911).

Mary first came to Banff in 1889, at the age of twenty, with Mary Vaux, a friend with similar interests in art and botany.[55] They left from Montreal and travelled by rail to Vancouver, staying at Glacier House on the way. There Mary met Dr Charles

Schaffer, a friend of the Vaux family from Philadelphia. Although he was a medical doctor with a private medical practice, Dr Schaffer's passion was botany. He had come to the Rockies for the wild flowers, which had been described by the Vauxes from their previous trips to Glacier. Although he was twenty-five years her senior, he and Mary had a love of flowers in common and, when they returned to Philadelphia, he asked her to marry him. They married late in 1889, and then returned each summer to Banff, Field, Glacier and Lake Louise to further their study of alpine botany.

Charles Schaffer's ambition was to publish the first book of the alpine flora of the Canadian Rockies. When he realised Mary's talent as an artist, he taught her to paint the specimens they collected with a botanist's eye for detail. 'He was emphatic that every petal, every stamen should be correct to the last and I was much more interested in grouping', she wrote ... 'any sketch that passed his eagle eye simply HAD to be correct.'[56]

In 1903 Charles Schaffer died of heart disease. He never saw his studies published. But Mary returned to the Rockies, primarily to complete her husband's work. It wasn't only that she had put so much time into the project through her illustrations, watercolour drawings and photographs; she'd also found the mountains to be a place of peace. Returning to where they had spent many happy hours offered her a space and a purpose in which to grieve. Her decision to return to the mountains, ostensibly to honour the work of her husband, was perhaps as much a desire to see her own hard work recognised. This work provided the connection between an acceptable notion of study and painting flowers, and the more remarkable trips that grew out of Mary's botanical collecting.[57]

Though Mary was engrossed in the subject of flowers, her knowledge was far more artistic than scientific, and she had trouble classifying anything beyond the more common specimens. To overcome her lack of botanical knowledge, she approached Stewardson Brown of the Academy of Natural Sciences of Philadelphia, offering him naming rights for the work. Brown agreed, and set to working through the existing collection. To extend the collection, Mary faced another challenge. Dr Schaffer's heart condition had limited the couple's collecting expeditions. And Mary made no secret of the fact that she was afraid of horses, bears and the wilderness in general. To her, all horses appeared 'tricky and vicious', and she had not previously ventured more than a few miles from the hotel.

Faced with the challenge of completing the collection, Mary realised that she would have to learn to ride. With a determination that would become characteristic, she sought out a guide to teach her. Billy Warren, then aged twenty-two, was a veteran of the

Boer War and an Englishman. He had arrived in Banff in 1902 and been given work by the pioneer guide and outfitter, Tom Wilson. Billy made a strong impression on Mary. She was drawn to his easygoing nature, his ability to converse with her and, above all, his kindness. Mary employed Warren to take charge of the longer wilderness trips and teach her the skills she needed to survive them, if she were going to finish the collection. Billy taught her to ride astride and 'rough it' in relative comfort: 'He gave us our very first lessons in sitting astride a horse and learning to jump a log without being shot over the head of our steed.'[58] They made several small pack trips: first overnight, then for three days and, finally, for five weeks. These Mary called 'a kindergarten of the at-first-despised camping life'.[59]

For Mary and her companion, Mollie Adams, who was the 'we' in Mary's narrative, these trips provided the opportunity to discover the 'secret of comfort, content and peace on very little of the world's material goods, to learn to value at its true worth the great un-lonely silence of the wilderness, and to revel in the emancipation from frills, furbelows and small follies'.[60]

Mollie was also from the Eastern United States and shared Mary's Quaker background. She had stronger scientific training and taught geology at Columbia College New York when she wasn't travelling.[61] Both women came from privileged, urban backgrounds and had never learnt how to keep house, let alone rough it in the backcountry. Mary described Mollie as a 'kindred spirit' and, between the two of them, there was never 'a riffle of disagreement in the thousands of miles we meandered'.[62] Through their first small trips, the women learnt to negotiate the swift rivers, steep passes, and clogged forests. Of crossing rivers, Mary was told, 'If your horse rolls over, cling to his mane or tail. Don't let go of him altogether. He may get out alive, you never will alone.'[63] Her inclusion of this advice signals her departure from the woman who was afraid of horses.

After a three-day trip to the Yoho Valley, a few days at Moraine Lake, seven days in the Ptarmigan Valley and, finally, a five-week trip to Saskatchwan country, they had collected enough material for Mary to finish the botany project. They had also gained enough skills to enjoy the sensation of camping beyond the sight and sound of the railway. The book that Mary and Charles had conceived, *Alpine Flora of the Canadian Rocky Mountains* (1907),[64] was completed three years after Charles Schaffer's death. For Mary its completion meant that she and Mollie Adams had no need to continue their small research trips with Billy Warren. Yet, as the popularity of the Banff area as a tourist attraction grew, many of the sites they'd enjoyed in solitude were being made accessible to tourism of a more general kind. As the tide of tourists, many of them women, flowed into the hotels, the area around the railway grew more and more manicured. Women travelled to the mountains to escape the restrictions society placed on single women in their role as daughters, sisters, aunts or potential wives,[65] and they followed the propaganda trail of the railway promoters, who saw in the incredible beauty of the area a way to pay for their railways.

Mary Schaffer was very much a part of this tourist experience. But what began as an activity that closely reflected her status as an upper-class woman of leisure changed into a lifetime's passionate pursuit of high places, of solitude and silence, beyond the tourist trail. Travelling through the backcountry of the Rocky Mountains, Mary experienced a freedom of movement and action not normally available to a woman of her class in any other environment. It was her wealth that allowed her to travel, yet it was also wealth that placed barriers between her body and the physical landscape. Gentility was a commodity that restrained physical movement.[66] Mary pursued physical movement, but when she wrote about her experiences, she aggressively defended her gentility and questioned its terms.

> Why must they settle so absolutely upon the fact, that the lover of the hills and wilderness drops the dainty ways and habits with the conventional garments and becomes something of courser mould? Can the free air sully, can the birds teach us words we should not

hear, can it be possible to see in such a summer's out-
ing, one sight as painful as the daily ones of poverty,
degradation and depravity of a great city?[67]

In 1903 Mary had met the geologist-explorer Sir
James Hector, whose tales of huge mountains and
unexplored valleys struck a deep chord in her. By
1906 she and Mollie Adams, with two seasons of

Mary Schaffer riding on the Kootanay Plains in 1906.
The Athabaska River is in the background. Mary's party
had to negotiate this river twice on their trip of 1907.
Mary is riding astride on an American stock saddle
and wearing a long divided skirt. Photo: Whyte Museum
of the Canadian Rockies.

camping experience behind them, were listening to the tales of hunters and trappers with their newfound knowledge of pack travel beyond settlement. They were told of a country of 'great beauty, of unnamed peaks and little known rivers'. They watched jealously as various gentlemen explorers mounted expeditions to 'find' and (re)name the peaks, passes, rivers and lakes. 'From the States came Allen and Wilcox, (men of course), gathered their outfits together and left us sitting on the railroad track following them with hungry eyes as they plunged into the distant hills; to listen just as hungrily to the camp-fire tales on their return.'[68] As they watched the men come and go with mounting frustration at their own immobility, Mary and Mollie decided that they too were capable of an extended backcountry exploratory trip.

> [T]here are times when the horizon seems restricted, and we seemed to have reached that horizon, and the limit of all endurance,—to sit with folded hands and listen calmly to the stories of the hills we so longed to see, the hills which had lured and beckoned us for years before this long list of men had ever set foot in the country. Our cups splashed over. Then we looked into each other's eyes and said: 'Why not? We can starve as well as they; the muskeg[69] will be no softer for us than for them; the ground will be no harder to sleep upon; the waters no deeper to swim, nor the bath colder if we fall in,'—so we planned a trip.[70]

Their first big trip, in the summer of 1907, was to last four months, until the snows turned them back down the mountains. Their aim was to find the headwaters of the Saskatchewan and Athabaska rivers. But Mary wrote of another objective, using the masculine rhetoric of exploration:

> Our aim was to delve into the heart of an untouched land; to tread where no human foot had ever trod before, to turn the unthumbed pages of an unread book, and to learn daily those secrets which dear Mother Nature is so willing to tell those who seek.[71]

She found it strange to be asked repeatedly why she was travelling into the backcountry. Her social circle could not understand why she did not have some settled destination for her journey. But Mary sought the mountains for other reasons than the thrill of arriving somewhere, or climbing a peak never before ascended. She sought a place that was governed by laws different from the society she had left behind, and she sought something deeper, more difficult to articulate.

> There are some secrets you will never learn, there are some joys you will never feel, there are heart thrills you can never experience, till, with your horse, you leave the world, your recognised world, and plunge into the vast unknown.[72]

Mary's desire to leave behind the built-up world of settlement and enter into the wilderness can also be understood in terms of her upbringing. Quaker philosophy stressed introspection and the revelation of God in nature. When she was in the mountains, Mary felt herself in a sacred place.[73] She sought those places to commune with God. Her exploration gave her the opportunity to be spiritually refreshed. Climbing into the mountains, she connected her body and soul with the land that reflected her creator. The mountains became a place where she could feel 'whole'. Everything she saw around her spoke of a bountiful and creative God.

> The great mountains hung with glaciers sweep away on both sides of the high valley, we plunge deep into colour. Fancy trying to guide a materialistic pony's feet that he may not crush all this splendour beneath his iron shoes, knee deep in the tall forget-me-nots (lithosperumum), whose blue eyes brush the rider's knee, he cranes his neck and snatches a mouthful of the most perfect crimson castilia or painter's brush you think you ever saw and you long to spank him.[74]

She might mourn their impact on the land from the perspective of the picturesque rather than an awareness of the damage being done to fragile alpine plants, but her tone changed to anger when she wrote of timber cutters who would burn a hillside of forest for the sake of an easy day's travel.[75]

*Hand-coloured lantern slide by Mary Schaffer of a saddle horse
moving through fallen timber, showing the difficult country
Mary rode through. She painted hundreds of lantern slides from
her trips. Photo: Whyte Museum of the Canadian Rockies.*

Mary used the same language as male explorers
moving through the Pacific and Australia; her books
and articles were a feminine interpretation of the
genre of explorers' journals.[76] Yet there were differences. She gave all the credit of exploration to her
guide, Billy Warren, and his partner, Syd Unwin,
whereas most explorers were heroic individuals in
their accounts, with rarely a mention of the guides.[77]
Mary detailed the impact her party had on the land,
a consideration that hardly appeared in the heroic
version. The rhetoric of the white male explorer
was more likely to describe the land in terms of
its potential production, rather than concern for its

conservation. Few acknowledged that the country they travelled through was named and known by the indigenous people, while Mary was frank that many of the places they visited were only found through information gained from the indigenous people. Though her presence was transitory, she was eager to understand the unmapped country they were finding their way through. And like Freda Du Faur, she discovered that looking at a view and moving through the view were two very different experiences.

Though Mary wasn't a climber and had no instinctive love of the process of climbing, she did climb several peaks in an effort to understand where she was and where she was going: 'Hoping to get a different view of the mountains seen from the Sang-Sangen Creek, the following day we climbed Wilcox Peak (10 050 feet)'.[78] When she wrote of 'the weary grind' on this climb, she described the moment when she must push her body beyond her limits to arrive at the summit. She wrote of 'laboriously' trudging up the mountain, trying to keep her guide in sight. She caught sight of him disappearing around a huge wall of rock. Her body carried her upwards until she was confronted by a sheer drop of two thousand feet: Wilcox Peak sheared away as if cut by a knife. Above her, a rock wall towered, while below her, space loomed. There was a two-foot ledge jutting out from the rock wall above her, and by this route she would reach the summit.

Her instinct was to panic: 'It was too much for my stock of alpine courage and I yelled for help'. Billy yelled back with the encouraging instruction that it was 'safe enough, hold up your head, don't look down!' She surprised herself and followed without question, placing trust in his assessment and in her body to perform the scramble. But unlike Freda, she took little pleasure in the challenge, and being 'scared stiff of rocks and precipices', she avoided high climbing whenever possible. She didn't record feeling exhilarated by the achievement of it; rather, nearly all her climbs were made to understand more fully the height, depth and breadth of the mountains through which she was travelling.

Memory lives in our bodies as much as in our mind. When I returned from the mountains, I carried in me insignificance. I did not return triumphant. Instead, what I brought back was imparted in that moment of standing on a snow bridge and peering down into the icy heart of the mountain. Its terrible cold made me tremble with the tenuousness of *me*. My body still carries the memory of the tug of the powerful undercurrent of a glacially fed river. Its cold embraced me, whispering of its icy heart in its pull and slide past my body. These moments take me back to a place where I felt the world through my

Mary Schaffer and Mollie Adams climbing rocks.
Both women are wearing pants. Photo: Whyte
Museum of the Canadian Rockies.

senses and where I carried with me, at every moment,
a knowledge of my own mortality.

To experience a sense of place is a very physical
sensation. It is a paring down of elements that sur-
round us and make us feel comfortable. In the mountains there are no illusions of safety, no separation

between the land and our own fragile humanity. Life is just life and can be gone in the slip of a foot, or the fall of a rock.

On their homeward journey in 1907, Mary, Mollie, Billy and Syd Unwin spent some time with Samson Beaver, a Stoney Indian and his family. After many weeks of hard travel in the high country, they had returned via the Kootenai Plains. As they rode through the yellowing poplars, Mary saw two tepees set back amongst the trees. This small group of Stoney people gave her her Indian name of 'Yehe-Weha', meaning 'mountain woman'.

The outfit camped near the family for four days. Mary took photos, with their permission, and the resulting images are very different from the stereo-typical photos of Indians with blank, stoic faces that reveal nothing of the person in the photo. Samson Beaver and his wife and child look confidently into the camera. Mary arranged the photo with a back-drop of trees and a posy of poplar leaves for the child. The overall impression is of a family framed by nature. That Mary managed to capture their humanity was a result of her relationship with this family and her skill as a photographer.

When they finally took their leave of the Saskat-chewan valley, Samson Beaver gave them a map, which was the key to their return the next season.

Mary Schaffer's photograph of Sampson Beaver,
his wife and daughter. Photo: Whyte Museum of the
Canadian Rockies.

Sampson had with much care traced the lake we
had tried so hard to find, which was supposed to lie
north of Brazeau Lake. He had been there but once
as a child of fourteen, and now a man of thirty,
he drew it from memory,—mountain, streams, and
passes all included. They had to be labelled for our
benefit, for he had probably never seen a geography
in his life, and it would be hard to remember for a
whole year that a very scribbly spot was a pass, and
that something that looked like a squished spider he
called a mountain.[79]

The map was remarkable for its accuracy. The Stoneys had resisted sharing the secret of the lake with the whites, as it was a good hunting ground. But knowing that Mary's party was not a hunting party, Samson had sketched the map and given a few details about the best way to reach the lake. The next summer Mary, Mollie and their two guides followed the map and arrived on the southwestern shore of the lake, about five miles from its mouth. Railway surveyor Henry McLeod had passed through in 1875, but Mary and Mollie were the first white women in the valley. They never claimed to be first to explore this lake; instead, Mary made it clear that Stoney Indians and Métis hunting parties had used the lake and valley.

On Mary's return to Mt Stephens House near Banff in 1907, an incident occurred that captured the dichotomy of her two worlds. As they rode back into the small settlement of Banff after four months in the mountains, she was mourning the loss of the freedom of the trail, rather than longing for the awaiting luxury of a hot bath, clean clothes and a feather bed at the hotel. On the trail into the settlement that day, she and the others came face to face with the conventions and prejudices she had been living away from for four months:

And then we struck the highway and on it a carriage with people in it! Oh! The tragedy of the comparison! The woman's gown was blue. I think her hat contained a white wing. I only saw it all in one awful flash from the corner of my right eye, and I remember distinctly that she had gloves on. Then I suddenly realised that our own recently brushed-up garments were frayed and worn, and our buckskin coats had a savage cast, that my three companions looked like Indians, and that the lady gazing at us belonged to another world. It was then that I wanted my wild free life back again, yet step by step I was leaving it behind.[80]

She clearly set up the contrast of her two worlds. In one glance she took in gloves, hat, gown, the man gazing openly at the party, and her arrangement of these details in comparison to her own dress only emphasised her familiarity with the codes of gentility and femininity.

The man in the carriage was Rudyard Kipling, who was also staying at Mt Stephens House, and recording his journey through the Rockies. He reported the encounter in his book, *Letters of Travel, 1892–1913* (1920):

As we drove along the narrow hill road a piebald pack-pony with a china-blue eye came round a bend, followed by two women, black-haired, bare-headed, wearing beadwork squaw jackets and riding straddle. A string of pack-ponies trotted through the pines behind them.

'Indians on the move?' said I. 'How characteristic!'

As the women jolted by, one of them very slightly turned her eyes, and they were, past any doubt, the comprehending equal eyes of the civilised white woman which moved in that berry-brown face.

... That same evening, in an hotel of all the luxuries, a slight woman in a very pretty evening frock was turning over photographs, and the eyes beneath the strictly arranged hair were the eyes of the woman in the beadwork jacket who had quirted the piebald pack-pony past our buggy.[81]

His representation was disturbingly voyeuristic. It was as if Kipling felt invited to be aroused by Mary's indigenous appearance; she was outside the boundaries of the conventional civilised white woman in her appearance and activity. His comments on the colour of the packhorse effectively justified his gaze as being directed upon a party of Indians[82]. Kipling refers to the pony's wall-eye as he turns the reader's attention towards the women; when he mentions Mary's eyes, it's the colour of the pony's eyes that we remember. His comment that the women were black-haired, bare-headed and rode astride seems to justify his unashamed gaze. He ends his description with the arresting and sexually charged image of Mary 'quirting', that is, whipping the piebald pony past his carriage.

In the light of this, Mary's desire to journey through the mountains, experiencing an independence of dress, mind and action, could be thought of as an escape from restriction and convention, to a place where she could live her 'wild free life'. In her story of the meeting, it was not until that moment on the road that she realises how much she wanted to live beyond the world signified by the Kiplings in their carriage.

The last major trip Mary wrote about was in 1911, when she returned to Maligne Lake with her sister-in-law, Carrie, and nine-year-old nephew Paul. Her account of the trail into Maligne Lake from the eastern side was liberally sprinkled with character sketches of the people they met, but had none of the sense of wildness that her previous accounts possessed. In the three years since her first trip into Maligne Lake, the country north and east of the Lake had been flooded with settlers and miners following the Grand Trunk Pacific railway, Canada's second transcontinental line. As the railway went through, the government, recognising the potential of the area's beauty as a tourist destination, established Jasper Forest Park along the line. In a clever effort to publicise the park, D. B. Dowling of the Geological Survey of Canada suggested to the Commissioner of Parks at Edmonton that Mary Schaffer return to the Lake and survey it. The plan was approved on two fronts. Firstly, it provided valuable information about a rapidly expanding area of settlement and, secondly, Mary Schaffer's fame as an accomplished woman explorer and writer would promote the region's natural attractions.[83]

The map Mary produced of the Lake and its surrounds was remarkable in its precision and professional presentation. It was not just a precise sketch of a landscape; rather, it was an impressive scientific survey. She had no formal training beyond the coaching Dowling had given her in log and compass surveying.[84] To produce a map of such detail and accuracy required a concentrated level of engagement with the topography of the land. It was tedious, slow work, but through it Mary explored every section of the Lake; it gave her an intimate awareness of the shape and form of a place she had longed to return to the first time she had seen it.

It was surely with a certain amount of irony that Mary undertook this work, for she must have realised that, by producing such a map, her beloved wilderness would no longer be untouched. The very act of exploring, of coming back and reporting what the land held, implicated her in the colonial expansion from which she sought escape. But, ultimately, working on the survey allowed Mary one more trip into the wilderness before it was transformed.

E. J. Hart, who collated her writings into the book, *A Hunter of Peace*, wrote that her letters in later years expressed strong opinions on the mountain exploits of others. He argued that it considerably frustrated her that others had undertaken similar adventures to her own out of a desire for glory and reputation, rather than for enjoyment, peace of mind and respect for the land. She wrote: 'My own work was done for the love of being in the open, not for the largest number of ascents, which seems a fungoid growth here ever since I came to the country'.[85] Mary describes her exploring as work, and although she needed access to an independent income to finance her trips, her writing of her experiences opened the mountains as a place where *women* might move as freely as men.

Dr Mary Percy Jackson was just one woman who was able to climb and walk in the area explored and surveyed by Mary Schaffer Warren. On 27 July 1930, on a holiday from her medical practice at Peace River, Mary Percy wrote to her parents from the train that was taking her to the Canadian Alpine Club camp at Mary Schaffer's beloved Maligne Lake: 'I'm all togged up in breeches and hobnailed boots, am carrying a rucksack and, I flatter myself, looking "the complete mountaineer". Honestly, I'm singing with excitement.'[86] Mary Percy Jackson climbed many of the mountains named by Mary Schaffer Warren, including Mount Mary Vaux and Mount Unwin, and she wrote with an infectious delight of the enjoyment she gained from her climbing. Her tone, in contrast to Mary Schaffer Warren and Freda Du Faur, was playful and revealed a confidence in her right to enjoy the space of the mountains as a woman:

> We zigzagged across steep patches of skidding scree, negotiated a snow cornice, were roped up and climbed up a patch of almost smooth rock and then were pushed and pulled round a corner of rock with singularly awkward footholds and about 1000 feet drop if you fell, and then did about a mile up steep snow, a good bit steeper than a house roof, up steps made by the guide—and along a fairly wide snow edge (about 18 inches) with a drop to eternity on either side and finally achieved the top. I've never been in such a blue funk in all my life. We came down a different way, much more snow, and we all sat down and tobogganed down nearly 1000 feet of it! A perfectly marvellous sensation till you come to thin snow and feel the rocks! I tore 6 holes in the seat of my breeches and my breeches got filled with snow, but it was great fun![87]

It was the writing of women such as Freda Du Faur and Mary Schaffer Warren that inspired a new generation of women, like Mary Percy Jackson, to imagine that they might also be able to climb in the mountains. Maureen Scott Harris, a Canadian writer, speaks of the difference between looking at a view and of moving beyond the lookout and becoming part of the view: 'When I'm within or on the land I don't experience it as prospect or view, at a distance; I'm in conversation with it, immersed, linked.'[88] It was this transition from looking at the view to being in conversation with the land that Mary Schaffer Warren and Freda Du Faur wrote about and, in doing so, they created the space for other women to imagine themselves in that journey.

After her last trip to Maligne Lake, Mary decided to spend the 1912 winter in Banff to see if she could stand the long cold season. Her expeditions out into the backcountry had taken the mountains from 'an ideal playground' to a place she wanted to call home. She enjoyed the winter and decided to stay. Then in June 1915, despite the great difference in their ages, Mary Schaffer married Billy Warren. They lived in Banff in the house that Billy built for her, and Mary became a pivotal personality in the community.[89] As she grew older, she travelled less frequently into the backcountry, but her memory of the places she'd visited remained strong, and people planning trips beyond the tourist trail sought her advice. Her obituary described her as Banff's greatest friend.[90]

The journey into the mountains is cyclical. It is about leaving and returning. Those who approach the mountains must shed the skin of their old life and adjust to a different rhythm. Mountains have traditionally been viewed as a very masculine space into which men go to test their masculinity, a place to conquer or be conquered. Yet women's accounts demonstrate that they too went to the mountains to test the boundaries of their capabilities. Like the frontier, the mountains provided a space in which women could engage with the land on a very physical level. The result was an opportunity to expand their understanding of themselves, physically, mentally and spiritually. As Mary and Freda climbed, travelled over high passes, or sought shelter from violent mountain storms, they pushed the boundaries of their safety and experienced there, if only for the shortest of times, a vision of their vulnerability, the smallness of their humanity in the face of an extreme physical landscape. When they returned to the buffer of 'civilisation', they wrote of leaving a part of themselves back in those wild high places.

But what does that mean—to leave a part of oneself somewhere else? Is it just an expression, a cliché?

When Elyne Mitchell wrote *Speak to the Earth* in 1945, she had already reflected on the experience of climbing a mountain. For Mitchell, climbing was about experiencing a physical intimacy with the land. She reflected on the way in which the memories of those who have climbed are held in the place itself:

> A mountain top does not lose its mystery in the intimacy of contact; what is lost is so amply outweighed in the gain of memories that have become some subtle part of the spirit of the peak.[91]

When she climbed, Elyne found she encountered a meeting of her spirit with 'the spirit of the peak'; it was as if the mountains cut into her and provided the steps for her body, mind and spirit to feel as one.

Even in the mountains, the strangest and most forbidding of places, women sought to ease their estrangement from the landscape. Through words they shaped their experiences and made sense of their desire to make these journeys. From the mountains of words they created, they took with them, perhaps, the knowledge that the mountains they climbed exist apart from their imagination, dreams and desires.

Speaking to earth

Elyne Mitchell

Chapter five

I know the land like the curves
Of my belly I hold it in my hands I hold it
In my head I know the lay of this land
I know its winds and its ways I know
This land and speak its language.[1]

Barbara Schott

On a summer evening in 1934, Elyne Chauvel looked out over the valley and up toward the mountains. It was her first visit to the Upper Murray cattle station, *Towong Hill*. Standing quite still, she breathed in the rising night air:

[A] wind from the future drifted down from the mountains and a prophecy emanated from the river and the dark valley floor. It gave me an absolutely intense feeling that the land was reaching out to me, taking me, claiming me—that in time I would become part of the whole vast land of mountains and valley, bush and flood plain, but that the land would be in my trust and that I would care for it all the days of my life. Even then, I felt a strange, small fear in the touch of the night air, but how could I, aged twenty, understand the immensity of the trust and of the love that I would give?[2]

Elyne would come to know the country of the Upper Murray and the mountain range above it as intimately as she knew the curves of her own body. Yet when she first came to *Towong Hill*, she came as a young woman, a stranger to the land. When she looked at a map of the country, she saw only 'an enigma of wandering lines that indicated barely imaginable spurs and mountains, rivers, creeks, and lakes. There was no knowledge then to give those lines intimacy.'[3] What lay before her was a daunting vastness of valley, foothills and mountains, a history beside which Elyne felt a stranger.

This first visit to *Towong Hill*, which had been associated with the Mitchell family since 1835, occurred before Elyne was engaged to Tom Mitchell. Although a stranger to this place, she framed her re-collection of that evening as the moment when the land reached out to her, and placed a claim on her that was beyond her relationship with Tom. It was the country she responded to, not the traditional domestic domain of the beautiful house and garden that would be hers if she chose to become Tom's wife. She never mentioned feeling as if the garden or house were embracing her as a home. Rather, her construction of that prophecy tied her to the different levels of the land: the mountains, the river, the valley floor 'spoke' to her. Her reconstruction of this moment stressed that she felt as strongly chosen by the land as by her husband Tom. In return for 'becoming part of the whole vast land', she would trust its ability to sustain her. Her fear was that she would be incapable of what she sensed the land would ask of her, and how much of her self would be sacrificed in labour and care of it. Perhaps more than any of the other women in this book, she continually sought to articulate how she saw herself in relation to the land.

> Somehow, for me to enter into a place, the strenuous giving of energy was necessary—there must be the feel of the land itself beneath my feet, or beneath the hooves of the horse I rode, the cool touch of sea or stream in which I swam, the feel of snow caressing my skis; there must be the giving of myself, my own energy, there must be this contact with earth and water or snow.[4]

She went on to say that out of her physical interaction with the land came this 'feeling of becoming part of a place'.[5]

Born in 1913, Elyne had inherited a freedom of movement, action and opportunity unknown to the women who had pioneered the land before her. The coming of the telephone and the increasing mechanisation of the country, which brought railways, roads and cars even to the more remote parts of Australia and Canada by the 1930s and 1940s, changed people's concepts of time and space. Elyne's experience of the land was buffered in ways unimaginable to women who lived on the land in the Nineteenth Century. Yet her experience, especially during the years of the Second World War, echoed that of women settlers of the earlier generation. The war brought a labour shortage on the land. Together with the rationing of petrol, as well as restrictions on train travel and many foods, this shortage slowed modernisation of the country, so that it resembled earlier times[6].

Elyne Mitchell was born Sibyl Elyne Keith Chauvel. She was the third child of Sir Henry (Harry) Chauvel and his much younger wife, Sibyl Keith Jopp. At eighteen, Sybil had married a soldier twenty years her senior; at twenty-one, she had two small boys and a husband who was rapidly rising up the Australian military ranks. For Elyne, her father's position as the Australian representative on the Imperial General Staff meant that her first six years were spent in England.[7] The family left Melbourne in 1914, just before the declaration of war. Elyne was six months old.

While the family was at sea, war was declared, and the fear of attack by a German ship was so great that the chief engineer made a lifejacket out of corks for the baby Elyne. It was in this uncertain atmosphere of war that Elyne spent her impressionable childhood, yet her recollections of these years were filled with beach excursions and country picnics. Writing of this as a woman in her seventies, she was struck by the lengths to which her mother went in a strange country in the middle of a war to give her children as normal a childhood as possible.[8]

The family returned to Australia in 1919 when Elyne was six years old. Her older brothers, Edward and Ian, were eleven and thirteen.

Elyne Mitchell and her mother, Sibyl Chauvel, 1920. Elyne was seven years old.

Elyne's Australian childhood was urban, punctuated by holidays to the beach or in the country. Her love of horses was inherited from her father, who had grown up on a station on the Clarence River and been taught to ride by the Aboriginal stockmen. As a child she longed to be old enough to go riding with her brothers and father during their holidays. One of the most significant moments of her early life occurred on a bush holiday during her eighth year:

In the long rides through the bush, the lazy midday rest with bright sun burning us, the billy boiling, and the ponies cropping grass beside us—happily being with Dad and my brothers—or in the sunset light, playing alone, something magnificent was given to me.[9]

There were, of course, formal riding lessons in the covered military school with other daughters of high-ranking officials, but it was to the experience of riding on the beach and through the bush that Elyne attributed a growing awareness of being drawn to the land as a source of meaning.[10]

Elyne Chauvel and Tom Mitchell met at the Melbourne Cup festival in 1932, at a stage in Elyne's life when she was very uncertain of herself socially. Fifty years later, she would write that the only place she felt confident was on the back of a horse. She reconstructs herself as seeking something beyond society and finding a glimpse of it while riding. But perhaps it was her fearless riding after the hounds with the Melbourne Hunt that so attracted the older and more experienced Tom Mitchell.

Unlike Elyne, Tom had been to university in England and travelled all over Europe, America and New Zealand on the international ski circuit. He was sophisticated, handsome, assured and the heir to one of Victoria's premier cattle and horse properties in the Upper Murray Valley. His background and lifestyle were very different from Elyne's sheltered and close family circle, which was dominated by other military families. She'd been in Melbourne, while Tom 'had been to Japan, crossed Siberia and Russia to Europe, and raced in the International Ski Races again.'[11] Nevertheless, Elyne was the daughter of Australia's most decorated and famous war hero, and a brilliant rider across country. She received an invitation to *Towong Hill* from Mrs. Mitchell, with a full understanding that 'it was really probable that Tom had invited me in order to see if his mother approved of me or not'.[12]

Evidently she did, for Tom and Elyne were married in 1935 in Melbourne. Elyne was twenty-two years old and very much in awe of her husband. Because of his love of skiing, she was determined to learn to ski, though it cost her in bruises, sprains and, later, a badly broken leg. She realised that in order to keep up with Tom she would not only have to ski, but ski well enough to compete in international races and become strong enough for long ski tours, carrying packs through the mountains. 'Tom had said—standing on the snow at Buller—that skiing was his life. I had to do well, not only to please him, but to have some sort of part in that life.'[13]

They spent their honeymoon in New Zealand and, although Elyne was 'intensely aware of the mountain world all around',[14] unlike Freda Du Faur twenty years before her, she had no desire to climb Mount

Cook. But she brought back from this trip a curiosity to explore the mountains that bounded *Towong Hill*. They loomed above as a place of 'immense challenge, of mystery and adventure'.[15]

Tom and Elyne returned to *Towong Hill* in January 1936. The tone in Elyne's memoir as she wrote of this period was flat. The day of their arrival Elyne was met by her mother-in-law with three boxes of labelled keys, and 'lists and lists in her handwriting'.[16] The responsibility of the big house and garden settled heavily upon her; it was a responsibility she had never wanted.

The main house on *Towong Hill* stood at the end of a long ridge, which rose a hundred and fifty feet from the rich river flats of the Murray. It occupied a commanding position with a view that swept up the river until the eye was confronted by the sheer wall of the western face of the Snowy Mountains, 'and all around, with the green flats lapping at their feet', Elyne wrote 'are the foothills'.[17] The house was built of striking red bricks that were made from the mud of the paddock down by the lagoon below the homestead. It had taken two years to build, from 1902 to 1904. Tom had been born there in 1906. It was a two-storey house, not typical of the country houses that Elyne had stayed in on family holidays in country Victoria. In her memory, it was intimidating and austere, with a somewhat cold, forceful personality.

When she first arrived, Elyne remembered it as being very dark, with the rooms kept shut up to prevent the harsh Australian light from ruining the furnishings. It was not a relaxed family home. Elyne's early memories of the house reflected her uncertainty about her own ability to run it or, at least, to run it in the way Mrs. Mitchell wished and envisioned. To escape, she turned to the activity of the station and rode out each day over the paddocks to take part in whatever work was underway.

Elyne's writing about the house and garden slowly changed over time.[18] There were two events that encouraged this process. While she was travelling in Europe and skiing with Tom, her mother replanned the garden. She removed Mrs Mitchell's labour-intensive flowerbeds, which were filled with annual displays of colourful plants that had to be replanted with the changing season, replacing them with flowering shrubs and perennials. The garden was thus easier to look after, yet still provided seasonal displays of colour.

Then, in 1954, a massive storm destroyed the garden's boundary of European trees. Though saddened by the loss of five beautiful trees and many of her favourite shrubs, Elyne decided not to replant: 'We discovered, once we could see out, and the great roots and trunks were removed, that we could have a terrace with a steep drop that could give a superb view of the mountains'.[19] After this the house and garden came to reflect her personality, and began to feature in her memoirs and fiction. Like Alice Duncan-Kemp, however, Elyne defined herself and her sense of place against the land, not as a reflection of the house or garden.

When Elyne first arrived at *Towong Hill*, she'd no experience of working the land. Though she sought involvement from the beginning, she remained only passively connected to the running of the station. She was a willing participant in mustering and droving, but her pony would be saddled for her at the beginning of the day, and her labour was never essential. She went out with the men because she wanted to. She was never expected to crutch sheep, or pull lambs from the wombs of ewes in the freezing cold of the morning, or put up hay in the rush to beat an oncoming storm.

It was the onset of the war that changed the way Elyne understood and responded to the land.[20] The acute crisis of rural labour meant that she became intimately involved in the work and decisions about the management of the sheep, cattle, thoroughbred horses and the land. It was through this work that Elyne came into a relationship with the land, which went beyond pleasure in its beauty. Notions of what women could and couldn't do on the land were so entrenched that her labour was unacceptable to Mr. Herbert, the manager of *Towong Hill*, until there was simply no one left except her to do the work: 'At last Herbie began to realise that he had to make use of every bit of available labour, not just for mustering but for every other job too'.[21]

Elyne had referred to the years before the war, from 1935 to 1939, as her 'Billabong years'.[22]

> The few years of riding all over the paddocks, riding and skiing in the mountains, happily mustering cattle, swimming in the river, were all in fact a preparation for the time when I had to live alone and care for the land and for the people who worked with it, and the animals it supported.[23]

This reference to Mary Grant Bruce's series about a young girl who lived on a cattle station in Victoria was important. Elyne's own writing picks up the legacy of Bruce's 'Norah', the 'Australian girl' created for a newly federated Australia. When Elyne wrote about her life on the land, she stepped into a space created by characters such as 'Norah', or even Ethel Turner's 'Judy', who were sure of their legitimacy in the Australian bush.

The war brought a dramatic change for Elyne. Instead of riding for pleasure, or moving over the land as a bushwalker, or skier, she now moved over it as manager and caretaker. She set rabbit baits, and learnt about soil. Rabbits had become a huge problem on *Towong Hill*, as they had across most of Australia in the 1930s.[24] The situation was worsened by a fire in 1939, which burnt *Towong Hill's* well-maintained and relatively rabbit-proof fences. With the war effort having taken all the men, and the station no longer able to afford to employ even one or two full-time rabbiters, it was inundated with rabbits. The only solution was to bait them.

Elyne learnt that in a dry summer the rabbits could do severe damage, not only eating feed for the stock, but eating it right down to the roots, so that the soil was 'left unbound by any living growth, brown and barren and somehow sour, unarmed against erosion.'[25] She watched as the rabbits burrowed into loose, dry hillsides, gradually weakening the topsoil until it fell in and was washed away with the first heavy rain. She baited them with black thistle roots soaked in sugar, flour and strychnine and scented with vanilla. With her younger sister Eve, she rode out into the paddocks and, as the battle raged over Singapore, where Tom was stationed with the 8th Division, they scratched with a hoe, and placed the sweet-smelling baits by the rabbit pads or on the mounds where the rabbits played.

She was an inheritor of a ravished land. All around her, everywhere she looked, she saw evidence of overstocking, of erosion, of a moving crop of rabbits destroying everything in their path.

As the sisters worked with the baits, thunder and lightning played out over the hills. The rain flayed the paddocks, but Elyne felt no escape from the tension within her. Later, she wrote that she did, in fact, find 'strength and hope in the perpetual cycle of the land'.[26] However, that day, cantering home in the rain, her pony reefing at the bit as wet reins slid through her hands, she felt only despair. Not only did she not know whether Tom had survived the battle over Singapore, but all around her the rain was washing the loose topsoil off, and the water was running over the ground with nothing to hold or collect it. The baits they'd set would be sodden and useless. Tomorrow they would have to repeat the whole process again in a race to beat the rabbits to the tender shoots of grass that would push up through the damp soil.

Out of this experience, Elyne would write in 1946 her least well-known book, *Soil and Civilisation*, which is one of the earliest calls for sustainable practices in an era when mechanisation was changing the face of farming in Australia.

We, in Australia, have indiscriminately denuded our land of its forests and allowed sheep and rabbits to eat out the roots of perennial grasses; but still, throughout the whole continent, there is no real understanding of the cause of sand-choked streams

and shallow rivers ... Nor will people connect the
drying up of springs with the removal of soil covering. 'Seasons have been bad' is the only reason given
—with no thought that man himself is changing
Australia's climate.[27]

Yet even in this state, the land still inspired her. She
wrote of how the drought and the rabbits revealed
the skeleton of the landscape around her. There was
no carpet of rich green to soften the hills. The flats
were not a moving sea of knee-deep feed. Instead,
the land was stripped of its hide and she could see its
bones. They entered her and remained in the precision of her memory.

This connection with the land enabled Elyne to
find a release from the tension of waiting and won-
dering whether Tom was alive, and anticipating the
outcome of the war. Through physical activity, she
made herself part of a larger whole. Her labour
produced in her an acknowledgement of the interdependence between people and the land, and it was
a solace, too, in those times of loneliness. She
recorded the bombing of Darwin, a time of great
uncertainty and shock for Australia, framed within
the tasks that were performed on that day. She, her
sister Eve and Mr. Herbert had to move five trouble-
some bulls, but the strenuous work of moving them
provided a physical counterpoint to the bombing
of Darwin.

Later, writing about this day, Elyne gave her audience a space to make sense of their own ordinary activities on that extraordinary day. Her writing underlined the importance of the home front; it legitimised the feelings of the majority of Australians, who waited, watched and worked through this defining time.

As the summer drew to an end, they moved mobs of sheep to fresh feed, crutched them to prevent fly strike and treated foot rot, along with the hundred other activities that make sheep-work so much more backbreaking than working cattle.[28]

> So every day, day after day, was full of work with sheep, much longer, harder hours than we had had during all the summer; and time went aching on into an eternity from which I seemed to be able to salvage so little. Yet slowly the deep satisfaction of contact with the land began to quicken my spirit. Though my uncertainty was a constant, rotting fear, I was beginning to see again some purpose in the land, a design far beyond the necessity of the nation's food, a deep underlying strength which comes from infinity to man through the medium of the land; not the inspired, far-leaping notion of infinity that is brought by high places, but one that gives full meaning to the pattern of our life.[29]

In those days of labour shortage, through being out on the land every day, observing it, watching it and learning from it, Elyne gained a new perspective and a deep underlying strength. Perhaps most importantly, she found some kind of peace in the endless cycle of life and the constant engagement one has with that cycle when in daily contact with the land. Physically, the land demanded labour; sweat would fall from her and return to the earth: 'No breath of wind dried the sweat, and the heavy air seemed weighed down to the earth.'[30] Her body was pummelled by the work.

She wrote of catching a 'killer' for the household meat supply out of a mob of ewes. Beneath the amphitheatre of the huge sky above, she moved into the mob, eyes trained on one fawn back, amongst thirty other fawn backs, and moving closer—pale sheep, blue sky, pale earth, the scrunch of her boots on the dried yellow feed. A lunge, and she had a hind leg, but then her boot caught in a rabbit hole and she was flung to the ground. A hundred drumming hooves tattooed her back, her mouth was full of the earth's dull sweetness and, in her hand, was the kicking leg of the struggling ewe.

Other days were spent in the yards, 'drafting' sheep. Elyne would stand at the end of a narrow race and watch the sheep as they were pushed through, swinging the drafting gate from side to side, separating them into mobs. The sound of their bleating would fill the air and block any other noise. Around her the air would be heavy with dust. Later in the day, she and Eve would escape to swim in the river.

> There we forgot the hot dustiness of the sheep-yards in the swift glide of the current past our limbs, its tug and swirl through our hair; we could forget the sheep as we watched four bright blue kingfishers swooping in and out of the willows.[31]

Her recollection of this time was marked by the extreme physicality of her work. She was interpreting the natural world around her through the receptor of her body, linking herself to the place in which she laboured in the absence of her husband—covered in the dust of the earth, then washed clean by the moving cycle of the river.

Autumn was filled with cattle work: bringing the fat cattle in and sending them off to market, weaning calves and mustering far paddocks in order to bring in young beasts to be fattened. This meant hard swift action. She rode her chestnut pony Razzer, who grabbed the bit and pulled like a steam train from the beginning of the day to the end. She wrote of the thrill and exhilaration of galloping after the cattle. Her body would respond to Razzer's stride, his sudden twists and turns, as he moved beside a galloping beast. Her hands were tight on the reins, low on her pony's neck, her concentration absolute as he ducked and swung, accelerating and spinning in two, three strides, following the movement of the beast.

This cattle work gave her another view of the land to overlay the knowledge gained through baiting rabbits, riding waterholes to check for bogged beasts, moving sheep, endless lambing, and raising vegetables in the garden. The more she worked, the more she knew, and in the knowledge came an understanding of the different layers of the land and how each had to be peeled back, lived in, smelt, felt, earned.

> The paddocks became like a map in my mind, drawn in sunlight and love. I was beginning to be able to feel, or imagine, the way a beast might break out of a mob, where or when a whole mob might suddenly swing and gallop. I learnt to watch and watch, and to use my imagination.[32]

Imagining the world through the eyes of the beasts enabled her to anticipate their movement and their reactions to the country around them. But for Elyne, this process had a greater significance as she transposed it into her writing, particularly her writing for children. She wove stories around this ability to imagine what the world might look like through the eyes of a horse, or dog, a kangaroo or dingo, or the quiet slow wombats. Her work during the war taught her to watch animals in a way that enabled her to anticipate their actions and understand their movement. Her ability to portray this in her children's stories had an added depth because of the detailed observations on which she based them.

Elyne's second book, *Speak to the Earth* (1945), was the record of her life in those days of fear and uncertainty. It was based on diaries she had kept for Tom as an account of her days during the war.

> I started to keep for him a faithful chronicle of his land. Should he sometimes think of how my time was spent, why so little writing was done, why so little reading, then that diary might suffice as a record of a manner of living. ... Now, as I write, that ever-increasing diary kept for Tom is on the desk before me, telling of the start of the long waiting, of all the anxiety for Australia and the increasing difficulty in properly looking after the land.[33]

Speak to the Earth had as its foundation at least two competing strands. There was the fear and uncertainty of the general outcome of the war and her continual anxiety regarding Tom's fate as a prisoner of war in a Japanese camp. So great was the tension that Elyne often wondered if the result of their work would be handed to the invading Japanese army. The other component was the land as constant, unchanging, and sustaining. The daily processes of living and working on the land required a service from her body, while her mind continually grappled with the personal and societal implications of a world at war:

> All work in the country runs to a broad, elastic routine which flows inexorably from appointed beginnings to appointed ends. If, in those first few days, my body was carried on and my mind left behind, Towong continued and the routine and needs of the land were there to grasp at as at something changeless.
>
> Yet the land is not changeless. Whole regions can be altered by fire or flood, by man's axe or by his engineering. But still the land endures … The land is a constant, imperious force in the world, without whose fertility civilization dies.[34]

Within the poetry of Elyne's connections with the land, there is a gritty realism that she stressed as part of the cycle of life and death on the land. Her world was an increasingly mechanised one, and much of her writing critiques the importance of maintaining and understanding the connection between 'civilised' societies and the land. Yet, for all her fervour in representing the importance of the agrarian world for the health of civilisation, she does so with a realism that stressed the connections between life and death and the health of the land and of societies. The cattle that she so loved to watch moving slowly across the flats, or stringing through the trees of the foothills, were destined for the beef market. When she looked at a beast, she learnt to see it in terms of how much beef it would produce as a carcass. When she selected a lamb from the mob of killers, it was in the knowledge that the breathing, kicking life that fought its capture would be stilled so she could eat. When she baited the rabbits, it was with the knowledge that they would die a slow and agonising death.

Throughout her writing she acknowledged these realities. For the land to recover, the rabbit had to be destroyed; in order that society be fed, the great red beasts must be killed; for her own family to be fed, the lamb had to die. Her understanding of these connections informed her lyricism. She could not enjoy the pleasure of galloping after a beast or of bringing a mob down from the hills without framing it within the final outcome of such a day: the trucks pulling up, and the beasts being loaded onto them and driven away.

After the success of *Speak to the Earth,* Elyne wrote *Soil and Civilization* (1946), a far more ambitious, political statement, which moved away from memoir, a style legitimised for her feminine voice. In *Soil and Civilization,* she attempted the large task of tracing the connections between the rise and fall of civilisations and their attention to the soil. As a book, it fell somewhere between philosophy and environmental science in its effort to understand the connections between western civilisation's historical reliance on the land and a more modern scientific approach to farming. Its message was to outline the danger a society faced in not understanding the connections between the body and soul, and the physical world that sustains these.

Written in the middle of the drought (1944–1945),[35] with the dust storms engulfing the country, it argued for an acknowledgement of the universal laws that govern life:

> Generations that have lived and died without feeling their own life cycles to be vitally linked with the cycles of the soil have no sense of the balance between growth and decay, death and re-creation.[36]

Elyne wrote of the natural progression of allowing market forces to dominate production on the land. She foresaw a time when the dairy cows that provide milk and the fowl that provide eggs and meat would be fed by processed foods.[37] She attacked the concept of one-crop farming, arguing instead for self-sufficiency and sustainability. She could not see the sense in a wheat farmer sowing thousands of acres of wheat and then driving to town to buy eggs, milk, bread and meat.

Elyne later wrote that she received a lot of criticism for this book, and indeed, its arguments against further mechanisation and modernisation of farming were not popular in post-war Australia. Yet they came out of her own observations of the degradation of the land, and an attempt to put into words the importance of acknowledging a civilisation's dependence on the land for its survival.[38] Her arguments don't sound as radical today, as the next generation grapples a rising of water tables, a salinity crisis and the repercussions of earlier land management policies.

Her next book, *Images in Water* (1947), was a return to the memoir genre. But if Elyne had learnt from the criticism of *Soil and Civilisation* that society was not yet ready to read a woman's arguments for land conservation, she still refused to drop her politics. *Images in Water* is more recognisably Mitchell, but it is just as passionate in its arguments, even if they are given through personal, poetical reflections. She wrote that justice in Australian society was not possible 'till we are in harmony with all that is and was this continent'.[39]

Although she doesn't preface this comment with any reference to indigenous ownership of the land, it seems an implicit attempt to tie the past and the future of Australian society together through looking after the land. This comment is typical of her uneasiness in directly confronting the theft of Aboriginal land. Elyne rarely mentions Aboriginal ownership, but in her fiction, she does portray Aboriginal people as having a sacred knowledge of land, which can be handed on to privileged white children, usually after they have passed through a series of tests based on their observation of nature and the land.[40]

When the war ended and Tom returned to *Towong Hill,* it came as a shock to Elyne that she was no longer expected to be involved with running the station:

> The welcome home present which I had bought for Tom was something I would have loved to own myself. It was a strong, handsome leather case to hang on one's saddle, containing good dagging shears, a sharpening stone, and a place to hold a bottle of fly oil. It never entered my thoughts that we would not continue to be as deeply involved in the running of Towong Hill as I had been, all these years.[41]

This present for Tom signals the extent to which Elyne had been changed through her efforts and struggles to keep the station running through the war. The work had come to define her; the gift represented who she had become: a woman who understood and could use the tools of the land. Somehow, it seemed that this was not what Tom wanted to return to. Writing in 1989, four years after Tom's death, in a memoir that is more intimate than her earlier works, Elyne reflected that she 'should have realised that men who had been starved and beaten could never grasp the desperation of the fearful struggle to keep their homes going and to keep up production in spite of there being almost no materials or labour'.[42]

In 1946 Elyne faced the challenge of having to fit into a different rhythm of the land and her place in it. In the ten years after the war, she and Tom had four children, the youngest born in 1955. She wrote of her changed place in the land as a mother. The days 'were quite different from the days when I left the homestead on horseback at 7:30 to go round the lambing ewes, or galloped to head an angry Short-horn bull, or shore lambs.'[43] There are hints in her autobiography, *Towong Hill* (1989), of how difficult this time was for her. No longer was she able to pack her skis, a bivouac, some chops and tea and walk up into the hills for a day of spring skiing as she had even during the hard work of the war. She had written of these experiences and how they fulfilled her need to connect with the mountains above the land that she worked. Before the children were born, she had relied on these times of escape and renewal, with only her Border Collie dog for company. In 1989 she wrote of her memory of those times:

> The comfort of the red blaze as my fire began to seep right into me—red blaze, bodily weariness being soothed by food, tall white gums, mountain 'cattle road', just bush around me.[44]

With motherhood came restrictions on her time and her mobility; even an hour away from the house was out of reach. 'Maybe I should not count so much on that ride and swim, that renewal with the earth'.[45] The demands on her time and energy in caring for young children required qualities different from those called for during the war. When she was physically engaged in the running of the station, she'd found renewal through her labour on the land. By contrast, her labour as a mother left her disconnected from the physical activity of the station and the land.

The death of Mr. Herbert shortly after the birth of her first child amplified this disconnection. He had been the manager of *Towong Hill* since the early 1900s, and the one who'd taught Elyne the skills she needed to work the sheep and cattle, to handle horses and dogs. It had been Herbie with whom Elyne had first ridden when she arrived at *Towong Hill* and Herbie who'd included her in its history by telling her stories of the early days of the station:

> In the days and weeks after we arrived back from our honeymoon, Mr Herbert, Charlie and George took me mustering cattle, or mustering the sheep ... and they began to weave their yarns around me ... Mr. Herbert was the one person, at least, who was glad that I was always 'down the paddocks'.[46]

After he died, there was no one who had been with her while she kept the station running during the war.

Then, in 1947, Tom Mitchell entered parliament, and thereafter 'was almost entirely taken up with politics and his constituents; I was left out of the workings of the station'.[47] Reading this statement alongside others that Elyne made about Tom and his relationship to the land, there seems to be a tension emerging between Tom's duty to the land and his ambitions outside of it. Elyne wrote that it came as something of a shock to her that Tom did not feel the same way about *Towong Hill* as she did:

> It was difficult for me to realize or understand that Towong Hill had gone on without Tom for a long time. He had actually spent most of the previous twenty years away from Towong Hill, first at school in Sydney and, after he had finished school, Mrs. Mitchell (as I have since learned) against her father's strong advice took Tom and Honnor to England.[48]

For Tom marriage to Elyne had meant settling down on the land that he had always known was and would be his home, but this moment had been put off once again by the war. Elyne felt keen disappointment as she learnt that Tom did not share her instinctive love of horses and riding and her recognition that such an activity connected her with the land. She had anticipated this time of transition from farmer to wife as she wrote *Speak to the Earth*, but it was more complicated than she had imagined.

Tom did come riding round the paddocks with me, sometimes, but I learnt, rather sadly, that he did not really like horses or riding. However, in those days, the only way to see the stock and the pastures was on horseback, and he would show me his willowing plans for the river banks[49] and took me riding round the newly acquired sheep, which were his own project.[50]

The way Elyne has phrased this observation of her husband emphasised the loneliness she felt after Tom's return. It was easier in the mountains, as they shared a love of skiing. Yet, even in the mountains, their different approaches to skiing often caused tension between them. On numerous occasions, Elyne wrote of just wanting to enjoy the mountains for their beauty and isolation, the closeness of the natural world, while for Tom, the mountains and skiing were more often about winning ski races.[51] This inability to share the way she felt about the land with Tom is something that is reflected in other women's writing about place. Her immersion in the processes of the land was something that Tom either did not understand or refused to become involved in. Her discontent at their inability to share what was so important to her echoes the sentiments of Susan Allison in British Columbia, who 'begged and begged' to go back to the Okanagan, where she had been so happy. Elyne's appreciation of the mountains seems closer to Freda's desire to climb for climbing's sake, to experience the fullness of her moment in the mountains, rather than for the 'mere notoriety' of reaching the top.

Elyne's observation of Tom's disconnection with the land made her more aware of her role as mother to her children, her capacity to give something of her own understanding of the land to them. It became important to her to impart this knowledge physically, by taking her children out into the land and moving over it with them, teaching them to observe and listen. She created wonderful tales of the place where they lived, implicitly realising the importance of stories. The Mitchell's first daughter, Indi, was named for the river with its source in the Snowy Mountains above *Towong Hill,* which had run through the history of the Mitchell family for two generations:

By the time Indi was two I started taking her out riding, in front of my saddle, sitting on a rolled up coat. ... Realizing that even if Indi remembered nothing of these early rides, they might create an attitude of mind—like all the picnics Mother used to take my brothers and myself that I barely remember at all—a longing for a world beyond houses and streets, a storehouse of glowing half-memories or impressions. So though I was not taking delivery of new store cattle, and counting them into their paddocks, and not in a wild gallop bringing in the mares, I was out on a pony in the beloved paddocks, and Indi might have first memories of these paddocks seen from her comfortable seat in front of my saddle.[52]

This effort that Elyne invested in Indi was repeated for each of her children as she took them camping, riding, swimming, seeking to give them a treasure to draw on, as they grew older. As well as taking them out into the land, she also taught them about it through stories, which she later published. The first and most famous of her stories for children was *The Silver Brumby* (1958). This series has given generations of Australian children a different way of looking at the Australian bush. Elyne's writing made connections between her young readers and the land. Like many of the stories she wrote for children, the idea for *The Silver Brumby* came to her from the land itself. 'For me, it is almost always the country that suggests the story'.[53] Unlike Tom's childhood, which had been so dominated by school, and later university in England, Elyne was determined to give to her children something of her sense of place in *Towong Hill*, in the mountains above and in the natural world around that she had gained in the hard war years:

There were four children to give some awareness of the natural rhythms of this country, awareness of the birds—their migrations, their types of flight, their calls—give them love for the vision of a frieze of kangaroos hopping rhythmically through the bush, try to quicken their joy in the scent of wild flowers in the mountains, the scent of stringybark blossoms coming in on the south wind at night ... Riding—being out in the bush, climbing up and down rugged hills, or in the paddocks—had given me such deep pleasure, and I have loved horses themselves so much, the very rhythm of their movements and the sound of their hooves, that I had hoped I would be able to help my children to have this depth of enjoyment.[54]

Elyne knew that a connection with the land was something that could be given and received through relationships with people. As she had been made part of the land through the efforts of Mr. Herbert, so she sought to tie her own children to the land through the immediacy of her stories. Her writing created an imaginative space in which not only they, but all those who read her books, could engage creatively with the landscape.

Elyne wrote *The Silver Brumby* (1958) 'for Indi who loves horses'.[55] The idea came to her when she was seven months pregnant with her fourth child. During stormy weather she was woken in the early hours of the morning by the wind in the chimney of the room. She could hear it whipping round the gables of the house, and she recalled that the air around her seemed filled with 'unease'. The storm had entered her dreams, and she had seen a vision of a mare and foal sheltered beneath an overhanging rock. She groped for a pencil by her bed and scrawled the beginning of a story that her daughter and generations of Australian children were to love. She wrote:

> Once there was a dark, stormy night in spring, when, deep down in their holes, the wombats knew not to come out, when the possums stayed quiet in their hollow limbs ... On this night, Bel Bel, the cream brumby mare, gave birth to a colt foal, pale like herself, or paler, in that wild, black storm night.[56]

As she entered this period of her life, where her responsibilities as a mother restricted her access to the mountains, she continued to create the link between her imagination and the land by writing about it. Through the *Silver Brumby* series, she gives her audience an imaginative space to access an intimacy with place.

In this series she told a story of the mountains interwoven with the animals and people who lived there. She brought to life the animals that she had watched and listened to as she moved through the country. In the opening paragraph of *The Silver Brumby*, there were all the elements of her observation. She had been on the rocky tors of the Ramshead range when the wind rose and roared its way eerily through the rocks, sending all in its path to seek the shelter of the deep valleys. She had watched a mare give birth, seen the last violent heave and the sudden gush of foal, seemingly all legs, from the body of the mare.

> He heaved up his head, stuck his long forelegs out in front of him, and gave a little snort of fear. Bel Bel pushed him up till he stood, his feet far apart, long legs trembling ...[57]

Elyne's portrayal of the behaviour of the brumby herd was based on her observation of mares and foals in the *Towong Hill* thoroughbred herd and on times spent in the mountains observing the brumby herds. The accuracy of her descriptions of herd behaviour and her characterisation of herd hierarchy was the result of a mixture of observation and imagination. Her descriptions of dominant stallions fighting, of young horses on the periphery of the herd, of the relationship between mares and foals were marked by a realism absent in so much children's literature in which animals are given human characteristics.

Elyne used the character of the mare, Bel Bel, to teach her young audience about the interconnections between the land, animals and humans. She intended that as Bel Bel taught Thowra, the silver brumby, her readers would learn how to listen and look in the bush:

Bel Bel ... taught them to recognize the track of a dingo ... to tell the wombat paths through the damp bush, and the narrow trail of the Evil One, the snake, over sand ...[58]

Throughout the series, the native animals were portrayed as the most intimately connected with the mountains and wise in the ways of the bush. Bel Bel taught Thowra to talk with and listen to the wise kangaroos, the grumpy wombats, the vague and silly emus and all the different birds of the mountains.

Elyne was writing of another language outside of speech. She described a language of finely drawn relationships, where the ability to understand the connections between the living things and the natural world provided the means of survival. She stressed the stupidity of some of the other horse characters that would not listen to the native animals and died because they were unable to read the signs of the land warning of bad weather, drought, flood, fire or the coming of people to the mountains. Elyne's stories portrayed the native animals as having the ability to read the land. Throughout the series, it was the horses that listened to the native animals that were able to learn about the mountains in all their different seasons. She characterised the horses that explored, knew and loved their environment as being successful in surviving the harsh land:

Thowra moved so quietly and carefully that a dingo bitch playing with her fat puppies in a patch of sunlight did not hear him coming. 'Never mind, old woman, I won't hurt your beautiful children,' he said to her. 'Tell me, have you seen sign of man near here?' 'A man on his two legs went towards the river a mile from here, leading a lame horse, late last night. You will smell his blood, maybe. He had cut his head.' ... Thowra nodded his thanks, snuffed at the pups, and said again, with much politeness, how beautiful they were.[59]

Elyne Mitchell's use of the horse as a vehicle to write about the land can be seen as a metaphor for white occupation and use of the mountains. She stressed that horses were not indigenous to the mountains, but through learning to 'read' the land, to listen and understand the messages that it carried —for example, signs in the weather or marks on the earth—these horses, like white people, could learn to 'belong' in the mountains. The strength of the character of Thowra and his mother Bel Bel came from their ability to blend into the natural world around them. It was this ability, more than physical strength, that made Thowra the 'king of the Cascade brumbies'.

Elyne used her books for children to write her relationship to place into a social discourse. In *The Silver Brumby*, she wrote as a mother for children, but the beliefs that informed the controversial *Soil and Civilisation* are still there; they are just set in an acceptable genre that would not draw criticism onto a woman of her generation.

Elyne's conservation activism was an important part of her life. As early as 1945, she was writing of the effect of the sharp hooves of sheep and cattle on the native pasture. She wrote of how the sight of sheep grazing the headwaters of the Tumut River affected her: '[I] felt it almost like a nightmare—all the thousands of little hooves treading in the sphagnum bogs, squeezing the sponginess that should hold the water.'[60] In *Soil and Civilization* (1946), she traced a direct link between soil erosion, the dropping water table and rising salinity, the introduction of hoofed animals and destruction of the forests:

> The slow-breeding [native] animals are soft-footed. They have no hooves to wear deep 'pads' towards waterholes, nor to press down the spongy, water-storing bogs, as have sheep and cattle, making the soil ever more impervious to moisture. The whole ecology of the country tended towards the preservation of the soil's stability.[61]

Elyne was a strong proponent of the Snowy Mountains becoming a national park. She saw a need for the protection of the land against overstocking and overgrazing, yet she also mourned a way of life—taking the cattle up into the mountains every spring, mountain musters, and bringing them back down again. In the *Silver Brumby* series, she celebrated both the introduced animals and the natural environment.

If Elyne made an implicit link between horses and white occupation of mountains in *The Silver Brumby*, her later work for children makes a more direct link between indigenous knowledge of the land and white children and adults as inheritors of that knowledge. In *Kingfisher Feather*, which she wrote for Harry, Honor and John in 1962, an old Aboriginal woman gives the two children in the novel a quest 'which brought them closer and closer to the heart of the mysterious, beautiful countryside'.

> Suddenly the old woman saw the family standing there ...
>
> 'From the Dream Time,' she muttered, pointing to both Sally and David, who could not quite make out what she had said ...
>
> 'Where have you come from and where are you going?' asked Sally ...
>
> 'I am the last' ... Her voice dropped to a whisper. 'Understanding lies in the mountains, and, if you have the courage, it is in the treasure of the snow. I am the last and I have never seen you at the Dragonfly Cave.'[62]

The children in this story are framed as the future, and because of their understanding of the bush and because their great-grandfather was kind to the local Aborigines, Mitchell portrays them as being chosen by the old Aboriginal woman, 'the last one', to inherit her knowledge. The generational connection to the land is important. Mitchell writes,

'Of course your grandfather was an exceptional man for his time, respecting and understanding the aborigines as he did. And he learnt about the bush from them as though he were a native of the land, not just first generation born here.' ... 'He couldn't really have known it as well, but he was believed to have done by everyone who lived around.'[63]

What Elyne never acknowledges is that the privileged position she has created for the white children was based on Aboriginal dispossession. The closest she comes to this is through her use of Judith Wright's poetry, which is taught to the children by their mother.

'The song is gone; the dance
is secret with the dancers in the earth,
the ritual useless, and the tribal story
lost in an alien tale.

Only the grass stands up
to mark the dancing ring; the applegums
posture and mime a past corroborree,
murmur a broken chant.'[64]

But unlike Judith Wright, who complicates her sense of place by acknowledging that it is based on stolen land, Elyne Mitchell portrays her connection to the land as received in some mysterious way from the indigenous people. There are moments of discomfort in Elyne's writing about Aborigines, but rather than acknowledging the destruction of a people and culture by her family, she constructs herself as the privileged receiver of some of their knowledge. The silence in Elyne's writing about how the land was won for the Mitchell family sits uncomfortably next to her appreciation of the braiding of land and identity. So although her writing sings the 'songlines' of the country in a new language, her silence on indigenous land ownership makes her complicit in the process of colonisation—the profits of which we all share.

In 1972 tragedy struck Elyne when her eldest son, her beloved Harry, was killed in a car accident in the Blue Mountains of New South Wales at the age of twenty-two. Once again she returned to the land. As she looked back at her diary over this time, she found it marked only by time. 'Lovely day' followed by '6 hours' or '5$\frac{1}{2}$ hours'. She worked on *Towong Hill* as she hadn't worked since the war:

The work went steadily on, and I was part of it as I had not been for years, deeply involved—woven into the world around me by the rhythm of the beautiful chestnut pony, the sound of the cattle, the brilliant light, the scent of dry grass at evening.[65]

The land held her grief in its 'unlonely silence', as she had known it would. Wherever she looked, she saw moments shared with Harry. But somehow in the action of working, of moving out into place, she was able to go on. Later, when she returned to this time through her writing, she was able to express the ways she had moved through her grief. She could describe the dulling of her pain through physical labour, and relief in being carried forward by the cycles of life on the land. But her diary holds no words and no images during this period; instead, her writing voice, her curiosity to make sense of her world through words, lay dormant.

Elyne Mitchell has given something unique to women's writing about place. Unlike so many of the women in this book, she stayed rooted on the one spot. Her life was lived out over the one piece of land. She travelled over it as a single girl, newly married woman, young mother, grieving mother, mature woman and matriarch widow after Tom's death in November 1985. She recorded her life against the same backdrop of country, and her interaction with it informed and shaped every part of her life. Her understanding of the land and her interpretation of the Australian bush have taught generations of young readers how to look at the bush, how to see the beauty and the mystery of its cycles. Her work was always informed by what we now call conservation, but she was of a generation in which it was hard for women to be heard as philosophers or conservationists. After the poor reception of *Soil and Civilisation,* she gave up the attempt to address these philosophical ideas directly; instead, she wrote books that taught children how to see that same bush as home, and how to receive her vision of the bush as part of their inheritance.

> If the land had to be 'sung' and a map of song lines created before the land existed for all to see, then my words may create a vision of the land I love. Memories, experience, effort and association with 'place' may make the essence of that place palpable, visible, strongly present.[66]

Elyne was able to make the mountains 'come alive' for her readers as they had for her. She was the inheritor of the hard-won threads of place gathered by early pioneer women. Her love of flowers is reminiscent of Georgiana Molloy. The freedom that she possesses as she rides into the mountains or writes about her experiences is inherited from Isabella Bird's radical demand to be allowed to ride astride and still maintain her femininity. Yet if she inherits these threads from earlier generations, she also inherits a blindness to her privileged position as 'caretaker' of the land, as a 'singer' of place. Though she slides over the complicity of her inheritance, her right to 'speak to the earth', Elyne's insight into the reasons for the land's suffering and her call for the conservation of wild places all signal her as a woman ahead of her time.

Core of my heart

Beneath these women's stories, stitched to and through them, are relationships. Women's writing about place reveals the connective tissue that holds their lives together. Revisiting place by writing about it revisits the intensity of these relationships.

In 1996 I paddled a kayak over 400 miles through Prince William Sound, Alaska. Blithely, happily, I paddled stroke for stroke with the man with whom I envisioned spending the rest of my life. The sound of laughter over water, the splash of paddles, even the sting of salt in my eye takes me to a place where mountains spring out of oceans and forests crowd the sea, a place where a loved one's face comes back into focus and I can once again hear the crinkle of his laughter.

When I first read the words of the women in this book about lost homes, lost lovers, lost children, I could respond to grief, but I could not understand the heaviness of their words, the inability of the pen and parchment to convey the burden of their loss. When Georgiana Molloy buried her baby and then another child in a strange new world, I could recognise grief in her letters to her mother and closest friends. But I did not know that grief can press so heavily that it encases you and muffles the sound you make—and I did not, could not, *will not* enter into the closeness, the darkness, the privacy of her grief. I could recognise the intensity of Marie Rose Smith who, in a single paragraph, wrote that she had buried twelve of her seventeen children. And I wept when I read of Elyne Mitchell's loss, and of her efforts to salve the pain in the physical exhaustion of farm work. Bereft of her normal eloquence, her bleak, halting description hinted at depths of pain that I knew nothing of. Only after my husband died could I make sense of the blankness in her diary entries— 'Work, $5\frac{1}{2}$ hours'—or in Mary Schaffer Warren's withdrawal from society to search the mountainsides for flowers. Only then could I connect with the emptiness that drove Freda Du Faur to place her head inside an oven and seek release. Not a sound did I make for six months. I spoke, but I could not hear my words.

But on the land, I could hear. The country of my grandmother and mother reclaimed me. It is the place I know I can come back to and be absorbed by, where I can sit on the rocks, watch the wind stir the leaves, watch the sun sink behind the hill and walk home without needing to blink away the tears.

Grief, then, is held in place. Over our land sits the grief that society tries to silence—the grief of displaced people. Like the stories of loss in these women's lives, the grief of lost places is difficult for an outsider to hear. Even Elyne Mitchell's writing, as engaged as it was with the interconnections between people and place, could not bring this grief into view. I walk the land of my childhood and wonder at who tended it before my family came here. My grandmother, who was almost identical in age to Elyne, never mentioned the indigenous owners of her land. She drew inspiration from its beauty, loved it and is buried in it but, though I know the places where the land bears her grief, I don't know the stories of the grief that went before.

This is a silence in our histories, which this generation must learn to hear. Reading the words of women who lived in the new land, we are left with these women's stories, which give us a richness of experience, a way of seeing place that is intimately related to personal and community identity. They also give us a point to acknowledge what our sense of place cost the indigenous people. This was not a question asked by many of the women in this book. Some, like Alice Duncan Kemp, acknowledged the impact of colonisation on Aboriginal people, but their perspective was clouded by the tired Darwinian justifications of a racial hierarchy. Others, like Elyne

Mitchell, trace connections between their love of place and an indigenous knowledge of country, but this patterning can hide the continuing grief of indigenous people and reinforces their displacement.

Perhaps Marie Rose Smith, who simply asked to be allowed to live her life out beside the creek that flowed from the mighty Rockies, shows us an acceptance of the ways our different communities are linked together. As her story crisscrossed the land and moved between cultures, she sought common ground between the indigenous people, the settlers and her own culture. The women in this book have all stretched beyond the boundaries of their skins, shrugged off their estrangement from the new world and, through their actions and words, built up the bones of home.

The philosopher Edward Casey asks: how do we get into place? He answers his question by arguing, 'In the very way by which we are always already there—*by our own lived body*'.[1] For Elyne Mitchell, her own body and her interaction with place were the source of her writing, an expression of the experience between her 'lived body' and the land. Her books demonstrated an understanding of the power of a place, the power of stories about places and of the importance of the interaction between people, the land and nature. Casey's insistence on the power of places outside time, space and culture sounds philosophically interesting, and intellectually challenging, yet he cannot capture the physicality of such a moment. But it is when we read these women's stories that we share that moment of lived intensity, their visceral response to place—whether on the beach with Georgiana Molloy, by the lake with Mary O'Brien, wrapped in bearskin and asleep on spruce branches in the mountains with Susan Allison, trudging up the glacier with Freda Du Faur, or even seeing lights in the night of the Channel Country with Alice Duncan-Kemp and being turned away from a hill by a force as real as a knife blade. Our visceral reading of these moments, our response to the image of Mary Percy Jackson galloping across the prairie, enveloped in sound—the thud of hooves and the creak of her saddle, the whistle of wind—and her attempt to explain what it felt like to be caught up in a land that was bigger than its representation on a map, establish a connection for us between place and a collective social memory.

Casey argued that the second essentialist trait of place (the first being the role of the lived body) was that 'places gather'. Places gather experiences and histories, languages and thoughts: 'places ... keep such unbodylike entities as thoughts and memories'.[2] For Mary Schaffer Warren the Rocky Mountains of Alberta held memories of her life, and all she had to do was look up at those distant peaks to release and relive those memories. Places hold all these stories.

'Land is culture before it is nature', wrote Simon Schama, and we in our post-modern society nod and agree; land is what *we* make it. Schama's book, *Landscape and Memory,* makes a persuasive argument about the relationship between nature and culture.[3] But there is an incessant whisper that unsettles my intellectual distance, a memory of standing on a glacier and looking into its icy heart. For Schama, landscapes are 'constructs of the imagination projected onto wood and water and rock'. Yet even as he argued this, he conceded that the idea of landscape was more complex than a simple deconstruction will allow. Once a place becomes imbued with a certain idea of landscape, what Schama calls a myth or vision, the actual place begins to muddle categories; metaphors become more real than their referents.[4] For Schama, place is reducible to culture.

Other writers, such as the American anthropologists Stephen Feld and Keith Basso, have encouraged a movement beyond 'facile generalisations about places being culturally constructed by describing specific ways in which places naturalize different worlds of sense'.[5] For the anthropologists, place has a physical reality beyond space and time, or as Casey puts it, 'the phenomenological fact of the matter is that space and time come together in place. Indeed they arise out of place itself.'[6] Casey was touching on the reality of the tangible qualities of place; you can both touch and feel place, yet the way you experience that place is influenced by the culture you see it through.

These two positions are not as mutually exclusive as they first appear, and in reading both, a middle ground can be found. Schama warns his reader of the complexity of myths in writing about land; he is cautious about the possibility of taking myth seriously without becoming 'morally blinded by [myths'] poetic power'.[7] For him this was a dilemma, which he resolved by acknowledging myth's importance to culture without backing away from his idea of the pre-eminence of culture overlaying all interpretations of the land.

In turn, Casey argues that place is the most fundamental form of embodied experience, the site of a powerful fusion of self, space and time.[8] This idea gives us philosophical access to some sort of comprehension of the reality of the relationship of the women in this book with the land. This relationship—between land and body—was fundamental to their interpretation of place, no matter how significantly that interpretation was refracted through the cultural lens of ideals of landscape and their society's limitations on them in that landscape. When Casey talks of place as an 'embodied' experience, he highlights the power of places upon our identity. 'I do not take place to be something physical', he writes; 'a place is not a mere patch of ground, a bare stretch of earth, a sedentary set of stones'.[9] Land as place, while culturally interpreted, maintains and similarly asserts upon culture a reality of its own.

The naturalist and writer, Barry Lopez, has grappled with the difficulty of writing about the different realities of the land. His writing acknowledges the importance of culture in understanding the land, while maintaining the land's separate existence to that culture.

As I traveled, I came to believe that people's desires and aspirations were as much a part of the land as the wind, solitary animals, and the bright fields of stone and tundra. And, too, that the land itself existed apart from these ... The physical landscape is baffling in its ability to transcend what we would make of it. It is as subtle in its expression as turns of the mind, and larger than our grasp; and yet it is knowable. The mind, full of curiosity and analysis, disassembles a landscape and then reassembles the pieces—the nod of a flower, the color of the night sky, the murmur of an animal—trying to fathom its geography. At the same time the mind is trying to find its place within the land, to discover a way to dispel its own sense of estrangement.[10]

It is this journey from estrangement to a sense of place that the women in this book have written. Their words have built up the bones of home. They provide a framing picture of their place(s), which we in Australia and Canada have inherited from them.

Or, as Elyne Mitchell described it, they were singing the song of the country, calling it into being. The writing of women in this book has recorded the journey to see a reflection of 'self' in new lands. Many of the women wrote to actively pass this hard-won knowledge on to their own children's generation.

My view is to the east. I look over the old orchard and out to a hillside of trees. The colours are those of late summer, not mid-autumn, as it is hot for April. On a northerly breeze, locusts drift in like acid rain. Their fecundity is an irresistible force. Outside, my children play where I played as a child in the big garden under the cedars and elms. They flit like butterflies, full of purpose, through imaginary worlds. The locusts hover, but the children are unaware of this descending army and they play on. This country is the core of my heart, and even though it is singed by drought and consumed by insects, I can still hear its promise of loss—but also of life.

Notes

Into the Wild

1   Elspeth Probyn, *Outside Belongings*, Routledge: New York, 1996, p6.
2   See Richard Waterhouse, 'Australian Legends: Representations of the Bush, 1813–1913', *Australian Historical Studies*, No. 115, October 2000, p218. Using images of rural women on the stage, Waterhouse has argued that the notion of separate spheres on the land was not as definitive as suggested.
3   See Jill Kerr Conway, *The Road from Coorain*, Albert Knoff: New York, 1987, especially the first chapter.
4   G. Whitlock & Russell McDougall (eds), *Australian/Canadian Literature in English: Comparative Perspectives*, Methuen: Sydney, 1987, p51.
5   See Janice Monk, 'Gender in the Landscape: expressions of power and meaning', in Kay Anderson and Fay Gale (eds), *Inventing Places: Studies in Cultural Geography*, Longman/Cheshire: Melbourne, 1992, p135. Monk identifies a connection between self and land in the expressions of women across race and culture in her study of American Indian, Mexican-American and Euro-American women in the landscape of the American Southwest.
6   See for example, N. Donkin (ed), *Always a Lady: Courageous Women of Colonial Australia*, Collins Dove: Melbourne, 1990; L. Frost, *No Place for a Nervous Lady: voices from the Australian bush*, McPhee Gribble/Penguin: Ringwood, Vic, 1984; L. Frost, *A Face in the Glass: The Journal and Life of Annie Baxter Dawbin*, William Heinemann: Melbourne, 1992; H. Heney, *Dear Fanny: Women's letters to and from New South Wales*, Australian National University Press: Canberra, 1985; A. McLeary, with T. Dingle, *Catherine: On Catherine Currie's Diary, 1873–1908*, Melbourne University Press: Carlton, 1998; M. Braidwood Mowle, in Patricia Clarke (ed), *A Colonial Woman: The Life and Times of Mary Braidwood Mowle*, Allen & Unwin: Sydney, 1986.
7   K. Holmes, *Spaces in Her Day: Australian Women's Diaries of the 1920s and 1930s*, Allen & Unwin: Sydney, 1995, p61. Holmes noted that one of the strongest distinctions in women's diaries was whether the writer lived in the city or a country town or on the

land. She argued that the land impacted rural women's writing by ordering their days to the rhythms and demands of the season.

8   The idea of a garrison mentality within the Canadian imagination has been discussed by N. Frye, *The Bush Garden: Essays on the Canadian Imagination*, House of Anansi: Toronto, 1972; D. Jones, *Butterfly on a Rock: A Study of the Themes and Images in Canadian Literature*, University of Toronto Press: Toronto, 1970.

9   K. Schaffer, *In the Wake of First Contact: The Eliza Fraser Stories*, CUP, Melbourne, 1995.

10 See Suzanne Falkiner and Alan Oldfield, *Lizard Island: The Journey of Mary Watson*, Allen & Unwin: Sydney, 2000, for an account of Mary's life.

11 The harvesting of the sea slug, or sea cucumber as it was sometimes known; these creatures were then boiled down and sold as a delicacy renowned for its aphrodisiac properties.

12 S. De Vries, *Strength of Spirit: Pioneering Women of Achievement from First Fleet to Federation*, Millennum Books: Sydney, 1995, Introduction.

13 See Peter Read, *Belonging: Australians, Place and Aboriginal Ownership*, Cambridge University Press: Cambridge, 2000.

14 'Mooraberrie', the Duncans' cattle station, is currently under a native title claim.

15 J. Wright, 'The Broken Links', republished in *Born of the Conquerors: Selected Essays*, Aboriginal Studies Press: Canberra, 1991, p30.

16 J. Wright, 'Two Dreamtimes (for Kath Walker)', in Isabel White, Diane Barwick, Betty Meehan (eds), *Fighters and Singers: The Lives of Some Australian Aboriginal Women*, Allen & Unwin: Sydney, 1985, xix–xxi. First published in Judith Wright, *Alive: Poems 1971–2*, Angus & Robertson: Sydney, 1973.

17 J. Wright, 'An Apology to the Koori and Murri People' in *Half a Lifetime*, 1999, p295.

18 See Peter Read for a longer discussion on this tension, *Belonging …* .

19 Barbara Schott, 'The Farmhouse Poems', in P. Banting (ed), *Fresh Tracks*, 1998.

Chapter One

1   Marie Harris, 'Interstate' in *Raw Honey*, Alice James Publishers: Cambridge, Mass, 1975.

2   Gaston Bachelard, *The Poetics of Space* (translated from French by Marie Jolas), Beacon Press: Boston, 1969, (1958), p5.

3   Alexandra Hasluck, *Portrait with Background*, (first pub. by Oxford University Press: Melbourne, 1955), Fremantle Arts Centre Press: Fremantle, 1990, p26.

4   This area is now Toronto.

5   Now Perth.

6   Virginia Watson Rouslin, 'The Intelligent Woman's Guide to Pioneering in Canada' in *Dalhousie Review*, Vol. 56, No. 2, Summer 1976, p322.

7   Hasluck, *Portrait with Background*, p15.

8   Lyn Barber, *The Heyday of Natural History: 1820–1870*, Johnathan Cape: London, 1980, p71.

9   Ibid, pp13–16.

10 There is a vast amount of published diaries, journals, etc. of educated women who kept their journals and wrote letters of their experience of the voyage to Australia and Canada.

11 Rouslin, 'The Intelligent Woman's Guide ...,' p322.

12 See Suzanne L. Bunkers & Cynthia A. Huff (eds), *Inscribing the Daily: critical essays on women's diaries*, University of Massachusetts Press: Amherst, 1996. Barbara Powell, 'Discourse and Decorum: Women's Diaries in Nineteenth Century Canada' in Uma Parameswaran (ed), *Quilting a New Canon: Stitching Women's Words*, Sister Vision, Black Women and Women of Colour Press: Toronto, 1996, pp335–345.

13 Mary O'Brien to friend Cara, *The Journal of Mary O'Brien*, Journal Forty-One, August 1830, Ontario Archives, MS 199–2.

14 For a discussion on genteel invalidism and the discrepancy between women's supposed natural weakness and their level of physical activity, see Marian Amies, 'The Victorian Governess and Colonial Ideals of Womanhood', in *Victorian Studies*, Vol. 31, No. 4, 1988, p542.

15 *Journal One*, September 2nd, 1828.

16 Ibid, September 10th, 1828.

17 Vivienne Rae-Ellis, *Louisa Anne Meredith: A Tigress in Exile*, St David's Park Publishing: Hobart, 1990 (first published 1979), p70.

18 Ibid, 65.

19 Mrs. Charles Meredith, *Notes and Sketches of New South Wales: during a residence in that colony from 1839 to 1844*, London: John Murray, 1846, p19.

20 *Journal Two*, October 10th, 1828.

21 Ibid.

22 Ibid.

23 *Journal Two*, October 13th, 1828.

24 *Journal Two*, October 16th, 1828.

25 *Journal Three*, November 4th, 1828.

26 The sap of the maple tree was collected to make maple sugar.

27 *Journal Five*, December 1st, 1828.

28 *Journal Thirteen*, March 7th, 1829.

29 *Journal Fourteen*, April 29th, 1829.

30 Ibid.

31 Ibid.

32 *Journal Twenty-Five*, December 11, 1829.

33 *Journal Twenty-Six*, January 1830.

34 William Lines, *An All Consuming Passion: Origins, Modernity and the Australian Life of Georgiana Molloy*, Allen & Unwin: Sydney, 1994, p93.

35 Hasluck, *Portrait with Background*, p59.

36 G. Molloy, cited in Lines, *An All Consuming Passion*, p93.

37 See Geoffrey Bolton, *Spoils and Spoilers: Australians make their environment 1788–1980*, Allen & Unwin: Sydney, 1994, pp40–41, for a discussion of Old World attitudes to clearing land of trees. Also, Lines, *An All Consuming Passion*, pp108–109.

38 Cited in Hasluck, *Portrait with Background*, p81, Letter to Helen Storey, March 1831.

39 See Elizabeth Webby, 'A Grave in the Bush', in Dennis Haskell (ed), *Tilting at Matilda: Literature, Aborigines, Women and the Church in Contemporary Australia*, Fremantle Arts Centre Press, 1994, pp30–38, for a discussion on the significance of burial and graves to settlers in their attempts to imaginatively and physically possess the land.

40 See Susan Hosking, 'I 'ad to 'ave me garden': A Perspective on Australian Women Gardeners,' in *Meanjin*, Vol. 47, No. 3, 1988, p439, for a discussion on the importance of gardens for women's identity, and pp445–447 for a discussion on Georgiana Molloy's garden.

41 Cited in Hasluck, *Portrait with Background*, pp81–82, Letter to Helen Storey, March 1831.

42 See Susan K. Martin, 'The Gender of Gardens: The Space of the Garden in Nineteenth Century Australia,' in Ruth Barcan and Ian Buchanan (eds), *Imagining Australian Space: Cultural Studies and Spacial Inquiry*, University of Western Australia Press: Nedlands, 1999, pp115–125, for a discussion on the gendered space of the garden.

43 Georgiana Molloy to her sister Elizabeth, in A. Hasluck, *Portrait with Background*, p73.

44 Gillian Whitlock, *The Intimate Empire: reading women's autobiography*, Cassell: London, 2000, p44; D. M. R. Bentley, 'Breaking the "cake of custom": the Atlantic crossing as a Rubicon for female emigrants to Canada?' in Lorraine McMullan (ed.), *Re(Dis)covering Our Foremothers: Nineteenth Century Canadian Women Writers*, University of Ottawa Press: Ottawa, 1990, pp91–122.

45 Arnold Toynbee, 'The Stimulus of Migration Overseas,' in *A Study of History*, Oxford University Press: London, 1955 (1935), p93.

46 Arnold Toynbee cited in G. Whitlock, *The Intimate Empire*, p44.

47 See Gillian Whitlock, *The Intimate Empire*, 2000, and David Bentley, 'Breaking the "cake of custom". …

48 See Emma Curtin, 'Gentility Afloat: Gentlewomen's diaries and the voyage to Australia, 1830–60,' in *Australian Historical Studies*, Vol. 26, No. 105, 1995, pp634–652, for a discussion on the changing expression of women's gentility on board ship.

49 Many women referred to flowers as dear friends. Louisa Meredith, writing from Tasmania in the 1840s, uses this expression, as did Susanna Moodie in Upper Canada. For a discussion on the connections between the metaphor of flowers and women in the landscape of nineteenth-century Australia, see Pam Hodge, *Fostering Flowers: Women, Landscape and the Psychodynamics of Gender in nineteenth century Australia*, unpublished Ph.D thesis, Edith Cowan University, Western Australia, 1998.

50 See Pam Hodge, *Fostering Flowers*, pp82–112, for a detailed analysis of Georgiana's pregnancies and childbearing experience.

51 Georgiana Molloy to Margaret Dunlop, 12 January 1833, cited in A. Hasluck, *Portrait with Background*, p103.

52 Ibid.

53 Ibid, p162, Georgiana Molloy to Captain Mangles, January 1838.

54 Ibid, p157.

55 Ibid, p154, Letter from Captain Mangles received by Georgiana in December 1836.

56 Ibid, p164, Georgiana Molloy to James Mangles, 25 January 1838.

57 *Journal One Hundred & One*, 26 April 1835.

58 Hasluck, *Portrait with Background*, p156, Georgiana Molloy to James Mangles, 25 January 1838.

59 Ibid, p164.

60 Lines, *An All Consuming Passion*, p124.

61 The land had been kept open and clear of thick undergrowth or heavy timber by Aboriginal fire stick farming. For a history of the use of fire in Australia, see Stephan J. Pyne, *Burning Bush: A Fire*

History of Australia, Allen & Unwin: Sydney, 1992 (first pub. 1991).

62 Lines, *An All Consuming Passion*, p266, Georgiana Molloy to James Mangles, 31 January, 1840.
63 A. Hasluck, *Portrait with Background*, p192.
64 A. Hasluck, *Portrait with Background*, p222, Georgiana to Captain Mangles, February 1841.
65 Ibid, p197, Georgiana Molloy to Captain Mangles, 31 January 1840.
66 Ibid, p198.
67 Ibid, pp197–8.
68 Ibid, p198.
69 Ibid, p202.
70 Ibid, p214, Georgiana Molloy to Captain Mangles, August, 1840.
71 Ibid, p220, Georgiana Molloy to Captain Mangles, 20 January 1841.
72 Ibid, p220, Georgiana Molloy to Captain Mangles, 20 January 1840.
73 See Pam Hodge, *Fostering Flowers*, p112.
74 See Cynthia Huff, 'Chronicles of confinement: reactions to childbirth in British women's diaries,' in *Women's Studies International Forum*, Vol. 10, No. 1, 1987, pp63–68, for a discussion on how women wrote about childbirth in their private writings in the nineteenth century.
75 *Journal Thirty-Nine*, July 7th, 1830.
76 *Journal Forty-Eight*, December 30th, 1830.
77 *Journal Forty-Seven*, November 27th, 1830.
78 *Journal Forty-Seven*, Letter to Cara, December 14, 1830.
79 The Journal before the missing one contains a note saying that Edward's mother in Ireland was anxious to be part of the group who received Mary's journals, so possibly it was not returned from Ireland or was lost en route.
80 *Journal Fifty-Two*, April 11th, 1831.
81 *Journal Fifty-Two*, April 14th, 1831.
82 *Journal Fifty-Three*, May 1st, 1831.
83 *Journal Sixty-Six*, end of March 1832.
84 *Journal Sixty-Seven*, April 1832.
85 *Journal Seventy*, May 11th, 1832.
86 *Journal Seventy-One*, July 1832.
87 *Journal Seventy-Three*, August 15th-16th, 1832.
88 *Journal Seventy-Three*, August 19th, 1832.
89 *Journal Ninety-Five*, October 22nd, 1834.
90 *Journal One Hundred & Ten*, August 1st, 1835.

Chapter Two

1   S. Allison (edited by M. A. Ormsby), *A Pioneer Gentlewoman in British Columbia: The Recollections of Susan Allison*, University of British Columbia Press: Vancouver, 1976, p21.

2   The Métis Nation grew out of the marriage of French Canadian men and Plains Indian women. They were allied to the French through language and religion and to the First Nation people by their economic and social life. 'First Nation' refers to the indigenous people of Canada, and 'Aboriginal' refers to the indigenous people of Australia.

3   Marcus Billson, 'The Memoir: New Perspectives on a Forgotten Genre,' in *Genre*, Vol. X, 1977, p259.

4   *A Pioneer Gentlewoman ...*, introduction by Margaret Ormsby, px.

5   Ibid, pxii.

6   Ibid, pxiii.

7   Ibid, pxiv.

8   Allison, *A Pioneer Gentlewoman*, p7.

9   Ibid, p9.

10 Ibid, p10.

11 Ibid, p20.

12 Ibid, p21.

13 Ibid, pxxvii.

14 Ibid, p21.

15 Bannock was bread made on the trail with flour, water and bacon fat.

16 Ibid, p21.

17 This scene of a bride going out into the wilderness with her husband and taking as their bed something of the land was found in Australia also. See Mrs. Campbell Praed, *Lady Bridget in the Never Never Land: A Story of Australian Life*, Hutchinson & Co: London, 1915, p153.

18 Allison, *A Pioneer Gentlewoman in British Columbia*, p35.

19 Ibid, p23/24.

20 Ibid, p27.

21 Ibid, p28.

22 Ibid.

23 Ibid.

24 Ibid.

25 Ibid, p44.

26 Ibid, p34.

27 Ibid, p40.

28 Ibid.

29 Ibid, p41.

30 Ormsby, Introduction, *A Pioneer Gentlewoman ...*, p1.

31 See Dee Brown, *Bury My Heart at Wounded Knee: An Indian History of the American West*, Pan Books: London, 1972, pp320–327.

32 Allison, *A Pioneer Gentlewoman ...*, p44.

33 Ibid, p41.

34 Ibid, p55.

35 Ibid, p47.

36 Ibid, p52.

37 Ibid, p55.

38 Ibid, p60.

39 Ibid, p62.

40 *Canadian Cattlemen Magazine*, Vol. 11–12, 1948–49.

41 Jock Carpenter, *Fifty Dollar Bride: Marie Rose Smith, A Chronicle of Métis Life in the Nineteenth Century*, Greys Publishing Ltd: Sidney, B.C., 1977.

42 Victoria Haskins, *My One Bright Spot: A Personal Insight into Relationships between White women and Aboriginal Women under the New South Wales Aboriginal Protection Board Apprenticeship Policy, 1920–1942*. Unpublished PhD thesis, University of Sydney, 1998, p4.

43 J. Kinsey Howard, *Strange Empire: a narrative of the North West*, Morrow: New York, 1952, p40.

44 Ibid, p43.

45 Smith, *Eighty Years on the Plains*, manuscript held in Glenbow Archives, Calgary, Canada (not dated), p64.

46 *Eighty Years on the Plains*, p1.

47 Ibid, p8.

48 Ibid, p21.

49 See Wallace Stegner, *Wolf Willow: A History, A Story, a Memory of the Last Plains Frontier*, Penguin Books: New York, 1962/1990, 'Half World: The Métis', pp57–64, for a detailed analysis of the Red River Carts and their role in the development of the Canadian west.

50 Smith, *Eighty Years on the Plains*, p14.

51 Ibid, p9.

52 Ibid.

53 The prairie as a pastoral garden has been a strong tradition in Canadian literature. See Walter Pache, 'English-Canadian Fiction and the Pastoral Tradition', in *Canadian Literature*, No. 86, Autumn, 1980, pp15–28 for a discussion on the roots of this

tradition in English literature. In Australia Coral Lansbury traces the romantic evocation of the bush back to an English literary tradition that transferred the English pastoral ideal of Arcadia to Australia; see Lansbury, *Arcady in Australia: The Evocation of Australia in Nineteenth Century English Literature*, Melbourne University Press: Melbourne, 1970.

54 *Eighty Years on the Plains*, p9.

55 Susan Jackel, *Images of the Canadian West 1872–1911*, unpublished PhD thesis, University of British Columbia, 1977. Jackel discusses William Butler's *The Great Lone Land: A Narrative of Travel and Adventure in the North West of America*, Sampson Low, Marston, Searle and Rivington: London, 1878 (8th edition), which was a narrative of travel, exploration and adventure across the Canadian prairie. The text was very influential from the 1860s to the 1920s, when it was published in its twentieth edition. Jackel traces the connections between the ideas in Butler's account and the way these have influenced the development of a settler society. Butler's *The Great Lone Land* was a eulogy for a dying race. He conceptualised the prairie as a wilderness that could become a garden through settlement.

56 There is a large volume of critical literature that addresses the idea of the prairie and its effect on the Canadian imagination. It is comparable with the amount written in Australia on the 'bush' and desert and their effect on the Australian imagination.

57 *Eighty Years on the Plains*, p2.

58 See Simon Ryan, 'Discovering Myths: The Creation of the Explorer in Journals of Exploration', in *Australian Canadian Studies*, Vol. 12, No. 2, 1994. Ryan argues that the publication of explorers' journals was an important source of myth-making about the new land.

59 *Eighty Years on the Plains*, p81.

60 *Eighty Years on the Plains*, p22.

61 Ibid, p11.

62 Ibid, p12.

63 Ibid.

64 Diane P. Payment, " 'La vie en rose'? Métis Women at Batoche, 1870 to 1920", in Veronica Strong-Boag and Anita Clare Fellman (eds), *Rethinking Canada: The Promise of Women's History*, Third Edition, Oxford University Press: Toronto, 1997, p207.

65 *Eighty Years on the Plains*, p34.

66 Ibid.

67 Ibid, p35.

68 Ibid, p36.

[69] Ibid, p66.

[70] Ibid, p70.

[71] Ibid, p72.

[72] Ibid, p73.

[73] Ibid.

[74] J. Carpenter, *Fifty Dollar Bride*, p22.

[75] See Payment, " 'La vie en rose'?", p206, for Métis population figures.

[76] This was an expression used by the fur-traders who followed the government agents into Indian Territory as they paid treaty money to the Indians. The traders would then sell the Indians whiskey and manufactured goods, which they paid for with treaty money.

[77] *Eighty Years on the Plains*, p79.

[78] Payment, " 'La vie en rose'?", p205.

[79] For a detailed discussion of the Chinook Wind and its effect on the climate and settlement in southern Alberta, see Sid Marty, *Leaning on the Wind: Under the Spell of the Great Chinook,* Harper Perennial: Toronto, 1996, pp27–38.

[80] Ibid, p35.

[81] Coulee is a deep gorge or gully. From the prairie they are invisible. For instance, the town of Pincher Creek is built in a coulee and only the tops of the houses are visible from the prairie around it.

[82] He would slit the loose skin below the neck and leave it hanging like a handle.

[83] Marie Rose bore seventeen children over twenty-six years, the first being born in 1878 and the last in 1904. Of her seventeen live births, only six of her children lived to middle age, a cause of much grief to her.

[84] *Eighty Years on the Plains*, p161.

[85] Ibid, p81.

[86] Ibid.

[87] Ibid, p82.

[88] Ibid.

[89] Ibid, p37.

[90] Ibid, p69.

[91] Ibid, p170.

[92] Carpenter, *Fifty Dollar Bride*, 1977, p87.

[93] *Eighty Years on the Plains*, p74.

[94] Ibid.

[95] Ibid, p76.

[96] Ibid, p78.

[97] Ibid, p79.

[98] Ibid.

[99] Ibid, p83.

[100] Ibid, p84.

[101] Ibid, p176.

[102] Mark O'Connor, in an interview in the *Bulletin* 1990, cited in Suzanne Falkiner, *The Writers' Landscape: Wilderness*, Simon and Schuster: Sydney, 1992, p130.

[103] P. Carter, *The Road to Botany Bay: An Exploration of Landscape & History*, Alfred A. Knopf: New York, 1988.

[104] B. Lopez, *Crossing Open Ground*, Vintage: New York, 1978/1989, p64.

Chapter Three

[1] M. Franklin, *Childhood at Brindabella: My First Ten Years*, Angus & Robertson: Sydney, 1963/1974, p20.

[2] Ibid.

[3] Ibid, p19.

[4] Walers were the foundation breed for the Australian Stock Horse. They were bred from thoroughbreds for speed, Arabian horses for endurance and Timor ponies for hardiness. For these characteristics they were a highly valued cavalry mount in the Indian wars, Boer War and First World War.

[5] *Childhood at Brindabella*, p18.

[6] Ibid, p19.

[7] Ibid, p18.

[8] Shelley Armitage, 'Rawhide Heroines: The Evolution of the Cowgirl and the Myth of America' in Sam B. Girgus (ed), *The American Self: Myth, Ideology & Popular Culture*, University of New Mexico Press: Albuquerque, 1981, p169.

[9] Penny Russell, 'Recycling Femininity: Old Ladies and New Women', in *Australian Cultural History*, No. 49, 1996, pp33–34. Kylie Winkworth, 'Women and the Bicycle: Fast, Loose and Liberated' in *Australian Journal of Art*, vol. 8, 1989/90, p105.

[10] Lucy Frost, *A Face in the Glass: The Journal and Life of Annie Baxter Dawbin*, William Heinemann: Melbourne, 1992, p65.

[11] Ibid.

[12] Ibid, p125.

[13] Mary O'Brien, *Journal Twenty-Five*, 29 November 1829.

[14] *Journal Twenty-Six*, December 17, 1829.

[15] Pat Barr, introduction to I. Bird, *A Lady's Life in the Rocky Mountains*, Virago: London (1880), 1982, pxviii.

[16] I. Bird, *A Lady's Life in the Rocky Mountains*, fly piece.

17 Ibid, p163.
18 Ibid, 162.
19 Ibid, 152.
20 Susan Armitage, 'Another Lady's Life in the Rocky Mountains' in Bonnie Frederick & Susan H. McLeod (eds), *Women and the Journey: The Female Travel Experience*, Washington State University Press: Pullman, Washington, 1993.
21 Ibid, p26.
22 Ibid, p27.
23 M. Hopkins, Introduction, *Letters from a Lady Rancher*, Glenbow Museum: Calgary, 1981, p4.
24 A democrat is a Canadian term for a buggy usually drawn by two horses.
25 *Letters from a Lady Rancher*, p5, (letter dated 21 September 1909).
26 Ibid.
27 Ibid, p6.
28 Ibid, p7.
29 Range was land not yet taken up by settlement.
30 Ibid, p11.
31 Ibid, p17.
32 There is a large body of literature on the effect of homesickness on settlers in a new land. In the eighteenth century, homesickness was treated as pathological. See Maureen Scott Harris, 'Being Homesick, Writing Home', in Pamela Banting (ed), *Fresh Tracks: Writing the Western Landscape*, Polestar Publishing: Victoria, BC, 1998, p253. Ronald Rees wrote about the physiological effect of homesickness on settlers on the prairie as being extremely dislocating, so that while people are physically in one world, they are imaginatively in another. See *New and Naked Land: Making the Prairies Home*, Western Producer Prairie Books: Saskatoon, 1988, p160.
33 *Letters from a Lady Rancher*, p149 (letter dated September 1911).
34 Ibid, p128 (letter dated May 1911).
35 A. Duncan-Kemp, *Our Channel Country: Man and Nature in South-West Queensland*, Angus and Robertson: Sydney, 1961, pp182–183.
36 Ibid, p121.
37 A. Duncan-Kemp, *Where Strange Paths Go Down*, W. R. Smith and Patterson Pty.Ltd.: Brisbane, 1952, p89.
38 *Our Channel Country*, p115.
39 See Henry Reynolds, *Black Pioneers: How Aboriginal and Islander People helped build Australia*, Penguin: Ringwood, Vic,

1990/2000, for a discussion on the importance of indigenous labour for the survival and success of white settlers.

40 Pamela Lukin Watson, *Frontier Lands & Pioneer Legends: How Pasturalists Gained Karuwali Lands*, Allen & Unwin: Sydney, 1998, pp29–30.

41 For the gender bias against women in the anthropological canon, see Marie de Lepervanche, 'Women, Men & Anthropology,' in Julie Marcus (ed), *First in their Field*, 1993, pp1–13. Also Julie Marcus, 'The Beauty, Simplicity and Honour of Truth: Olive Pink in the 1940s', in *First in their Field*, pp111–135. For a wider discussion of the history of women writing about other cultures and the inherent problem of anthropology as a discipline for women, see a collection of feminist essays edited by Ruth Behar and Deborah A. Gordon, *Women, Writing, Culture*, University of California Press: Berkeley, 1995.

42 *Our Channel Country*, p5. Alice's and her sister's experience of being raised by an Aboriginal nurse was not uncommon in outback Australia.

43 A. Duncan-Kemp, *Our Sandhill Country: Nature and Man in South Western Queensland,* Angus and Robertson: Sydney, 1933, p69.

44 Ibid, p140.

45 A Duncan-Kemp, *Where Strange Gods Call*, W. R. Smith and Patterson, Pty. Ltd.: Brisbane, 1968, p184.

46 Ibid, p19.

47 *Our Channel Country*, p42.

48 Ibid.

49 Dr Mary Percy Jackson, *Suitable for the Wilds—Letters from Northern Alberta, 1929–1931.* Edited and with an introduction by Janice Dickson McGinnis, University of Toronto Press: Toronto, 1995, p10.

50 Sally Ledger, 'New Woman' in Lorna Sage (ed), *The Cambridge Guide to Women's Writing in English*, Cambridge University Press: Cambridge, 1999, p465 and Cecily Devereux, 'New Woman, New World: Maternal Feminism and the New Imperialism in the White Settler Colonies', in *Women's Studies International Forum*, Vol. 22, No. 2, March 1999, pp175–184.

51 J. Dickin McGinnis in M. Percy Jackson, *Suitable for the Wilds,* Introduction, 1995, p19.

52 Ibid, p13.

53 M. Percy Jackson, ibid, p98 (letter dated 20 September 1929).

54 A caboose is a sleigh drawn by a horse, but with a little cabin on top with benches and a stove.

[55] J. Dickin McGinnis, ibid, pp23–25.

[56] Ibid, p33.

[57] Dr M. Percy Jackson, ibid, p79 (letter dated 29 August 1929).

[58] Margo Culley, Introduction, in Margo Culley (ed), *A Day at a Time: The Diary Literature of American Women from 1764 to the Present*, The Feminist Press: New York, 1985, p22. Culley argues that as a reader of women's private writings, it is important to identify the 'silences' of the text. What women 'did not, could not or would not write sometimes shrieks from the page'.

[59] *Suitable for the Wilds*, p75 (letter dated 31 July 1929).

[60] J. Dickson McGinnis, ibid, p22.

[61] Dr M. Percy Jackson, ibid, p65 (letter dated 6 July 1929).

[62] Ibid, p75 (letter dated 31 July 1929).

[63] Ibid, p78.

[64] Ibid.

[65] Ibid, p79 (letter dated 4 August 1929).

[66] Ibid, p126 (letter dated 12 November 1929).

[67] Ibid, p104 (letter dated 19 September 1929).

[68] Ibid, p107 (letter dated 17 October 1929).

[69] Ibid, p107 (letter dated 29 January 1930).

[70] Ibid, p163.

[71] Ibid, p122 (letter dated 11 November 1929).

Chapter Four

[1] Freda Du Faur, *The Conquest of Mount Cook & Other Climbs: An Account of Four Seasons' Mountaineering on the Southern Alps of New Zealand*, George Allen & Unwin: London, 1915, p219.

[2] See Donna Haraway for her discussion on the boundary of the body not ending with the skin, 'A Manifesto for Cyborgs: Science, Technology, and Socialist Feminism in the 1980s', *Socialist Review*, 80, 1985, p89. See also Elspeth Probyn, *Outside Belongings*, Routledge: London, 1996, p6.

[3] Margaret Somerville, *Body/Landscape/Journals*, Spinifex: Melbourne, 1999, p12. Somerville discussed her discovery of the body/place connection in her work of transcribing and editing Aboriginal stories of places. She battles with her understanding of how her own body can 'discover' this connection. It is not until she takes a walk down into some deep gorges that she is able to begin to articulate the body/place connection, to repair the mind/body split.

4 Sara Mills, *Discourses of Difference: An Analysis of Women's Travel Writing and Colonialism*, Routledge: London, 1991, Introduction.

5 Ibid, 21.

6 For a more detailed biographical account of Eccleston Du Faur and his relationship with Freda, see Sally Irwin, *Between Heaven and Earth: The Life of a Mountaineer, Freda Du Faur*, White Crane Press: Victoria, 2000, pp10–14 and also pp34–47.

7 John Woolley arrived in Sydney in 1852 to take up the position of rector at the University of Sydney and became the Professor of Classics. In *Between Heaven and Earth*, pp15–26.

8 Ibid, p56.

9 F. Du Faur, *The Conquest of Mount Cook*, 1915, p26.

10 Ibid.

11 Ibid, p27.

12 Ibid.

13 Ibid, p29.

14 Ibid.

15 Ibid, p32.

16 Ibid, p35.

17 Ibid, p198.

18 Ibid, p42.

19 Ibid, p36.

20 Ibid.

21 Ibid, p37.

22 Ibid, p64.

23 Ibid.

24 Ibid, p66.

25 Ibid, p71.

26 Ibid, p57.

27 Freda trained with Murial Cadogan at the Dupain Institute in Sydney. The Dupain Institute was run by George Dupain, father of photographer Max Dupain. Cadogan devised an intensive exercise program for Freda, which included special exercises to strengthen her arms and abdominal muscles, and increase flexibility and stamina. *Between Heaven and Earth*, p130.

28 *The Conquest of Mount Cook*, p87.

29 Ibid.

30 Ibid, p102.

31 Ibid, p103.

32 Ibid.

33 Ibid, p104.

34 Ibid.

[35] Ibid, p108.

[36] Ibid, p218.

[37] David Mazel (ed), *Mountaineering Women: Stories by early climbers*, Texas A & M University Press: College Station, 1994, p19. Mazel contends that it was not until the 1978 all-female Annapurna expedition led by Anita Blum that women climbers consciously repudiated the patriarchal model in favour of what he called a sort of egalitarian communialism.

[38] *The Conquest of Mount Cook*, p153.

[39] For Freda's views on different guides, see *Between Heaven and Earth*, pp209–218.

[40] For more information on Murial and Freda's relationship, see *Between Heaven and Earth*, pp232–300.

[41] *Australian Dictionary of Biography*, 1898–1939, p349.

[42] *Between Heaven and Earth*, p209.

[43] See *Between Heaven and Earth* for more details of her life after climbing.

[44] *A Lady's Life in the Rocky Mountains*, p34.

[45] Ibid, p109.

[46] Ibid.

[47] Although the climb is today considered not much more than a walk-up mountain, there are several difficult sections that the party had to rope together to negotiate.

[48] Ibid.

[49] Mountain Jim's real name was Jim Nugent, and he was the only man with whom Isabella came close to having a romantic sexual relationship. Pat Barr, Introduction, *A Lady's Life in the Rocky Mountains*, pxvi–xvii.

[50] *A Lady's Life in the Rocky Mountains*, p118.

[51] Sid Marty, *Leaning on the Wind, Under the Spell of the Great Chinook*, p15.

[52] E. J. Hart, 'Yahe-Weha—Mountain Woman: The Life and Travels of Mary Schaffer Warren, 1861–1939', Introduction to Mary Schaffer, *A Hunter of Peace: Mary T. S. Schaffer's Old Indian Trails of the Canadian Rockies, with her heretofore unpublished account 1911 Expedition to Malaigne Lake*, introduced and edited by E. J. Hart, Whyte Musuem of the Canadian Rockies, Banff, Alberta, (1911) 1980, p2.

[53] This trip was a popular one for the more adventurous Eastern families. They usually sailed from San Francisco up to the beginning of the Klondike gold trail. See also Mary Hitchcock, *Two Women in the Klondike: the story of a journey to the goldfields of Alaska*, Knickerbockers Press: New York, 1899.

54 'Yahe-Weha …', p3.
55 Elsie Park Gowen, 'A Quaker in Buckskin: Mary Schaffer was a Pioneer Explorer whose story is linked with Jasper Park' in *Alberta Historical Review*, Vol. 5, No. 3, Summer, 1957, p2.
56 'Yahe-Weha …', p6.
57 John Thomson, 'Lure of the Rockies' in *The Brooklyn Eagle*, June 7th 1911.
58 M. Schaffer, *Old Indian Trails in A Hunter of Peace* 1911/1980, p17.
59 *Old Indian Trails*, p16.
60 Ibid.
61 Ibid.
62 Cyndi Smith, *Off the Beaten Track: Women Adventurers and Mountaineers in Western Canada*, Coyote Books: Jasper, 1989, p57.
63 *Old Indian Trails*, p26.
64 Stewardson Brown, *Alpine Flora of the Canadian Rocky Mountains*, illustrated by Mrs. Charles Schaffer, G. P. Putnam's Sons: New York, 1907.
65 For a discussion of the broader reasons for women seeking to travel, speaking generally, see Dea Birkett, *Spinsters Abroad: Victorian Lady Explorers*, Victor Gollancz Ltd: London, 1991, 'Points of Departure', pp1–40.
66 Leonore Davidoff and Catherine Hall, *Family Fortunes: Men and Women of the English Middle Class, 1780–1850*, University of Chicago Press: Chicago, 1987, p403.
67 *Old Indian Trails*, p73.
68 *Old Indian Trails*, p17.
69 *Muskeg* is a broad term used to describe boggy, swampy ground. It often looks as if it is firm but, when stepped upon by horse or human, it is shown to be a deep mud hole.
70 *Old Indian Trails*, p17.
71 Ibid, p18.
72 Ibid, p19.
73 'A Quaker in Buckskin …', p3.
74 M. Schaffer, *My Garden*, unpublished manuscript of a talk Mary gave in 1910, held at Whyte Museum, Banff.
75 *Old Indian Trails*, p36.
76 See Simon Ryan, 'Discovering Myths: The Creation of the Explorer in Journals of Exploration', in *Australian-Canadian Studies*, Vol. 12, No. 2, 1994.
77 For other accounts of women explorers, see, in Canada, Mina Hubbard's account of her expedition through Labrador in Eastern

Canada: *A Woman's Way through Unknown Labrador*, 1908. In Australia, see Alison Cadzow, 'Footnoting: Landscape, Space and Writing in the Exploration Diary of Caroline Creaghe,' in *Southerly*, 1996–97, Summer, 56:4, pp219–233.

78 Ibid, p47.
79 M. Schaffer, *Old Indian Trails*, p73.
80 Ibid, p78.
81 Rudyard Kipling, *Letters of Travel, 1892–1913*, Dominion edition, Macmillan: London, 1920, 188.
82 Piebald (black with white patches) and skewbald (brown with white patches) ponies were a standard stereotype to represent Indians.
83 'Yahe-Weha …', p11.
84 Ibid.
85 Ibid, p13.
86 M. Percy Jackson, *Suitable for the Wilds*, 1995, letter dated 27 July 1930, p225.
87 Ibid, letter dated 30 July, 1930, p227.
88 Maureen Scott Harris, 'Being Homesick, Writing Home' in Pamela Banting (ed), *Fresh Tracks: Writing the Western Landscape*, Polestar Publishing: Victoria B.C. 1998, p253.
89 The house was called *Tarry-a-while* and now operates as a bed and breakfast—maintaining Mary's love of hospitality and entertaining young travellers.
90 'Mrs. Wm Warren, Banff Old Timer & Explorer of Rockies Passes' in *Crag & Canyon*, Banff, Alberta, Banff National Park, Friday January 27th, 1939; Whyte Museum of the Canadian Rockies.
91 Elyne Mitchell, *Australian Alps*, Angus & Robertson: Sydney, 1942 (reprinted 1946, this edition1962), p92.

Chapter Five

1 Barbara Schott, *The Farmhouse Poems,* cited in Pamela Banting, *Fresh Tracks: Writing the Western Landscape*, Polestar Publishing: Victoria, 1998.
2 E. Mitchell, *Towong Hill*, 1989, p5.
3 E. Mitchell, *Images in Water*, Angus & Robertson: Sydney, 1947, 97.
4 E. Mitchell, *Chauvel Country: The Story of a Great Australian Pioneering Family*, Macmillan: Melbourne, 1983, p188.
5 Ibid.
6 Geoffrey Bolton, *Spoils and Spoilers: Australians Make their Environment 1788–1980*, Allen and Unwin: Sydney, 1981, p145.

Bolton argued that under the combined impact of the Depression and Second World War, progress in rural Australia was halted between 1930 and 1945.

[7] On his arrival in London, Harry Chauvel found he had been given command of the 1st Australian Light Horse Brigade. One of the first battles he fought on their behalf was to insist they be disembarked in Egypt, instead of in England, where they would have been encamped 'fetlock deep in water' on Salisbury Plain. For more information on Sir Harry Chauvel and the military campaigns in Egypt, see E. Mitchell, *Chauvel Country*, also E. Mitchell, *The Light Horse: The Story of Australia's Mounted Troops*, 1978, E. Mitchell, *Light Horse to Damascus*, Hutchinson: Melbourne, 1971, a children's book on the battles of the light horse in Egypt that recounts many of the stories told to her by her father. For a military history of Sir Harry Chauvel's career, see A. J. Hill, *Chauvel of the Light Horse: biography of General Sir Harry Chauvel, G.C.M, K.C.B.*, Melbourne University Press: Carlton, 1978.

[8] *Chauvel Country*, p40.

[9] Ibid, p85.

[10] A covered school was an enclosed arena usually with sand or bark footing.

[11] *Chauvel Country*, p134.

[12] Ibid, p138.

[13] Ibid, p179.

[14] Ibid, p152.

[15] Ibid, p164.

[16] Ibid, p152.

[17] E. Mitchell, *Australia's Alps*, Sydney: Angus & Robertson, 1946, p1.

[18] See Katie Holmes, *Spaces in Her Day*, 1995, pp54–60, for a discussion on the importance of gardens in women's expression of their 'selves'.

[19] *Towong Hill*, p67.

[20] Tom Mitchell joined the Australian 8th Division in July 1940, from E. Mitchell, *Chauvel Country*, p246.

[21] Ibid, p258.

[22] See Brenda Niall, *Seven Little Billabongs: The World of Ethel Turner and Mary Grant Bruce*, Melbourne University Press: Carlton, 1979, for a discussion on the influence of Mary Grant Bruce's character, Norah, from the *Billabong* series on images of Australian girlhood. Elyne mentioned how much she loved to read the *Billabong* series as a young girl. *Chauvel Country*, p93.

23 *Towong Hill,* p10.
24 For a study of the impact on the land by the introduction of rabbits, see Eric Rolls, *They All Ran Wild: the story of pests on the land in Australia,* Angus and Robertson: Sydney, 1969
25 *Speak to the Earth,* 1945, p8.
26 Ibid.
27 E. Mitchell, *Soil and Civilization* [sic], Angus & Robertson, Sydney, 1946, p3.
28 Crutching is shearing the hind legs and rear end of the sheep to prevent dags from forming in the wool, which increased the risk of fly strike. Sheep were attacked by flies, which laid their eggs in the wool, where they hatched into maggots that fed on the flesh of the sheep. Fly strike occurred more frequently in hot humid conditions. The flock must be vigilantly watched to prevent this, as a fly-struck sheep could be dead in as little as twelve hours. Once a sheep was 'struck', it had to be caught, the wool clipped away and milk oil applied to the maggot-infested area. Foot rot also had to be treated by catching the sheep and clipping back the infected hooves.
29 *Speak to the Earth,* p21.
30 Ibid, p9.
31 Ibid, p32.
32 *Towong Hill,* p19.
33 Ibid, p7.
34 Ibid, p6.
35 *Spoils and Spoilers,* p135.
36 *Soil & Civilization,* p24.
37 Ibid, p4.
38 Ibid, p46.
39 *Images in Water,* p94.
40 See E. Mitchell, *Kingfisher Feather,* Hutchinson: London, 1962.
41 *Towong Hill,* p45.
42 Ibid, p46.
43 Ibid, p47.
44 Ibid, p26.
45 Ibid, p95.
46 *Chauvel Country,* p155/6.
47 *Towong Hill,* p48.
48 Ibid, p11.
49 Tom planted stands of Basket willows in an attempt to stem the erosion of the riverbanks. Basket willows have since become an environmental disaster all over eastern Australia, where they were planted extensively from the 1930s to the 1960s. Their roots clog

the water system and they will grow from a broken twig fallen on the ground.

50 *Towong Hill*, p11.
51 *Chauvel Country*, p205.
52 *Towong Hill*, p51.
53 Ibid, p98.
54 Ibid, p71/69.
55 E. Mitchell, *The Silver Brumby*, Hutchinson: London, 1958.
56 Ibid, p11.
57 Ibid, p12.
58 *The Silver Brumby*, p20.
59 Ibid, p135.
60 E. Mitchell, *The Snowy Mountains*, Rigby: Melbourne, 1980, p95.
61 *Soil & Civilization*, p29.
62 *Kingfisher Feather*, Hutchinson: London, 1962, p13.
63 Ibid, 27.
64 Ibid, 86.
65 *Towong Hill*, p142.
66 Ibid.

Core of My Heart

1 Edward S. Casey, 'How to Get from Space to Place in a Fairly Short Stretch of Time' in Steven Feld and Keith H. Basso (eds.), *Senses of Place*, School of American Research Press: Santa Fe, NM, 1996, p21. My emphasis.
2 Ibid, p25.
3 S. Schama, *Landscape and Memory*, HarperCollins: London, 1995.
4 Ibid, p61.
5 Feld and Basso, 'Introduction', *Senses of Place*, p8.
6 Casey, 'How to get from Space to Place ...', p36.
7 S. Schama, *Landscape and Memory*, p134.
8 'How to Get from Space to Place ...', p27.
9 Ibid, p26.
10 B. Lopez, *Arctic Dreams: Imagination and Desire in a Northern Landscape*, The Harvill Press: London, 1998 (1986), Preface.

List of illustrations

Chapter Five

Select bibliography

List of Institutions where research was carried out

Archives of British Columbia, Victoria, BC.
Glenbow Archives, Calgary, Alberta.
Mitchell Library, Sydney.
Ontario Archives, Toronto, Ontario.
Whyte Museum of the Canadian Rockies, Banff, Alberta.

PRIMARY SOURCES

Newspapers and Journals

Crag and Canyon, Banff, Alberta, 1937.
The Brooklyn Eagle, 1911, New York.
The Canadian Alpine Journal, 1907–1914.

Unpublished Material

Adams, Mollie, Laggan to Maligne Lake and Tete Jaune
    Cache and Return, Diary June 8th to September 20th, 1908,
    Whyte Museum of the Canadian Rockies, Banff.
Allison Family Papers, *Various Manuscripts, Reminiscences,*
    & Correspondence, Provincial Archives of British Columbia,
    Victoria. (Ref. A1636, Add. MSS. 2692.)
—— *Some Reminiscences of a Pioneer of the Sixties.*
    (Ref. B9771.)
—— *What I know of Ogopogo.*
—— *When the River Rose.*
—— *Incowmasket.*
Hopkins, Monica, Fonds—Manuscript, diary, letters.
—— *My Garden*, 1910 Clevious Museum, Calgary.
O'Brien, Mary, Papers, Ontario Archives.
—— *Scenes From Our Life in British Columbia No 1—On*
    the Okanagan Lakes.

Sharples, Carrie, Diary of a trip to Jasper Park, Rocky Mountains, Canada, May 29th to August 16th, 1911.

Smith, Marie Rose, Papers, Glenbow Museum Calgary.

—— Manuscript, *Eighty Years on the Plains*.

Warren, Mary, Schaffer Collection, Whyte Museum of the Canadian Rockies, Banff.

—— Map of Maligne Lake, drawn by Mary Schaffer Warren on grid paper.

—— Map of Maligne Lake, with names of mountains and justifications of them.

—— Map of Maligne Lake, from survey by Mary Schaffer Warren.

Published Materials

Australia

Atkinson, Louisa, *A Voice From the Country*, Mulini Press: Canberra, 1978.

—— *Excursions From Berrima: and a trip to Manaro and Molonglo in the 1870s*, Mulini Press, 1980.

—— *Tom Hellicar's Children*, Mulini Press: Canberra, 1983.

—— *Debatable Ground; or the Carlillawarra Claimants*, Mulini Press: Canberra, 1992.

—— *Cowanda: The Veteran's Grant—an Australian Story*, Mulini Press: Canberra, 1995 (1859).

Bates, Daisy, *The Passing of the Aborigines: a lifetime spent among the Natives of Australia*, Murray: London, 1938.

Blackburn, Julia, *Daisy Bates in the Desert*, Secker and Warburg: London, 1994.

Boswell, Anabella, *Annabella Boswell's Journal*, edited with introduction by Morton Herman, Angus and Robertson: Sydney, 1965.

Brent of Bin Bin, *Gentleman at Gyang Gyang: A tale of the Jumbuck pads on the summer runs*, Angus and Robertson: Sydney, 1956.

Brusdon, Jyoti, (ed), *I Love a Sunburnt Country: The Diaries of Dorothea Mackellar*, Angus and Robertson: Sydney, 1990.

Burn, David, *Narrative of the Overland Journey of Sir John and Lady Franklin and Party from Hobart Town to*

Macquarie Harbour, 1842, George Mackaness (ed), Australian Historical Monograph, 1955.

Byles, Marie, *By Cargo Boat and Mountain: the unconventional experiences of a woman on tramp around the world*, Seeley Service: London, 1931.

Clacy, Mrs. Charles (Ellen), *A Lady's Visit to the Gold Diggings of Australia in 1852–53*, Patricia Thompson (ed), Lansdowne Press: Melbourne, 1963, (1853).

Clarke, Patricia, *Pioneer Writer: The Life of Louisa Atkinson, novelist, journalist, naturalist*, Allen and Unwin: Sydney, 1990.

—— *A Colonial Woman: the life and times of Mary Braidwood Mowle*, Allen and Unwin: Sydney, 1986.

Cohen, Bill, *To My Delight; the autobiography of Bill Cohen the grandson of the Gumbangarri*, Aboriginal Studies Press for the Australian Institute of Aboriginal Studies, 1987.

Conway, Jill Kerr, *The Road from Coorain, an Australian Memoir*, William Heinemann, Australia 1989/1990.

Cowan, Peter (ed), *A Faithful Picture: the letters of Eliza and Thomas Brown at York in the Swan River Colony 1841–1852*, Fremantle Arts Press: Fremantle, 1977.

Crawford, Evelyn, *Over My Tracks: A Remarkable Life*, as told to Chris Walsh, Penguin: Ringwood, Vic. 1993.

Du Faur, Freda, *The Conquest of Mount Cook & Other Climbs: An Account of Four Seasons' Mountaineering on the Southern Alps of New Zealand*. George Allen & Unwin Ltd: London, 1915.

Duncan-Kemp, Alice, *Our Sandhill Country: Nature and Man in South Western Queensland*, Angus and Robertson: Sydney, 1933.

—— *Where Strange Paths Go Down*, W. R. Smith and Patterson Pty. Ltd.: Brisbane, 1952.

—— *Our Channel Country: Man and Nature in South-West Queensland*, Angus and Robertson: Sydney, 1961.

—— *Where Strange Gods Call*, W. R. Smith and Paterson, Pty. Ltd.: Brisbane, 1968.

Gunn, Mrs. Aeneas, *We of the Never Never*, Hutchinson: London, 1907 (7th edition).

—— *Little Black Princess*, Angus and Robertson: Sydney, 1983 (1905).

Franklin, Miles, *My Brilliant Career*, William Blackwood & Sons: Edinburgh, 1901.

—— *All That Swagger*, Angus and Robertson: Sydney, 1940 (1936).

—— *My Career Goes Bung: purporting to be the Autobiography of Sybella Penelope Melvyn*, Georgian House, 1946.

—— *Childhood at Brindabella*, Angus and Robertson: Sydney, 1963.

Frost, Lucy, *A Face in the Glass: The Journal and Life of Annie Baxter Dawbin*, William Heinemann: Melbourne, 1992.

Frost, Lucy (ed), *The Journal of Annie Baxter Dawbin, 1858–1868*, University of Queensland Press: St Lucia, 1998.

Fullerton, Mary E., *Bark House Days*, Heath Cranton Ltd.: London, 1931.

Furphy, Joseph, *Such is Life*, Angus and Robertson: Sydney, 1991 (1903).

Hanrahan, Barbara, *The Scent of Eucalyptus*, University of Queensland Press: St Lucia, 1973/1993.

Hasluck, Alexandra, *Portrait with Background: A life of Georgiana Molloy*, Oxford University Press: Melbourne, 1955.

Heney, Helen (ed), *Dear Fanny: Women's Letters to and from NSW*, Australian National University Press: Canberra, 1985.

Henning, Rachel, *The Letters of Rachel Henning* (ed), David Adams, Penguin Books: Ringwood, Vic., 1977 (first published 1951–52).

Hill, A. J., *Chauvel of the Light Horse: biography of General Sir Harry Chauvel, G.C.M, K.C.B.*, Melbourne University Press: Carlton, 1974.

Irwin, Sally, *Between Heaven and Earth: The Life of a Mountaineer, Freda du Faur, 1882–1935*, White Crane Press: Victoria, 2000.

Kennedy, Marnie, *Born a Half Caste*, Australian Institute of Aboriginal Studies: Canberra, 1985.

Lawson, Henry, 'A Double Buggy At Lahey's Creek', *Joe Wilson & His Mates*, in *A Camp-Fire Yarn: Henry Lawson Complete Works*. Compiled and edited by Leonard Cronin. Lansdowne: Sydney (1900), 1984.

Lines, William, *An All Consuming Passion: Origins, Modernity and the Australian Life of Georgiana Molloy*, Allen and Unwin: Sydney, 1994.

Makim, Gene, *Get Up on His Shoulder: A History of Campdrafting in NSW and Queensland*, privately published, Gene Makim: Wilberforce, NSW, 1997.

Martin, Catherine, *An Australian Girl*, Pandora: London (first pub. 1890), 1988.

Meredith, Mrs. Charles (Louisa), *Notes and Sketches of New South Wales: During a Residence in that Country from 1841–1852*, John Murray: London, 1846.

Mitchell, Elyne books (listed by date of publication):

—— *Australian Alps*, Angus and Robertson: Sydney, 1942.

—— *Speak to the Earth*, Angus and Robertson: Sydney, 1945.

—— *Soil and Civilization*, Angus and Robertson: Sydney, 1946.

—— *Images in Water*, Angus and Robertson: Sydney, 1947.

—— *Flow River, Blow Wind*, Australiasian Publishing Co: Sydney, 1953.

—— *Black Cockatoos Mean Snow*, Hodder and Stoughton: London, 1956.

—— *The Silver Brumby*, Hutchinson of London, 1958.

—— *Kingfisher Feather*, Hutchinson of London, 1962.

—— *Winged Skis*, Hutchinson of London, 1964.

—— *Jinki, Dingo of the Snows*, Hutchinson of London, 1970.

—— *Light Horse to Damascus*, Hutchinson of London, 1971.

—— *Light Horse: The Story of Australia's Mounted Troops*, Macmillian: Melbourne, 1978.

—— *The Colt from Snowy River: A Brumby Story*, Hutchinson: Melbourne, 1979.

—— *The Snowy Mountains*, with photography by Mike James, Rigby, Melbourne, 1980.

—— *Chauvel Country: The story of a Great Australian Pioneering Family*, Macmillan: Melbourne, 1983.

—— *Discoverers of the Snowy Mountains*, Macmillian: Melbourne, 1985.

—— *A Vision of the Snowy Mountains*, Macmillian: Melbourne, 1988.

—— *Towong Hill: Fifty Years on an Upper Murray Cattle Station*, Macmillan: Melbourne, 1989.

Praed, Mrs. Campbell, *My Australian Girlhood: sketches and impressions of Bush life*, T. Fisher Unwin: London, 1902.
—— *Lady Bridget in the Never Never Land: A Story of Australian Life*, Hutchinson and Co: London, 1915.

Pritchard, Katherine Susannah, *Coonardoo* (1923), Angus and Robertson: Sydney, 1996.

Rae-Ellis, Vivienne, *Louisa Anne Meredith: A Tigress in Exile* (1979), St David's Park Publishing: Hobart, 1990.

Roe, Paddy, *Gularabula: Stories from the West Kimberly*, (edited by Stephen Muecke), Fremantle Arts Centre Press: Fremantle, 1983.

Salter, Elizabeth, *Daisy Bates: The Great White Queen of the Never Never*, Corgi Books: London, 1973 (1971).

Shann, E.O.G., *Cattle Chosen: The Story of the First Group Settlement in Western Australia, 1829 to 1841* (1926), Facsimile edition, University of Western Australia Press, W.A., 1978.

Spender, Dale (ed), *The Penguin Anthology of Australian Women's Writing*, Penguin: Ringwood, 1988.

Stirling, Amie Livingstone, *Memories of an Australian Childhood, 1880–1900*, Schwartz Publishing: Melbourne, 1980.

Telfer, William Jr., *The Wallabadah Manuscript: recollections of the early days*, New South Wales University Press: Kensington, 1980.

Wallace, Judith, *Memories of a Country Childhood*, University of Queensland Press: St Lucia, 1977.

West, Ida, *Pride Against Prejudice*, Australian Institute of Aboriginal Studies Press: Canberra, 1987.

Wright, Judith, *Born of the Conquerors: Selected Essays*, Aboriginal Studies Press: Canberra, 1991.
—— *Half A Lifetime*, Patricia Clarke (ed), Text Publishing: Melbourne, 1999.

North America

Allison, Susan, *A Pioneer Gentlewoman in British Columbia: The Recollections of Susan Allison*, Margaret A. Ormsby (ed), University of British Columbia Press: Vancouver, 1976.

Benham, Gertrude, E, 'The Ascent of Mt. Assinboine', in *Canadian Alpine Journal*, Vol. 1, No. 1, 1907.

Bird, Isabella Lucy, *The Englishwoman in America*, University of Wisconsin Press: Madison, 1966 (first published 1856).

Bird, (Bishop), Isabella, *A Lady's Life in the Rocky Mountains*, John Murray: London, 1880.

Bird, Isabella, *A Lady's Life in the Rocky Mountains* (1879), with introduction by Pat Barr, Virago Press: London, 1982.

Black, Martha, *Martha Black: Her Story from the Dawson Gold Fields to the Halls of Parliament.*, Alaska Northwest Publishing Co: Edmonds, WA, 1976.

Butler, William, *The Great Lone Land: A Narrative of Travel and Adventure in the North West of America*, Sampson Low, Marston, Searle and Rivington: London, 1878 (8th edition).

Carpenter, Jock, *Fifty Dollar Bride: Marie Rose Smith, A Chronicle of Métis Life in the Nineteenth Century*, Greys Publishing Ltd: Sidney, B.C., 1977.

Cather, Willa, *O Pioneers!* (1913), Readers Digest Association, 1990.

Cooper, James Fenimore, *The Pioneers*, Airmont Publishing Co, 1823/1964.

Degraf, Anna, *Pioneering on the Yukon 1892–1917*, Archon Books: Hamden Connecticut, 1992.

Gates, Florence, *Back to the Coteau Hills*, Modern Press: Saskatoon, 1980.

Gowen, Elsie, Park, 'A Quaker in Buckskin: Mary Schaffer was a pioneer explorer whose story is linked with Jasper park,' in *Alberta Historical Review*, Vol. 5, No. 3, 1957.

Healy, W. J., *Women of the Red River: Being a Book written from the Recollections of women surviving from the Red River Era*, Russell, Lang & Co: Winnipeg, 1923.

Hall, Mrs. Cecil (Mary), *A Lady's Life on a Farm in Manitoba*, W.H. Allen & Co: London, 1884.

Harris, Marie, *Raw Honey*, Alice James Publishers: Cambridge, MA, 1975.

Henshaw, Julia W., 'The Mountain Wildflowers of Western Canada' in *Canadian Alpine Journal*, Vol. 1, No. 1, 1907.

Henshaw, Julia, W., 'The Orchidaceau of the Rocky & Selkirk Mountains' in *Canadian Alpine Journal*, Vol. 1, No. 2, 1908.

Hitchcock, Mary, E., *Two Women in the Klondike: The Story of a Journey to the Gold Fields of Alaska*, Knickerbocker Press: New York, 1899.

Hopkins, Monica, *Letters From A Lady Rancher*, Glenbow Museum: Calgary, 1981.

Hubbard, Mrs. Leonidas (Mina), *A Woman's Way Through Unknown Labrador*, The McClure Company: New York, 1908.

Inderwick, Mary, E., 'A Lady & Her Ranch' in *Alberta Historical Review*, Vol. 15, no. 4, Autumn 1967.

Jackson, Dr. Mary Percy. *Suitable for the Wilds: Letters from Northern Alberta, 1929–1931*, edited with Introduction by Janice Dickin McGinnis. University of Toronto Press: Toronto, 1995.

Jameson, Anna, Brownwell, *Winter Studies & Summer Rambles in Canada*, McClelland & Stewart: Toronto (1838), 1990.

Johns, Ethel, 'A Graduating Climb' in *Canadian Alpine Journal*, Vol. 2, No. 2, 1908.

Kipling, Rudyard, *Letters of Travel, 1892–1913*, Dominion edition: London, 1920.

Langton, Annie, *A Gentlewoman in Upper Canada: The Journals of Annie Langton*, edited by H. H. Langton, Clarke, Irwin & Co. Ltd, 1950.

MacCarthy, Mrs. A.H., 'Over the Wilson & Duchesnay Passes' in *Canadian Alpine Journal*, Vol. 2, No. 2, 1910.

Moodie, Susanna, *Roughing it in the Bush: Or Life in Canada*, Carl Ballstadt (ed), Carleton University Press: Ottawa (1852), 1988.

—— *Roughing it in the Bush: or Life in Canada. A Critical Edition*, Elizabeth Thompson (ed), The Tecumseh Press: Ottawa (1852) 1997.

Morris, Elizabeth Keith, *An Englishwoman in the Canadian West*,. J. W. Arrowsmith Ltd: Bristol; Simpkin Marshall: London, 1913.

McClung, Nellie, L., *Clearing in the West: My Own Story*, Thomas Allen Limited: Toronto (1935), 1964.

McClung, Nellie, L., *The Stream Runs Fast: My Own Story*, Thomas Allen & Son: Toronto, 1965.

McGinnis, Vera, *Rodeo Road: My Life as A Pioneer Cowgirl*, Hastings House: New York, 1974.

Nelson, Klondy, *Daughter of the Gold Rush*, Random House: New York, 1955.

O'Brien, Mary, *The Journals of Mary O'Brien 1828–1838*, Audrey Saunders Miller(ed), Macmillan: Toronto, 1968.

O'Neill, Moira, 'A Lady's Life on a Ranche', in *Blackwoods Magazine*, January 1898, Vol. 163.

Ostenso, Martha, *Wild Geese*, Grosset & Dunleap: New York, 1925.

Parker, Elizabeth, 'The Alpine Club of Canada' in *Canadian Alpine Journal*, Vol. 1, No. 1, 1907.

Parker, Elizabeth, 'Report of Secretary' in *Canadian Alpine Journal*, Vol. 1, No. 1, 1907.

Schaffer, Mary, T. S., *A Hunter of Peace: Mary T.S. Schaffer's Old Indian Trails of the Canadian Rockies, with her heretofore unpublished account, 1911, Expedition to Maligne Lake*, introduced & edited by E. J. Hart, Whyte Musuem of the Canadian Rockies, Banff, Alberta (1911), 1980.

—— 'Flora of the Saskatchewan & Athabasca River Tributaries' in *Canadian Alpine Journal*, Vol. 1, No. 2, 1908.

—— 'Untrodden Ways' in *Canadian Alpine Journal*, Vol. 1, No. 2, 1908.

—— 'Haunts of the Wild Flowers of the Canadian Rockies' in *Canadian Alpine Journal*, Vol. 3, 1911.

—— 'The Finding of Lake Malinge' in *Canadian Alpine Journal*, Vol. IV, 1912.

Smith, Cindi, *Off the Beaten Track: Women Adventurers and Mountaineers in Western Canada*, Coyote Books: Jasper, 1989.

Stearns, Sharon, *Hunter of Peace, A Play*, Scirocco Drama: Victoria, B.C, 1993.

Storrs, Monica, *God's Galloping Girl: The Peace River Diaries of Monica Storrs, 1929–1931*, W.L. Morton (ed), University of British Columbia Press: Vancouver, 1977.

Thoreau, Henry, *The Portable Thoreau*, Penguin Books, 1947 (Walden, 1854).

Traill, Catherine Parr, *The Backwoods of Canada*, Michael Peterman (ed), Carleton University Press: Ottawa (1836), 1997.

—— 'Flowers & Their Moral Teaching' in *Journal of Canadian Fiction* Vol. II, No. 3, Special Issue 1973 (1st pub. in *The British American Magazine*, May 1863, p55).

Walker, Frank, 'Map of Overland Trail to the Klondike' from *Alberta Historical Review*, Vol. 7, No. 1, Winter 1959.

Warren, Mary Schaffer, article review of *Old Indian Trails*, 'Lure of the Rockies' from *The Brooklyn Eagle*, June 7th 1911.

Vaux, Mary M., 'Camping in the Canadian Rockies' in *Canadian Alpine Journal*. Vol. 1, No. 1, 1907.

—— 'Observations on Glaciers in 1910' in *Canadian Alpine Journal*, Vol. III, 1911.

York, Lillian C., *Petticoat Pioneers of the South Peace: The Life & Stories of Fifteen Pioneer Women of the South Peace*, The Northern Lights College Community Education, 1979.

SECONDARY SOURCES

Books

Agnew, John, and James Duncan (eds), *The Power of Place: Bringing Together Geographical and Sociological Imaginations*, Unwin Hyman: Boston, 1989.

Armitage, Susan, and Elizabeth Jameson (eds), *Writing the Range: Race, Class and Culture in the Women's West*, University of Oklahoma Press: Norman, 1997.

Atwood, Margaret, *The Journal of Susanna Moodie, Poems by Margaret Atwood*, Oxford University Press: Toronto, 1970.

—— *Survival: A Thematic Guide To Canadian Literature*, Anansi Press: Toronto, 1972.

Bachelard, Gaston, *The Poetics of Space*, translated from the French by Maria Jolas, Beacon Press: Boston, 1969.

Banting, Pamela (ed), *Fresh Tracks: Writing the Western Landscape*, Polestar Publishing: Victoria BC., 1998.

Barber, Lyn, *The Heyday of Natural History: 1820–1870*, Jonothon Cape: London 1980.

Barthes, Roland, *Mythologies*, selected and translated by Annette Lavers, Jonathon Cape: London, 1972.

Behar, Ruth, and Deborah A. Gordon (eds), *Women Writing Culture*, University of California Press: Berkeley, 1995.

Berndt, Ronald, and Catherine H. Berndt, *End of an Era: Aboriginal Labour in the Northern Territory*, Australian Institute of Aboriginal Studies: Canberra, 1987.

Benstock, Sharri, *The Private Self: Theory and Practice of Women's Autobiographical Writings*, London: Routledge, 1988.

Benterrak, Kim, Stephen Muecke, Paddy Roe, *Reading the Country: Introduction to Nomadology*, Fremantle Arts Press: Fremantle, 1984.

Birkett, Dea, *Spinsters Abroad: Victorian Lady Explorers*, Victor Gollancz Ltd,: London, 1991.

Bolton, Geoffrey, *Spoils and Spoilers, Australians Make Their Environment, 1788–1980*, Allen and Unwin: Sydney, 1981.

Bowden, Ros, *Women of the Land: Stories of Australia's Rural Women*, as told to Ros Bowden, ABC Books, Sydney, 1995.

Brown, Dee, *Bury My Heart At Wounded Knee: An Indian History of the American West*, Pan Books: London, 1971.

Bunkers, Suzanne L. and Cynthia A. Huff (eds), 'Introduction' in *Inscribing the Daily: Critical Essays on Women's Diaries*, University of Massachusetts Press: Amherst. 1996.

Burgess, Marilyn, and Gail Guthrie Valaskakis, *Indian Princesses & Cowgirls: Stereotypes from the Frontier*, OBORO: Montreal, 1995.

Buss, Helen M., 'Pioneer Women's Memoirs: Preserving the Past/Rescuing the Self' in *Reflections: Autobiography & Canadian Literature*, K. P. Stich (ed), University of Ottawa Press: Ottawa, 1988.

—— 'Women & the Garrison Mentality: Pioneer Women Autobiographers and their Relation to the Land' in *Re(dis)covering Our Foremothers: 19th C Canadian Women Writers*, Lorraine McMullen (ed), University of Ottawa Press: Ottawa, 1990.

—— *Mapping Our Selves: Canadian Women's Autobiography in English*, McGill-Queen's University Press: Montreal, 1993.

Cameron, John, (ed), *Changing Places: re-imagining Australia*, Longueville Books: Sydney, 2003.

Carter, Paul, *The Road to Botany Bay: An Exploration of Landscape and History*, Alfred A. Knopf: New York, 1988.

—— *Living in a New Country: history, travelling and language*, Faber: London, 1992.

Casey, E. S. *Remembering: A Phenomenological Study*, Indiana University Press: Bloomington, 2000.

—— *The Fate of Place: A Philosophical History*, University of California Press: Berkeley, 1997.

Checkland, Olive, *Isabella Bird, 'And a Woman's Right to Do What She Can Do Well'*, Scotland Cultural Press: Aberdeen, 1996.

Culley, Margo (ed), *A Day At A Time: The Diary Literature of American Women from 1764 to the Present*, The Feminist Press: City University of New York, 1985.

Cunningham, Chris, *Blue Mountains Rediscovered: Beyond the Myths of Early Australian Exploration*, Kangaroo Press: Kenthurst, NSW, 1996.

Davidoff, Leonore and Catherine Hall, *Family Fortunes: Men & Women of the English Middle Class, 1780–1850*, The University of Chicago Press: Chicago, 1987.

De Vries, Susanna, *Strength of Spirit: Pioneering Women of Achievement from First Fleet to Federation*, Millennium Books: Sydney, 1995.

Dillard, Annie, *Pilgrim at Tinker Creek*, Cape: London, 1975.

Dixson, Miriam, *The Real Matilda: Women and Identity in Australia, 1788–1975*, Penguin: Ringwood, Vic, 1995.

Dixson, Robert, *The Course of Empire: Neo-Classical Culture in NSW, 1788–1860*, Oxford University Press: Melbourne, 1986.

Duncan, James and David Ley (eds), *Place/Culture/Representation*, Routledge: London, 1993.

Dyhouse, Carol, *Girls Growing up in Late Victorian and Edwardian England*, Routledge: London, 1981.

Ehrlich, Gretal, *The Solace of Open Spaces*, Penguin Books: New York, 1985.

—— *Islands, The Universe Home, Home*, Penguin Books: New York, 1991.

Fairbanks, Carol and Sara Brooks Sunberg, *Farm Women on the Prairie Frontier: A Sourcebook for Canada & the US*, The Scarecrow Press, Inc: Metuchen, N.J., 1983.

Fairbanks, Carol and Bergine Haakenson (eds), *Writings of Farm Women 1840–1940: An Anthology*, Garland Publishing: New York, 1990.

Falkiner, Suzanne, *The Writer's Landscape: Wilderness*, Simon and Schuster, Sydney, 1992.

Falkiner, Suzanne and Alan Oldfield, *Lizard Island: The Journey of Mary Watson*, Allen & Unwin: Sydney, 2000.

Feld, Stephan and Keith H. Basso (eds), *Senses of Place*, School of American Research Press: Santa Fe, 1996.

Ferrier, Carole (ed), *As Good as a Yarn with You: Letters between Miles Franklin, Jean Devanny, Marjorie Barnard, Flora Eldershaw, Eleanor Dark*, Cambridge University Press: Cambridge, 1992.

Ferres, Kay (ed), *The Time to Write: Australian Women Writers 1890–1930*, Penguin Books: Ringwood, Victoria, 1993.

Foster, David, *Crossing the Blue Mountains: Journeys through two centuries, from naturalist Charles Darwin to novelist David Foster*, Duffy and Snellgrove: Sydney, 1997.

Frost, Lucy (ed), *No Place for a Nervous Lady: Voices from the Australian Bush*, McPheeGribble/Penguin: Melbourne, 1984.

Frye, Northrop, *The Bush Garden: Essays on the Canadian Imagination*, House of Anansia: Toronto, 1971.

Gaard, Greta (ed), *Ecofeminism: Women, Animals and Nature*, Temple University Press: Philadelphia, 1993.

Garden, Don (ed), *Created Landscapes: Historians and the Environment*, compiled by Sue Hodge, The History Institute, Victoria, 1993.

Gayton, Don, *Landscapes of the Interior: Re-explorations of Nature & the Human Spirit*, New Society Publishers: Gabriola Island, BC, 1996.

Gilchrist, Gail, *The Cowgirl Companion: Big Skies, Buckaroos, Honky Tonks, Lonesome Blues & other Glories of the True West*, Hyperion: New York, 1993.

Glacken, Clarence, J., *Traces on the Rhodian Shore: Nature and Culture in Western Thought from Ancient times to the end of the eighteenth century*, University of California Press: Berkeley, 1967.

Goldie, Terry, *Fear and Temptation: The Image of the Indigene in Canadian, Australian, New Zealand Literatures*, McGill-Queens University Press: Montreal, 1989.

Goodman, David, *Gold Seeking: Victoria and California in the 1850s*, Allen and Unwin: Sydney, 1994.

Green, Jack, *Pursuits of Happiness: The Social Development of Early Modern British Colonies and the Formation of American Culture*, University of North Carolina Press: Chapel Hill, 1988.

Griffiths Tom, *Hunters and Collectors: the Antiquarian Imaginations in Australia*, Cambridge University Press, 1996.

Grimshaw, Patricia, Marilyn Lake, Ann McGrath and Marilyn Quartly, *Creating a Nation 1788–1990*, McPheeGribble: Ringwood, 1994.

Grimshaw, Patricia, with Susan Janson, and Marian Quartly, *Freedom Bound I: Documents on Women in Colonial Australia*, Allen and Unwin: Sydney, 1995.

Hampsten, Elizabeth, *Read This Only to Yourself: The Private Writings of Midwestern Women 1880–1910*, Indiana University Press: Bloomington, 1982.

Harris, Barbara J., *Beyond Her Sphere: Women & the Professions in American History*, Greenwood Press: Westport, Connecticut, 1978.

Harrison, Dick, *Unnamed Country: The Struggle for a Canadian Prairie Fiction*, University of Alberta Press: Edmonton, 1977.

Havely, Cicely Palser, *This Grand Beyond: The Travels of Isabella Bird Bishop*, Century Publishing: London, 1984.

Hawkes, Terrence, *Structuralism and Semiotics*, Methuen: London, 1977.

Holmes, Katie, *Spaces in Her Day: Australian Women's Diaries of the 1920s and 1930s*, Allen and Unwin: Sydney, 1995.

Holthaus, Gary, *Wide Skies: Finding a Home in the West*, University of Arizona Press: Tucson, 1997.

Hoorn, Jeanette (ed), *Strange Women: essays in art and gender*, Melbourne University Press: Carlton, 1994.

Howard, John Kinsey, *Strange Empire: a Narrative of the North West*, Morrow: New York, 1952.

Inglis K. S., *The Australian Colonists: An Exploration of Social History, 1788–1870*, Melbourne University Press: Melbourne, 1974.

Isaacs, Jennifer, *Pioneer Woman of the Bush and Outback*, Lansdowne Press: Willoughby, 1990.

Jackel, Susan (ed), *A Flannel Shirt & Liberty: British Emigrant Gentlewomen in the Canadian West*, University of British Columbia Press: Vancouver, 1982.

Jameson, Elizabeth and Susan Armitage (eds), *Writing the Range: Race, Class & Culture in the Women's West*, University of Oklahoma Press: Norman & London, 1997.

Johnston, Jean, *Wilderness Women: Canada's Forgotten History*, Peter Martin Assoc. Ltd: Toronto, 1973.

Jones, D. G., *Butterfly on Rock: A Study of Themes and Images in Canadian Literature*, University of Toronto Press: 1970.

Jordan, Teresa and James R. Hepworth (eds), *The Stories that Shape Us: Contemporary Women Write About the West*, W. W. Norton & Company: New York, 1995.

Kadar, Marlene (ed), *Reading Life Writing: An Anthology*, Oxford University Press: Toronto, 1993.

Keenlyside, Francis, *Peaks and Pioneers: The Story of Mountaineering*, Lansdowne Press: Melbourne, 1975.

Kolodny, Annette, *The Lay of the Land: Metaphor as Experience and History in American Life and Letters*, University of North Carolina Press: Chapel Hill, 1975.

—— *The Land Before Her: Fantasy and Experience of the American Frontiers, 1630–1860*, University of North Carolina Press: Chapel Hill, 1984.

LaBastille, Anne, *Women & Wilderness*, Sierra Club Books: San Francisco, 1980.

Lansbury, Coral, *Arcady in Australia: The Evocation of Australia in Nineteenth Century Literature*, Melbourne University Press: Melbourne, 1970.

Lawson, Elizabeth, *Louisa Atkinson: The Distant Sound of Native Voices*, English Department, University College, Australian Defence Force Academy, Occasional Paper, No. 15, June 1989.

Leed, Eric, J., *The Mind of the Traveler: From Gilgamesh to Global Tourism*, Basic Books, 1991.

Light, Beth and Joy Parr (eds), *Canadian Women on the Move 1867–1920*, co-published by New Hogtown Press and The Ontario Institute for Studies in Education: Toronto, 1983.

Lines, William, J., *Taming the Great Southland: A History of the Conquest of Nature in Australia*, Allen and Unwin: Sydney, 1991.

Lopez, Barry, *Arctic Dreams: Imagination and Desire in a Northern Landscape*, The Harvill Press: London, 1998.

—— *Crossing Open Ground*, Vintage Books: New York, 1978/1989.

—— *About This Life: Journeys on the Threshold of Memory*, The Harvill Press: London, 1998/1999.

Magarey, Susan, Sue Rowley and Susan Sheridan (eds), *Debutante Nation: Feminism Contests the 1890s*, Allen and Unwin: Sydney, 1993.

Marcus, Julie, *Yours Truly: Olive M. Pink*, The Olive Pink Society: Canberra, 1991.

Marcus, Julie (ed), *First in their Field: Women and Australian Anthropology*, Melbourne University Press: Carlton, 1993.

Marriott, Alice, *Hell on Horses & Women*, University of Oklahoma Press: Norman, 1953.

Marshall, Paul (ed), *Raparapa Kularr Martuwarra: All right, now we go 'side the river, along that sundown way: stories from the Fitzroy River Drovers*, Magabala Books: Broome, 1988.

Massey, Doreen, *Space, Place and Gender*, Blackwell Publishers: Cambridge, 1994.

Martin, Stephen, *A New Land: European Perceptions of Australia 1788–1850*, Allen and Unwin: State Library of NSW, 1993.

Marty, Sid, *Leaning on the Wind: Under the Spell of the Great Chinook*, Harper Perennial: Toronto, 1995.

Mazel, David (ed), *Mountaineering Women: stories by early climbers*, Texas A. and M. University Press: College Station, 1994.

McDougall and Gillian Whitlock (eds), *Australian /Canadian Literature in English: Comparative Perspectives*, Methuen: Melbourne, 1987.

McGrath, Ann, *Born in the Cattle: Aborigines in the Cattle Country*, Allen and Unwin: Sydney, 1987.

McMullen, Lorrain (ed), *Re (dis)covering Our Foremothers: Nineteenth Century Canadian Women*, University of Ottawa Press: Ottawa, 1990.

Mellor, Mary, *Feminism and Ecology*, New York University Press: New York, 1997.

Mills, Sara, *Discourses of Difference: An Analysis of Women's Travel Writing and Colonialism*, Routledge: London, 1991.

Modjeska, Drusilla (ed), *Inner Cities: Australian Women's Memory of Place*, Penguin: Ringwood, Vic., 1989.

—— *Exiles at Home: Australian Women Writers 1925–1945*, Angus and Robertson: Sydney, 1981.

Moreton-Robinson, Aileen, *Talkin' up to the White Woman: Indigenous Women and Feminism*, University of Queensland Press: St. Lucia, 2000.

Moses, Daniel Day and Terry Goldie (eds), *An Anthology of Canadian Native Literature in English*, Oxford University Press: 1998.

Moynihan, Ruth B., Susan Armitage and Christiane Fisher Dichamp, *So Much To Be Done: Women Settlers on the Mining & Ranching Frontier*, University of Nebraska Press: Lincoln & London, 1990.

Myres, Sandra, L., *Westering Women & the Frontier Experience 180–1915*, University of New Mexico Press, 1982.

Nash, Roderick, *Wilderness and the American Mind*, Yale University Press: New Haven, 1967/1982.

Neuman, Shirley, and Smaro Kamboureli (eds), *Amazing Space: Writing Canadian Women Writing*, Longspoon/Newest: Alberta, 1996.

New, W. H., *Land Sliding: Imagining Space, Presence and Power in Canadian Writing*, University of Toronto: Toronto, 1997.

Niall, Brenda, *Seven Little Billabongs: The World of Ethel Turner and Mary Grant Bruce*, Melbourne University Press: Carlton, 1979.

Nicolson, Marjorie Hope, *Mountain Gloom and Mountain Glory: The Development of the Aesthetics of the Infinite*, Cornell University Press: Ithaca, New York, 1959.

Penn, William S. (ed), *As We Are Now: Mixblood Essays on Race and Identity*, University of California Press: Berkeley, 1997.

Pesman, Ros, *Duty Free: Australian Women Abroad*, Oxford University Press, Melbourne, 1996.

Peterman, Michael A., *Susanna Moodie & Her Works*, University of Toronto Press: Toronto, 1980.

Plumwood, Val, *Feminism and the Mastery of Nature*, Routledge: London, 1993.

Poirer, Thelma, *Cowgirls: 100 Years of Writing the Range*, Red Deer College Press: Alberta, 1997.

Probyn, Elspeth, *Outside Belongings*, Routledge: London, 1996.

Pyne, Stephen J., *Burning Bush: A Fire History of Australia*, Allen and Unwin: Sydney, 1992 (1991).

Quantic, Diane Dufva, *The Nature of Place: A Study of Great Plains Fiction*, University of Nebraska Press: Lincoln & London, 1995.

Read, Peter, *Returning to Nothing: The Meaning of Lost Places*, Cambridge University Press: Melbourne, 1996.

—— *Belonging: Australians, Place and Aboriginal Ownership*, Cambridge University Press: Vic, 2000.

Rees, Ronald, *New & Naked Land: Making the Prairies Home*, Western Producer Prairie Books: Saskatoon, Saskatchewan, 1988.

Reynolds, Henry, *The Other Side of the Frontier: Aboriginal Resistance to the European Invasion of Australia* (1981), Penguin Books: Ringwood, 1982.

—— *Black Pioneers: How Aboriginal and Islander People helped build Australia*, Penguin: Ringwood, Vic, 1990/2000.

Robinson, Janet, *The Magnificent Mountain Women: Adventures in the Colorado Rockies*, University of Nebraska Press: Lincoln & London, 1990.

Robinson, Jane, *Wayward Women: A Guide to Women Travellers*, Oxford University Press: New York, 1990.

Roe, Jill (ed), *My Congenials: Miles Franklin and Friends in Letters, Vol. 1, 1879–1938*, Collins/Angus and Robertson: Sydney, 1993.

Rolls, Eric, *A Million Wild Acres: Two Hundred Years of Man and an Australian Forest*, Nelson, 1981.

Rose, Deborah Bird, *Dingo Makes us Human: Life and Land in Aboriginal Culture*, Cambridge University Press: Cambridge, 1992.

—— *Nourishing Terrains: Australian Aboriginal Views of Landscape and Wilderness*, Australian Heritage Commission: Canberra, 1996.

Russell, Penny, *A Wish of Distinction: Colonial Gentility and Femininity*, Melbourne University Press: Melbourne, 1994.

Ryden, Kent C., *Mapping the Invisible Landscape: Folklore, Writing & the Sense of Place*, University of Iowa Press: Iowa City, 1993.

Schaffer, Kay, *Women and the Bush: Forces of Desire in the Australian Cultural Tradition*, Cambridge University Press: Cambridge, 1988.

—— *In the Wake of First Contact: The Eliza Fraser Stories*, Cambridge University Press: Melbourne, 1995.

Schama, Simon, *Landscape and Memory*, HarperCollins Publishers: London, 1995.

Schiebinger, Londa, *The Mind has no Sex? Women in the Origins of Modern Science*, Harvard University Press: Cambridge, Mass, 1989.

—— *Nature's Body: gender in the making of modern science*, Beacon Press: Boston, 1993.

Sears, John F., *Sacred Places: American Tourist Attractions in the Nineteenth Century*, Oxford University Press: New York, 1989.

Seddon, George, *Landprints: Reflections on Place and Landscape*, Cambridge University Press: Melbourne, 1997.

Shepard, Paul, *Nature and Madness*, University of Georgia Press: Athens, 1982/1998.

Sheridan, Susan, *Along the Faultlines: Race and Nation in Australian Women's Writing, 1880s–1930s*, Allen and Unwin: Sydney, 1995.

Shields, Carol, *Susanna Moodie: Voice & Vision*, Borealis Press: Ottawa, 1977.

Silverman, Elaine Leslau, *The Last Best West: Women on the Alberta Frontier, 1880–1930*, Eden Press: Montreal, 1984.

Simpson-Housley, Paul and Glen Norcliffe (eds), *A Few Acres of Snow: Literary & Artistic Images of Canada*, Dundurn Press: Toronto, 1992.

Smith, Bernard, *European Vision and the South Pacific 1768–1850, A Study in the History of Art and Ideas*, Oxford University Press: London, 1960.

Smith, Sidonie, *A Poetics of Women's Autobiography: marginality and the fictions of self representation*, Indiana University Press: Bloomington, 1987.

Somerville, Margaret, *Body/Landscape/Journal*, Spinifex: Melbourne, 1999.

Soule, Michael E., and Gary Lease (eds), *Reinventing Nature? Responses to Postmodern Deconstruction*, Island: Washington, D.C., 1995.

Stegner, Wallace, *Wolf Willow: A History, A Story & a Memory of the Last Plains Frontier*, Viking Press: New York, 1955.

Strong-Boag, Veronica, and Anita Clair Fellman (eds), *Rethinking Canada: The Promise of Women's History* (third ed.), Oxford University Press: Toronto, 1997.

Swain, Tony, *A Place for Strangers: Towards a History of Australian Aboriginal Being*, Cambridge University Press: Cambridge, 1993.

Tacey, David, *ReEnchantment: The New Australian Spirituality*, HarperCollins: Sydney, 2000.

Thomas, Nicholas, *Colonialism's Culture*, Princeton University Press: New Jersey, 1994.

Thompson, Elizabeth, *The Pioneer Woman: A Canadian Character Type*, McGill-Queen's University Press: Montreal, 1991.

Thurston, John, *The Work of Words: The Writing of Susanna Strickland Moodie*, McGill-Queens University Press: Montreal, 1996.

Torgovnick, Marianna, *Gone Primitive: Savage Intellects, Modern Lives*, University of Chicago Press: Chicago, 1990.

Taun, Yi-Fi, *Space and Place: The Perspective of Experience*, Edward Arnold: London, 1977.

Turner, Frederick, *Beyond Geography: The Western Spirit Against the Wilderness*, Viking Press: New York, 1980.

Ward, Russel, *The Australian Legend*, Oxford University Press: Melbourne, 1958.

Watson, Pamela Lukin, *Frontier Lands and Pioneer Legends: How Pastoralists gained Karuwali Land*, Allen and Unwin: Sydney, 1998.

Wiebe, Ruby, *The Scorched-Wood People: a novel*, McClelland and Stewart, 1977.

White, Isobel, Diane Barwick, Betty Meehan (eds), *Fighters and Singers: The Lives of Some Australian Aboriginal Women*, George Allen and Unwin: Sydney, 1985.

Whitlock, Gillian, *The Intimate Empire: Reading Women's Autobiography*, Cassell: London, 2000.

Woloch, Nancy, *Women & the American Experience*, McGraw-Hill Inc: New York 1984.

Articles in Books and Journals

Amies, Marion, 'The Victorian Governess and Colonial Ideals of Womanhood', in *Victorian Studies*, No. 4, Vol. 31. 1988, pp537–565.

Anderson, Linda, 'At the Threshold of the Self: Women and Autobiography', in Moira Monteith (ed), *Women's Writing: A Challenge to Theory*, The Harvester Press: Great Britain, 1986.

Armitage, Shelley, 'Rawhide Heroines: The Evolution of the Cowgirl & the Myth of America' in *The American Self: Myth, Ideology, & Popular Culture,* Sam B. Girgus (ed), University of New Mexico Press: Albuquerque, 1981.

Armitage, Susan, 'Another Lady's Life in the Rocky Mountains' in *Women & the Journey: The Female Travel Experience,* Bonnie Frederick & Susan H. McLeod (eds), Washington State University Press: Pullman, Washington, 1993.

Bach, Evelyn, 'A Traveller in Skirts: Quest & Conquest in the Travel Narratives of Isabella Bird' in *Canadian Review of Comparative Literature,* September-December, 22: 3–4, 1995, pp587–600.

Ballstadt, Carl, 'Proficient in the Gentle Craft' in *Copperfield,* 5 1974 pp99–109 Bashford, Alison, 'Is White Australia Possible?' Race, colonialism and tropical medicine,' in *Ethnic and Racial Studies*, Vol. 23, No 2, March 2000, pp248–271.

Billson, Marcus, 'The Memoir: New Perspectives on a Forgotten Genre', in *Genre*, Vol. X, 1977.

Bird, Delys, 'Born for the Bush': An Australian Women's Frontier' in *Australian and New Zealand Studies in Canada*, No. 2, Fall, 1989.

—— 'The Spirit of the Place: women writers of the West', in *Women's Writing*, Vol. 1, 1998.

Bloom, Lynn Z., (1992) 'Utopia & Anti-Utopia in 20th C Women's Frontier Autobiographies' in *American Women's Autobiography: Fea(s)ts of Memory*, Margo Culley (ed), The University of Wisconsin Press: Madison.

Bordo, Jonathon, Peter Kulchyski, John Millory and John Wadland (eds), *Wilderness: Journal of Canadian Studies*, Special Edition, Vol. 33, No. 2, Summer 1998.

—— 'Picture and Witness at the Site of Wilderness' in *Critical Inquiry*, Vol. 26, Winter 2000.

Buss, Helen M., 'The Dear Domestic Circle: Frameworks for the Literary Study of Women's Personal Narratives in Archival Collections', in *Studies in Canadian Literature*, Vol. 14, No. 1, 1989, pp1–17.

—— 'A Feminist Revision of New Historicism to Give Fuller Readings of Women's Private Writing', in *Inscribing the Daily: essays on Women's Diaries*, Suzanne L. Bunkers and Cynthia A. Huff (eds), University of Massachusetts Press: Amherst, 1996.

Casey, E. S. 'How to get from Space to Place in a fairly short stretch of time: Phenomenological Prolegomena', in Keith Basso and Stephen Feld (eds), *Senses of Place*, School of American Research Press: Santa Fe, New Mexico, 1996.

Cadzow, Allison, 'Footnoting: Landscape, Space & Writing in the Exploration Diary of Caroline Creaghe' in *Southerly*, 1996–97, Summer, 56:4, pp219–33.

Conway, Margaret, 'Sundays Always Make Me Think of Home: Time & Place in Canadian Women's History' in *Rethinking Canada: The Promise of Women's History*, Veronica Strong-Boag and Anita Clair Fellman (eds), Copp Clark Pitman Ltd: Toronto, 1986.

Cook, Ramsey, 'Imagining a North American Garden: Some parallels & Differences in Canadian & American Culture' in *Canadian Literature*, No. 103, Winter 1984.

Crozier, Michael, 'The Idea of the Garden', *Meanjin*, Vol. 47, No. 3, Spring 1988.

Curtin, Emma, 'Gentility Afloat: gentlewoman's diaries and the voyage to Australia, 1830–60', *Australian Historical Studies,* Vol. 26, No. 105, 1995, pp634–652.

Daniels, Kay, 'Women's History', in *New History: Studying Australia Today*, G. Osbourne and W. F. Mandle (eds), Allen and Unwin: Sydney, 1982.

Davison, Graham, 'A Sense of Place', in Bain Atwood, (ed.), *Boundaries of the Past*, The History Institute, Vic, 1990.

Devereux, Cecily, 'New Woman, New World: maternal feminism and the new imperialism in the white settler colonies', *Women's Studies International Forum*, Vol. 22, Issue 2, March 1999.

Dodd, Kathryn., 'Cultural Politics & Women's Historical Writing' in *Women's Studies International Forum*, Vol. 13, Nos. 1/2, 1990, pp127–137.

Evans, Ray, 'Don't You Remember Black Alice, Sam Holt?: Aboriginal Women in Queensland History', *Hecate*, Vol. 8, 1982, pp6–21.

Fitzsimon, Trish and Susan Ward, 'Girls of the Bush: Tracking an Enigma Across Films, Fictions, Memories and Histories', in *Screening the Past: Aspects of Early Australian Film*, Ken Berryman (ed), National Film and Sound Archive: Canberra, 1995.

Flanagan, Richard, 'Wilderness & History' in *Public History Review*, Vol. 1, 1992.

Francis, Douglas, R., 'Changing Images of the West' in *Journal of Canadian Studies*, Vol. 17, No. 3, Autumn 1982.

Frank, Gelya, 'Becoming the Other: Empathy & Biographical Interpretation' in *Biography*, No. 8, Vol. 3, 1985, pp189–210.

Grimshaw, Patricia, 'Man's Own Country: Women in Colonial Australian History', in N. Grieve and A. Burns (eds), *Australian Women: New Feminist Perspectives*, Oxford University Press: Melbourne, 1986.

—— 'Writing About White Women in New Societies: Americans in Hawaii, Anglo-Australians in Colonial Victoria', in *Australasian Journal of American Studies*, Vol. 9, No. 2, December, 1990.

Grimshaw, Patricia and Julie Evans, 'Colonial Women on Intercultural Frontiers: Rosa Campbell Praed, Mary Bundock and Katie Langloh Parker', in *Australian Historical Studies*, Vol. 27, No. 106, April 1996.

Haraway, Donna, 'A Manifesto for Cyborgs: Science, Technology and Socialist Feminism in the 1980s', in *Socialist Review*, No. 80, 1985, pp65–107.

Hamilton, Paula, 'Inventing the Self: Oral History as Autobiography', *Hecate*, Vol. 16, 1990.

Holmes, Katie, 'Diaries as Deshabille? The Diary of Una Falkiner: A Careful Dressing', Susan Magarey, Caroline Guerin and Paula Hamilton (eds), *Writing Lives: feminist biography and autobiography*, Special edition, in *Australian Feminist Studies*, No. 16, Summer, 1992.

—— 'Diamonds of the Dustheap': Women's diary writing between the wars,' in *Wallflowers and Witches: Women and Culture in Australia, 1910–1945*, Maryanne Dever (ed), University of Queensland Press: St Lucia, 1994.

Holth, Tor, 'Some Glimpses of Pastoral Settlement in the Victorian Alps', in *Cultural Heritage of the Australian Alps*, Australian Alps Liaison Committee: Canberra, 1992.

Horne, Julia, 'Travelling Through the Romantic Landscapes of the Blue Mountains', in *Australian Cultural History*, No. 10, 1991.

Hosking, Susan, 'I 'ad to 'ave me Garden': A Perspective on Australian Women Gardeners' in *Meanjin*, Vol. 47, No.3, 1988.

Huff, Cynthia, 'Chronicles of Confinement: Reactions to Childbirth in British Women's Diaries', in *Women's Studies International Forum*, Vol. 10, No. 1, 1987.

Jacobs, Jane M., 'Earth Honouring: Western Desires and Indigenous Knowledges,' in Alison Blunt and Gillian Rose (eds), *Writing Women and Space: Colonial and Postcolonial Geographies*, The Guilford Press: New York, 1994.

Kingston, Beverly, 'The Lady and the Australian Girl: Some thoughts on Nationalism and Class', in Greive, Norma, and Ailsa Burns, *Australian Women: New Feminist Perspectives*, Oxford University Press: Melbourne, 1989.

Lake, Marilyn, 'Building Themselves up Apros: Pioneer Women Reassessed', in *Hecate*, Vol. 7, No. 2, 1981.

—— 'The Politics of Respectability: Identifying the Masculinist Context' in *Historical Studies*, Vol. 22, No. 86, April 1986.

—— 'Frontier Feminism and the Marauding White Man,' in *Journal of Australian Studies*, No. 49, 1996.

Latour, Bruno, 'Do you believe in reality? News from the trenches of the Science wars', in *Pandora's Hope: Essays on the Reality of Science Studies*, Harvard University Press: Cambridge, Mass, 1999, pp1–23.

Lepervanche, Marie de, 'Women, Men and Anthropology,' in Julie Marcus (ed), *First in their Field: Women and Australian Anthropology*, Melbourne University Press: Melbourne, 1993, pp1–13.

Marcus, Julie, 'The Beauty Simplicity and Honour of Truth: Olive Pink in the 1940s', in Julie Marcus (ed), *First in their Field: Women and Australian Anthropology*, Melbourne University Press: Melbourne, 1993, pp11–135.

Mantle, Nan, 'Shifting in the Saddle,' in *Journal of Australian Studies*, No. 49, 1996.

Martin, Susan, K., 'The Gender of Gardens: The Space of the Garden in Nineteenth Century Australia', in Ruth Barcan and Ian Buchanan (eds), *Imagining Australian Space: Cultural Studies and Spacial Inquiry*, University of Western Australia: Nedlands, 1999.

McGuire, Margaret, 'The Legend of the Good fella Missus', in *Aboriginal History*, Vol. 14, No. 2, 1990, pp124–151.

McGrath, Ann, 'Travels to a Distant Past: The Mythology of the Outback', in *Australian Cultural History*, No. 10, 1991.

McQuilton, John, 'Comparative Frontiers: Australia and the United States', in *Australiasian Journal of American Studies*, Vol. 12, No. 1, July 1993.

Monk, Janice, 'Gender in the Landscape: expressions of power and meaning', in *Inventing Places: Studies in Cultural Geography*, Hay Anderson and Fay Gale (eds), Longman/Chesire: Melbourne, 1992, pp123–138.

Montrose, Louis, 'The Work of Gender in the Discourse of Discovery', in Stephan Greenblatt (ed), *New World Encounters*, University of California Press: Berkeley, 1995.

Moss, John, 'Gender Notes: Wilderness Unfinished', in *Journal of Canadian Studies*, Vol. 33, No. 2, Summer 1998, pp168–177.

Murphy, John, 'The Voice of Memory: History, Autobiography & Oral Memory' in *Historical Studies*, Vol. 22, No. 87, October 1986.

Myerhoff, Barbara and Jay Ruby, 'Introduction' in *A Crack in the Mirror: Reflective Perspectives in Anthropology*, Jay Ruby (ed), University of Pennsylvania Press: Philadelphia, 1982.

Neuman, Shirley, 'Life-Writing' in *Literary History of Canada: Canadian Literature in English*, Vol. 4, W. H. New (general ed), University of Toronto Press: Toronto, 1990, pp333–70.

Newton, Janice, 'Domesticating the Bush', in *Journal of Australian Studies*, No. 49, 1996.

Pache, Walter, 'English-Canadian Fiction & the Pastoral Tradition' in *Canadian Literature*, No. 86, Autumn 1980.

Payment, Diane P., 'La vie en rose? Métis Women at Batoche, 1870 to 1920' in Veronica Strong Boag and Anita Clare Fellman (eds), *Rethinking Canada: The Promise of Women's History*, Oxford University Press: Toronto, 1997.

Pickering, Maggie, 'Looking Through the Fawnskin Window: white women's sense of place on the frontier in Australia and Canada' in *Australian Historical Studies*, No. 118, 2002, pp223–239.

Pigot, John, 'Women and the Bush: Hilda Rix Nicholas and the myth of the female artist in Australia', in Jeanette Horne (ed), *Strange Women: essays in Art and Gender*, Melbourne University Press: Carlton, 1994, pp53–64.

Ramson, William, 'Wasteland to Wilderness: Changing Perceptions of the Environment' in D. J. Mulvaney (ed), *The Humanities and the Australian Environment*, Highland Press: Canberra, 1991.

Read, Peter, 'The Look of the rocks and the grass and the hills: a rural life site on the South Coast of New South Wales', in *Voices*, Vol. II, No. 2, Winter, 1992.

Riddert, 'Watch the White Women Fade: Aboriginal and White Women in the Northern Territory, 1870–1940' in *Hecate*, Vol. 4, No. 2, 1993, pp73–92.

Richards, Cameron, 'Bush Frontier Rhetoric', in *Journal of Australian Studies*, No. 49, 1996.

Ricou, Laurence R., 'Empty as Nightmare: Men & Landscape in Present Canadian Prairie Fiction' in *Mosaic*, Vol. 1, No. 2, 1973, pp143–160.

Rose, Deborah Bird, 'Exploring an Aboriginal Land Ethic', in *Meanjin*, Vol. 47, No. 3, 1988, pp378–387.

Rouslin, Virginia Watson, 'The Intelligent Woman's Guide to Pioneering in Canada' in *Dalhousie Review*, Vol. 56, No. 2, Summer 1976.

Rowley, Sue, 'Inside the Deserted Hut: The Representation of Motherhood in Bush Mythology', in *Westerly*, No. 4, Vol. 34, December 1989.

—— 'The Journey's End: Women's Mobility and Confinement', in *Australian Cultural History*, No. 10, 1991.

Russell, Penny, 'Recycling Femininity: Old Ladies and New Women', in *Australian Cultural History*, No. 49, 1996, pp31–51.

Ryan, Simon, 'Discovering Myths: the Creation of the Explorer in Journals of Exploration' in *Australia-Canadian Studies*, Vol. 12, No. 2, 1994.

Schaffer, Kay, 'Colonizing Gender in Colonial Australia: The Eliza Fraser Story' in Alison Blunt and Gillian Rose (eds), *Writing Women and Space: Colonial and Postcolonial Geographies*, The Guilford Press: New York, 1994.

Scott, Joan W., 'The Evidence of Experience', in *Critical Inquiry*, Vol. 17, 1991, pp770–797.

Shapiro, Stephan A., 'The Dark Continent of Literature: Autobiography' in *Comparative Literature Studies*, Vol. 5, No. 4, 1968, pp421–454.

Shaw, Bruce, 'Heroism against White Rule: The "Rebel" Major', in Eric Fry (ed), *Rebels and Radicals*, George Allen and Unwin: Sydney, 1983.

Sinclair, Paul, 'Shared Places', in *Island*, Spring/Summer, No. 72/73, 1997.

Stanley, Liz, 'Recovering Women in History from Feminist Deconstructionism' in *Women's Studies International Forum*, Vol. 13, Nos. 1–2, 1990, pp151–157.

Stock, Brian, 'Reading, Community and a Sense of Place' in *Place/Culture/Representation*, J. Duncan and D. Ley (eds), Routledge: London, 1993.

Stouck, David, 'Secrets of the Prison-House: Mrs. Moodie & the Canadian Imagination' in *Dalhousie Review*, Vol. 54, No. 3, Autumn 1974.

Tinkler, John, 'Canadian Cultural Norms & Australian Social Rules' in *Canadian Literature*, No. 94, Autumn 1982.

Waterhouse, Richard, 'Australian Legends: Representations of the Bush, 1813–1913', in *Australian Historical Studies*, No. 115, October 2000, pp201–221.

Welter, Barbara, 'The Cult of True Womanhood: 1820–1860', in *American Quarterly*, Vol. 18, 1966.

Winkworth, Kylie, 'Women and the Bicycle: Fast, Loose and Liberated', in *Australian Journal of Art*, Vol. 8, 1989/90.

Unpublished Sources and Thesis

Hodge, Pam, Fostering Flowers: Women, Landscape and the Psychodynamics of Gender in Nineteenth Century Australia, PhD Thesis, Edith Cowan University: Western Australia, 1998.

Goodall, Heather, 'An Intelligent Parasite: A.P.Elkin and White Perceptions of the History of the Aboriginal People of New South Wales', in *Australian Historical Conference*, 1982 (unpublished).

Haskins, Victoria, My One Bright Spot: A Personal Insight into Relationships between White Women and Aboriginal Women under the New South Wales Aboriginal Protection Board Apprenticeship Policy 1920–1942, PhD Thesis, University of Sydney, 1998.

Jackel, Susan, Images of the Canadian West, 1872–1911, PhD Thesis, University of British Columbia, 1977.

McArdle, Kristin, Time Immersed in Space: a moving synthesis of ecological history, Masters Thesis, University of Sydney, 1997.

Pickering, Maggie, Free Our Dreams: The Politics of Aboriginal Literature, Unpublished Honours Thesis, University of Sydney, 1995.

—— Core of My Heart, My Country: Women's Sense of Place and the Land in Australia and Canada, 1828–1950, PhD Thesis, University of Sydney, 2001.